GERMANY
AFTER CAPITALISM

New Democracy - Old Principles:
The Wagenknecht-Doctrine

RALPH T. NIEMEYER

iUniverse, Inc.
Bloomington

Germany after Capitalism
New Democracy - Old Principles: The Wagenknecht-Doctrine

iUniverse books may be ordered through booksellers or by contacting:

iUniverse
1663 Liberty Drive
Bloomington, IN 47403
www.iuniverse.com
1-800-Authors (1-800-288-4677)

ISBN: 978-1-4697-6517-4 (sc)
ISBN: 978-1-4697-6516-7 (hc)
ISBN: 978-1-4697-6518-1 (e)

Printed in the United States of America

iUniverse rev. date: 2/18/2012

To Nadine, Till, Sarai, Lara-Berneen, Raulano-Isaac and Adrian-Leonid, for our children to for the world according to what they deem feasible, humane and in tune with nature.

"A government is not the expression of the will of a people but what a people can bear with."

– Kurt Tucholsky

Instead of a Foreword

In 1989 hard core "Stalinists" overnight became the best ever imaginable capitalists who managed to privatise the entire economy in Eastern Europe. Nowadays, we observe how the "Masters of the Universe" suddenly become anti-globalisation activists raising the question whether we shall trust the populist approach by George Soros and Warren Buffett one more time or whether we should become suspicious as their sudden reasoning may be a way for them to try to avoid imprisonment?

The difference between Socialism and Capitalism is that 23 years ago the Socialists accepted to be dictated the conditions of their surrender while today the capitalistic elite dictates their rescuers their conditions.

Shall we believe German Chancellor Angela Merkel in her plea to get things right and try a bit of Keynesianism while others like EU Commission President José Manuel Barroso jump onto ATTAC's bandwagon demanding better regulation of exactly those financial monsters he and his bureaucrats fed with every liberalisation, privatisation and deregulation they pushed through over the past years?

The financial crisis that started out as something the main stream media owned by the rich and glory referred to as a "credit crunch" on August 11, 2007, bringing down Bear Sterns as well as Northern Rock is only a symptom but not the cause of our economic problems.

An economic model that forces the real economy, our manufacturing industries, to produce only for profit and not for the actual demand leads to the production of an incredible amount of trash that implies wanton destruction of natural resources and climatic calamity.

The present economic system is evidently anti-economical as it destroys economic capacity with all the negative consequences for the vast majority of citizens on this planet as well as nature.

Time is ripe for a new economic system that will reverse these negative effects and that in contrast to the collapsing neo-classical model is mathematically coherent and economically sound while it is based on inclusion and proper management of resources.

Anti-Globalisation activists always postulate that "A different World is possible". I would rather say that a different world is not possible, but a different economic system is.

Read where we are heading once we have taken the power by democratic means in an as peaceful way as possible applying to the standards Nelson Mandela set forth by saying that the question of violence in a political struggle was not to be answered by the suppressed but by the oppressor.

Ralph T. Niemeyer, on 9th November 2011, the night, "Reichskristallnacht" of 1938 is to be remembered as well as the fall of the "Berlin Wall" in 1989.

PART 1

HOW COULD IT EVER GET THAT BAD?

I

THE INEVITABLE CLASH

The End of the Euro & a failed coup d'état in Germany

Neue Deutsche Mark notes and coins in the amount of 5 billion reportedly had already been printed and stored in Frankfurt in mid 2010 and were distributed across Germany over the Christmas holidays at the end of 2011 in dozens of convoys of German forestry administration vehicles armoured and accompanied by *Bundeskriminalamt* (BKA) bodyguards. The new, old, currency was rolling over German *Autobahnen* while the citizens had their Christmas dinner, many of them goose, but about 12 million had neither presents to exchange with their loved ones nor any kind of delicious meal in a cosy home. The outcast of Europe's richest nation were lining up in front of soup kitchens, infamously called *Tafeln* that churches and upper-middle class society clubs like Lion's Club or other organisations provided for in an effort to pacify their conscience.

During the Christmas holidays a scandal about federal German president, Christian Wulff, who got stricken-in by his connections to as powerful as dubious financial scam artists culminated in a witch hunt by conservative as well as left-leaning media who tried to topple him citing amoral behaviour when availing of advantageous interest conditions for the mortgage of his personal home.

Nevertheless, the president didn't do the combined "Fourth Power" that is controlled by five major publishing houses and private owners, the favour to resign over rather ridiculous and legally irrelevant charges but spoke wisely about the dangers of xenophobic sentiment in our society and the

3

scandalous infliction of state security services with Neo-Nazi – terrorist gangs.

It transpired that the media campaign that had been orchestrated by right wing publishing house Springer and the hard-core capitalist Bertelsmann – Group in liaison with the liberal appearing SPIEGEL magazine that for quite some time favours the Green Party, in the first place was meant to distract from the real scandals, the harsh social injustices as well as the rise of ultra – right wing terrorism sponsored by the state and secondly the president-bashing was designed to force him to step down and make room for a more conservative and tougher person such as finance minister Wolfgang Schäuble or the 2010 presidential hopeful Joachim Gauck, who the Social Democrats and Greens tried to push through but who had not found the support of the socialist DIE LINKE because of the man's deep-rooted anti-communism.

The office of German Bundespräsident is largely ceremonial and never had real powers but the moral impetus with which Mr Gauck, a former priest who although being an outspoken critique of the regime in the DDR (German Democratic Republic in the former East) had been in some way privileged and was allowed to travel with his family to Western Germany, could speak should not be underestimated. He, although his own possible infliction with East-Germany's secret service, the STASI, had always remained a mystery, made clear that he believes in capitalism and branded the Occupy-activists as idiots.

Instead, he is warning of leftist movements making it obvious why the state that had sponsored right wing and fascist groups needs him now in the office currently occupied by Christian Wulff. In that sense one can call the media bashing of Bundespräsident Wulff a kind of attempted Coup d'état.

One should investigate the case under the aspect of high treason against the federal president. One can imagine how Mr Gauck would pave the way for a Chancellor Carl Theodor von und zu Guttenberg who stumbled over his copy-paste –style in his thesis in March 2011 and resigned from his post as German war minister but ever since is enjoying continued support in

Germany's aristocracy and among leading industrialists, not the academic circles, though.

It has transpired that Mr Wulff in a speech in Lindau at Lake Constance on 24 August 2011 outright criticised the buying up by the ECB of state debts as well as the ESFS as an unfair transfer of debts and risks to future generations leaving room for speculation whether he would sign the laws into effect that the Bundestag had voted for in autumn of 2011. Mr Wulff said: "Whoever attempts to cushion the results of burst speculation bubbles by money or guarantees is transferring the obligations to the young generation and by this creates a heavy burden for future. All those who advocate this, act under the motto 'after me there will be apocalypse anyhow, so who cares?!'".[1]

Although the German president can not really block legislation to become effective but he can delay it by sending a law to the federal constitutional court in Karlsruhe where it could take months if not years to come to a conclusion. This might have frightened the coalition government of Chancellor Angela Merkel as well as the owners and powerful circles in Germany which also control the German media.

To ring the editors in chief of Germany's largest tabloid, BILD Zeitung, and ultra-conservative daily paper DIE WELT, threatening them with legal action if they went ahead with their campaign has been Mr Wulff's biggest mistake and probably not his only one. He apologized for his un-presidential behaviour, but for the German media that is not good enough. They still demand his resignation although other than his nervous reactions he has not been proven guilty of any crime, not even a serious misconduct which would be the only reasons for impeachment under German law.

Instead, media circles in Germany now threaten to reveal intimate details of the past of the president's wife. The speculation alone that there could be something true in this shows a new 'quality' and ever more brutal handling of issues once considered private. When we correspondents in Bonn heard about the various chancellor's love affairs and there had been many rumours about almost every chancellor, even Mr Kohl, we would not make this become a matter of political considerations and comments.

---

1   "Wer heute die Folgen geplatzter Spekulationsblasen allein mit Geld und Garantien zu mildern versucht, verschiebt die Lasten zur jungen Generation und erschwert ihr die Zukunft. All diejenigen, die das propagieren, handeln nach dem Motto: Nach mir die Sintflut." Original quote of German Federal President Christian Wulff on 24 August 2011 in Lindau.

This attitude of self-restricted, not censured, reporting has changed entirely when Berlin became the capital.

Never has the office of German president had played such a significant role other than when a weak Mr Hindenburg gave in to the German industrialists and aristocrats who threw their support behind the NAZIs. Mr Wulff, instead could now, that it has become clear that he lost all his former 'friends', become a really independent federal president, maybe the first one of it's kind in Germany.

79 years ago, Adolf Hitler, although he had never won the majority in any elections (in July 1932 it had been some 37% for his NSDAP, in the next elections in November of the same year it had already been a sharp decline by 8% leaving the NAZI-party financially almost ruined and demoralised as members de-fluxed to other parties) all of a sudden was supported by banks and leading industrialists of the 'Düsseldorfer Club' such as steal magnate Krupp and the Quandt family (who benefited tremendously from slave labour in the concentration camps and today build BMWs). Even today these circles have a say in throwing in Germany's upper class's support for a candidate for the chancellorship

One of the bankers, Kurt von Schröder, who organised a meeting on 4th January 1933 in his house in Köln with centrist former Reichschancellor Franz von Papen who by supporting Hitler saw a chance for a comeback for himself after he had been outmanoeuvred by Reichspresident von Hindenburg and his former friend, the present Reichschancellor Schleicher who only stayed in office for 57 days, had been among those who had been heavily benefiting from the aftermath of the financial crisis of 1929.

Mr. von Schröder had become one of the heavyweights of Germany's banking scene which together with the heavy industry and their shareholders must have seen a possibility for an economic recovery for Germany when playing the nationalistic card by supporting Adolf Hitler rather than being further dragged into the financial turmoil of the rest of the world.

"Globalisation" although not called like that in those days was sealed to be over in that night.

It is always said that the depression of 1929 had created an ungovernable situation in Germany in the 1930ies which is only partly correct. There would have been ways out of the crisis, but of course not by repeating the same mistakes over and over again.

Like today, the financial and economic crisis was swinging up and down and the political leadership was swiveling between left and right but the German upper class decided to try it with Fascism and suppression rather than any alternative economic model which could have averted the worst. But, the interest of the Krupp's, Quandts and Schröders lay in profit maximisation and not in solving the crisis as this would have meant to apply drastic changes in the economy, stirring away from speculation driven capitalism.

When the Industrie Club Düsseldorf decided to bring Hitler to power, things had already brightend up. At the beginning of 1933, the German stock market in Frankfurt am Main had left it's worst times behind and already closed 30 points higher again while unemployment had dropped by one million in January 1933.

Chancellor Schleicher just had issued a 500 million Reichsmark public employment program but the fruits of his idea were already credited to the new choice of Germany's elite, the WWI private and freshly baked Reichschancellor Adolf Hitler who in a coup d'état after his SA brigades had planted an arson attack on the Reichstag building on 27th February 1933 quit the alliance with Franz von Papen's Centrists and then could take the whole power with all the horrific consequences we know today from history books.

It can be worthwhile not only to read the political and military history of the 20th century but also about it's financial history.

The alternative is also clearly visible, a new democracy under Sahra Wagenknecht whose political thinking and philosophy I know by heart and which in many conversations I learnt from her over now 17 years. In the following I will try to explain the core of her ideas for a democratic and economically sound, fair, just, social and humane society. Therefore a few parts of this book are leaning onto her book *Freiheit statt Kapitalismus*.

Bank-co-Rrupt

While in Berlin, German Chancellor Angela Merkel pushed through the EFSF – up-grade, the "Occupy Frankfurt" movement was also picking up again to have an ever more intensified protest that culminated in another march on 15th October when 50,000 took to the streets of financial-Germany's headquarters.

Threatened with the order to leave the park in front of the European Central Bank (ECB) where some 350 activists camp as during day time a few thousands come to visit on 29th October unless the permission by the authorities is extended, the mostly young women and men organized grass roots democratic, but somewhat less chaotic than one would expect, events.

Every day an 'Asamblea' is being held in form of a gathering where by acclamation or show of hands, every single step is being decided democratically. The discipline of the young women and men in their early twenties can be called extraordinary although little rivalries sometimes derail the debate for a while, like in other political debates in Berlin and Brussels, too.

But, the young generation, in a strong contrast to the EU council, doesn't lose the focus although they are at the same time unable to define exact political goals or even structure their demands, yet.

The only other ones who do not lose the focus are Deutsche Bank AG and insurance firm Allianz AG who in joint cooperation had developed the idea of the insurance structure for the EFSF. They suggested a 1.5 ratio for the simple reason that these 2 trillion Euros would cover exactly the exposure Deutsche Bank AG has stemmed with its mere 30 billion € core-capital. Now as it is about trillions and not billions any longer the checks and balances reveal that even the best full-kasko - insurance by the newly – illegally, so far - enhanced EFSF won't solve the Euro-crisis. Through the back door, the Euro-zone's finance ministers in the manner of scam artists, increased the 'rescue' facility by 'optimizing' the volume of the fund for which all parliaments have given the green light.

"Could Greece's next rescue payout go straight into the pockets of London hedge funds?" asked the International Herald Tribune (IHT) on it's front page on 11th January 2012. And, in Germany, sentiment over further bail-outs and rescue missions for the financial sector are gaining ground not only among "Occupy" activists but the ordinary citizen, the 'real' 99%.

Just when Greece is expecting to be handed the next life-line of 30 billion Euros from the European Union and International Monetary Fund investment banks and hedge fund are betting on a major payout into their pockets.

"With stakes so high, investors are betting that Europe will go the extra mile to keep debt stained Greece afloat, and if the price to do that means that taxpayer funds end up bolstering the returns of a few hardy speculators – then, as far as they are concerned, the better", the IHT writes.

But, all this is depending on Greece's ability and willingness to accept harsh austerity criteria and barbaric social cuts.

In the meantime, the New York Times reported that hedge funds threaten to sue the Greek government at the European Court for Human Rights in Strasbourg should a deliberate state bankruptcy force hedge funds to write off parts or all of their demands.

Greek's Prime Minister Loukas Papademos suggested that the government in Athens could as well force creditors to a debt cut by a simple law referred to as 'collective action clauses' and refinance all of it's debts in this manner.

German SPIEGEL Magazine on 19th January 2012 asserted that the likelihood that the funds that are awash with virtual money are going to sue Greece is rising with every delay of the release of the rescue funds to the Greek government.

In South America, hedge funds and big private speculators had in the past won such cases against governments, but so far nobody ever had claimed speculation and profit maximisation to be guaranteed a 'human' right.

Amnesty International would probably find it hard to list such a case as a violation of fundamental rights although it is clear that in this regard Hungary, for instance, probably would have a clean bill of health.

And, as one speaks about engaging in humanitarian wars against Syria and Iran, one may wonder when Abs€Urdistan will be bombed by some hedge funds that aren't being paid back by Greece, Portugal, Spain, Ireland and Italy.

Technically, what our democratically elected leaders were up to amounts to the same tricks the 'masters of the universe', the investment bankers, hedge fund junkies and private equity sharks applied: a tool is being used to package a risk and make from a quite limited amount of cash a multiple of it. By once more defrauding the taxpayers only a few weeks of time have been bought during which more and more risks are transferred from the banks to the public hand, ultimately the citizen who will find hospitals, schools, libraries, universities, theatres and concert halls be closed.

But, as the end is nearing with France being the next economy to fall bankrupt even these lubricous trillion-fold umbrellas sooner than expected again reached their limits. The plan- and senseless activities by the EU's governments increasingly became a threat to the European idea, the solidarity among member states and the wellbeing of the citizens of Europe. Only way out would have been to liberate public finances from the dictate of the private capital markets. This means that EU member states ought to refinance themselves at a public European bank at low interest rates.

By circumventing the private banks who themselves refinance at the ECB at a very low interest rate but give away that money for exorbitant rates to governments a lot of unnecessary costs will be saved. At the same time it is of utmost importance to take away the 'casino-tokens' from the rich upper class by banning all investment banking, the introduction of a Europe-wide wealth tax for ultra rich and last but not least a significant hair cut of at least 60-75% of those debts.

One knew two years ago, in spring 2010, that Greece will never be able to pay back it's debt that had been accumulated by recklessly importing top shelf products and arms from Germany while 'investment' banks such as Goldman Sachs and Deutsche Bank speculated with Greek sovereign debts, but nobody cared. The EU Commission, all groups in the European Parliament as well as the European Central Bank could have known as even we journalists had written about the dangers and asked the democratically elected leaders questions about the very issue, but either the questions were avoided or simply not being addressed. Persons who have persistently avoided answering my questions were exactly those who now seem to be the most worried leaders who are still in charge. EU Commission President José Manuel Barroso always referred to his 'Economic and Monetary Affairs' Commissioners, Joaquin Almunia (at least he by education is an economist and could have been able to tackle an issue) or his successor Olli Rehn.

Truth is that 187 days before August 11, 2007, when the first credit crunch made the crisis visible, at that time Economic Affairs Commissioner Almunia once more avoided a specific question I put to him regarding the piling up of Southern and Eastern European debts. And, in January 2011, when being asked why the "Six Pack" of 'Economic Governance' didn't contain anything about a suffering by private banks, Mr Barroso referred my question to Mr Rehn who then said that "it was not in the interest of the EU Commission to let banks suffer". At the same time the two conspired together with EU finance ministers already over new 'rescue' packages for the PIGS (Brussels terminology for Portugal, Ireland, Greece and Spain) that again only benefited the banks and lead to Greece being indebted by 20 billion Euros more than at the beginning of the crisis.

The question arises how much longer one should stay at the sidelines and pretend that one trusts the democratic functioning of our leaders when it becomes more and more evident every day that not only a few warning signals were misread but that deliberately European law is being broken by those leaders who also seem to ignore any morals and the founding principles of the European Community that had always inspired any developments since the Treaty of Rome in 1957. Now that we are confronted with the rest of the Euro-zone being up for a haircut while everything else will stay as it is, the problem will not only persist but grow even bigger as he next countries, Portugal and Italy, eventually also France and last but not least Germany, won't have any chances any longer to refinance their obligations. Germany's exit strategy in introducing it's Neue Deutsche Mark will lead to hyperinflation across the former Euro-zone and also in Germany as the German export-strategy will no longer work leaving huge over-capacities behind while domestic demand in Germany won't be able to bridge the gap due to smashed purchasing power and low wages that are on the levels of the early 1980ies.

That's why, in order to rescue the EURO, we would have had to go much further and put into motion a completely different system of refinancing state-debts allowing for tapping governments the funds at the ESFS (European 'IMF') or at the ECB. Critics are quick to cite inflationary risks but there won't be more money being printed than it is right now as we would save the enormous amount of interests we are currently handing over to private banks that are still the mediators or brokers and nothing else in this stupid game.

Truth is, and neither Mr Barroso nor Mr Rehn want to admit it, that we would have not only less inflation because we would save a lot of useless interest payments that only end up in the pockets of ultra rich shareholders of those banks who again inflate the financial casino with that superfluous liquidity but also regain the heart of every democracy: control over our institutions. If we want to save the European idea we have to get our act together and stop listening to those 'leaders' that are willingly sacrificing the European idea on the altar of profit maximisation of banks. The International Herald

Tribune (IHT) noted on 21st October 2011 that the "historical ironies are considerable. Germany, for example, divided and in ruins after the war it fought to dominate Europe, is reunited and dominating Europe now, but without arms and with deep reluctance."

If one asks the young activists in the "Occupy Frankfurt" camp, they don't see this, yet, but some sense that in a way Germany has economically achieved where Hitler's terrorism had failed 70 years earlier. And, now, like Hitler, who had killed almost everybody in Europe, Germany lost it due to a literal overkill.

Deutsche Bank AG rescued itself

When I heard that the EU Council was getting "tough" on banks I only thought that it was like letting Monkeys mind a Banana Plant.

The October 2011 EU Council's so heroically found decision, it appears, had finally gotten to the bottom of the barrel making the banks agree to a 50% haircut on Greek debts and ordered an increase of 1% of the capital requirements raised from – nominal – 8 to now 9%. Sounds great but the reality check reveals that banks won't suffer. First of all, the bolstered ESFS – 'kasko'-insurance will blow up the fund's liabilities to up to 2 trillion Euros. Banks that had bought state obligations and get into trouble can draw the guarantee while placing comfortably their toxic assets with the taxpayer.

This idea was born by German insurance giant Allianz AG in close cooperation with Deutsche Bank AG. German officials and members of parliament admitted yesterday publicly that the exact structure of the new legislation is too complex to understand for them.

They hardly know what they were doing when voting this into effect.

Secondly, the financial merry-go-round will continue and the wheel will become bigger the faster it spins as banks will not be banned from speculating with state debt and also the banning of CDS trading will only become effective in November 2012, so in yet another year during which the banking industry will probably have eaten up all of the 2 trillion EFSF cake. EU Council, EU Commission and MEPs who failed to be tough with banks immediately will be left to blow out the candles.

As the 50% participation of banks does inlcude the principal as well as the accumulated interest payments the banks demand from Greece, this means that de-facto the banks do not lose any cent from the amounts they once invested in Greek bonds. But, very comfortably, the banks will now be able to sell their toxic Greek bonds to ESFS while the ECB is from now on bound not to buy up state bonds any longer from a state, but from any bank! The loss of interest will then be compensated by the ESFS that will have to cover the first 20% of such loss.

Thirdly, the much celebrated increase of the – nominal – capital requirement to 9% comes as along as a joke as long as "BASEL III" remains in effect. International regulations known as BASEL I and BASEL II that existed since end of the 1980ies required a minimum of 8% cash reserve for credits being issued by banks. In 2010 BASEL III, that favoured private banks and major corporations while making it more and more difficult for SMEs to re-finance themselves, came into force.

Naïve observers might conclude that with an 8% minimum capital requirement a bank could issue a loan of 12.50 € from every Euro it holds on deposit. If a bank holds 30 billion Euros on deposit it could hand out loans or gamble with toxic assets for 375 billion Euros one would think. More wouldn't be possible unless the bank either increases it's share capital or thesauruses gains or issues new stocks. But, the reality check reveals that above assumption is totally wrong as Deutsche Bank AG for example in the year 2007, when the current crisis began on 11th August, held 30 billion Euros on deposit but span a wheel of some 2 trillion Euros. That's why the ESFS – insurance needs to cover exactly that exposure.

This was possible by reducing it's capital requirement by loopholes in the BASEL II regulation that allow a bank to decide themselves whether a loan or financial instrument such as a derivative is considered risky or safe. Depending on this judgement at the sole discretion of the bank, a reduced capital requirement may apply. For assets or guarantees and instruments for banks in OECD countries as well as AAA rated investment institutions such as insurance companies a reduced risk level of 20% of the 8% minimum capital requirement is being considered sufficient.

In other words, when the totally trustworthy Lehman Brothers investment bank (R.I.P.) took a loan of 1 million Euros from another bank said credit line was only considered a risk of 200,000 € on the active side of the balance sheet of the lending bank for which it only had to fulfil the 8% minimum capital requirement in this case 16,000 € which only amounts to 1.6% of the 1 million Euros.

This may illustrate why the surprising collapse of this honourable institution had the potential of a financial Tsunami because the logic counter-calculation results in a multiplication factor of 62.5 meaning that with 1 € of on deposit 62.5 € of credit can absolutely legally be generated between banks and financial institutions rated A by the partners in crime, the so called rating agencies.

It becomes clear why the real economy has been hit that bad because of this insane mechanism when one realises that BASEL I had ruled that credit lines handed out to companies had to be valued at 100% risk-level making such less lucrative and more expensive for banks. This is why all private banks reduced their engagement in the classical core business task any bank should have: to supply the real economy with liquidity.

The new capital requirement of 9% for banks as the EU Council demanded this morning will only become effective if the tricks previously applied and known as "BASEL I, II and III" are no longer an option. But, that would mean that for instance Deutsche Bank AG which still only holds a core capital of 30 billion Euros won't be able to stem 2,000 billion Euros that it shows on the balance sheet any longer. That, indeed, would be an intriguing thought, wouldn't it?

Following the decision of the German Bundestag to support the EFSF rather sooner than later doomed the Euro-zone's real economy and eventually also in Germany. Since beginning to get "rescued" Greece accumulated 20 billion Euros in additional debt, also because the real economy collapses under draconic austerity measurements brought in by the 'Troika' and, secondly, because the government in Athens still has to re-finance itself through private banks who pocket exorbitant interest payments.

Even Germany would be bankrupt within a split of a second if the federal government all of a sudden had to pay 10 or 15 % interest for it's obligations. Interest rates are skyrocketing when investment bankers and rating agencies decide to lower a country's rating.

Public banks should instead of private banks be put into the position to re-finance the states. Of course, there shouldn't be anything like endless credit-lines. But, in order to consolidate public finances one ought to finish with the European-wide tax-dumping competition that led to a death – spiral. Instead, a harmonised tax system not only involving VAT but foremost corporate taxes and the taxation of excessive wealth would secure the funding of governments.

Mr Barroso's jumping onto ATTAC's bandwagon comes along like a joke when one looks at the estimated 55 billion Euros per year that such a financial transaction tax would raise. In any case, such tax would be priced-in and not do any harm to speculation.

What would also be needed is the re-capitalisation of banks that because of their misbehaviour as well as the debt cut got into difficulties. Those banks, of course, would then be owned by the public hand and serve the real economy by handing out loans and taking deposits.

For issuing a banking licence to the EFSF one would only need a single decision by the EU member states which should by the same token decide to close down the casino and introduce a European-wide wealth tax.

On top of that it would be required to shut down the casino and not only impose a little levy or financial transaction tax, an idea that EU Commission President José Manuel Barroso borrowed from ATTAC. It is absurd to let speculators make huge profits by risky gambling and whenever it goes wrong have the taxpayer foot the bill.

And, one should also repatriate the funds that went astray by multi millionaires who hide their illegitimate trillions in Switzerland and other black-holes of the offshore markets. Over the past years not only the public debts exploded but also private wealth and both for the same reason. If one wants to reduce debt one also needs to reduce privately accumulated wealth. The key is to identify the right ones who defrauded society by their ruthless greed.

The opposite is happening, though. EU institutions are obviously willing to pay for being fooled, transpired at the beginning of January 2012. Double Dipping is considered unethical according to international business guidelines but EU institutions ignore such standards as they allow Deutsche Bank AG, Credit Suisse S.A. and Société Générale S.A. not only to 'advise' the EFSF in placing freshly emitted papers which already amounts to letting monkeys mind a banana plant but even pay the aforementioned institutions huge fees.

Deutsche Bank AG which together with Goldman Sachs to a large degree is indirectly responsible for the Greek disaster as the institutions were issuing and trading Credit Default Swaps and by this blew up the Greek state debt so that it grew by 20 billion *after* the rescuing had commenced, had also advised the EFSF in previous emissions for five and ten years. Now, the

EFSF issued 3 year – papers for 3 billion Euros proceeds of which shall benefit Portugal and Ireland.

It is especially delicate to have Deutsche Bank AG pocket huge consultancy fees as all the smart investment bankers from Frankfurt are doing is protecting their own exposure. That's why Allianz AG and Deutsche Bank AG had construed the guarantee mechanism in a way that it covers up to 2 trillion Euros, the exact figure one finds on the balance sheet of Deutsche. EU institutions either don't get it or are partners in crime to pay for being fooled.

EU internal market Commissioner Joaquin Almunia is said to block the planned merger of NYSE Euronext and Deutsche Börse AG in February over fears that a derivative trading monopoly would be created. Well, the sick model itself is not being debated only it's structure, so Deutsche Bank AG can continue conning public banks and state governments while Deutsche Bank AG during the crisis year 2012 reports a pre-tax profit of 5.4 billion Euros, mainly made by it's investment banking division.

That's why activists from 'Occupy Frankfurt' and 'Occupy Deutsche Bank' together with many other Occupy-movements in the US and around the globe held simultaneous demonstrations on 15th January 2012.

Money printing license

Another funny idea of EU Commission President José Manuel Barroso has been to label Euro-bonds "stability-bonds" which implies that Brussels can dictate member states how to govern themselves. It would have been interesting to watch which parliament would surrender it's classical rights, especially the right to control the budget and fiscal authority, first. Euro bonds, however these will be called, would not have solved the crisis but intensify it as the austerity programs will become a predicament for the implementation of a regime of 'technocrats' from Athens to Rome and Lisbon who will push through brutal cuts amid an institutionalisation of the recession provoked by declining tax revenue

A radical reform of the financial markets is overdue that would force banking business back to it's roots. For two reasons the global banking system in the past didn't behave like an uncontrollable money spinning wheel of fortune that it has become nowadays. First of all, every bank had to make sure it maintained it's liquidity and for that reason lodged a certain amount of the deposits it took at the central bank. In case the bank wanted to expand their business it could only do so in the frame in which the central bank granted a credit-line.

Secondly, all banks, in order to guarantee their own solvency had to back up their exposure by some core capital, a method by which many smaller banks still operate even today. But, the 'global players' of the financial markets are in different spheres. "Investment banking" divisions became ever more creative when inventing ever more complex "innovative financial instruments" in order to enable them to create liquidity virtually out of nothing. Under present regulations, which the EU Commission does not even consider to be cancerous, banks can create more or less innovative core capital out of artificial transactions that in reality are nothing but self-feeding credit-lines. Assuming that an "investment bank" that somehow belongs to a major bank lodges at a subsidiary of said bank 1 million US Dollars and in exchange for that receives a credit-line of 62.5 million US Dollars at the inter-bank – rate of 3%. In order to guarantee the interest payments the "investment bank" buys US treasury bonds in the amount of 32.5 million US Dollars that are bearing an interest of 5%.

30 million are left aside over which the "investment bank" has full control and the return on any investment out of such will be net and is a risk-free present. Thanks to this financial perpetuum mobile banks and other financial institutions can finance an ever greater volume of credit-lines which feed a blasé of ever more "innovative" financial vehicles that have no meaning and stand in no relation to the real economy. On top of that these "investment banks" can sell to each other and buy from another these financial instruments at ever higher rates and by this have ever bigger profit margins. Imagine how two banks create on that basis more and more credit-volume and for this buy stocks of a major corporation, let's say steel company Arcelor. Assuming that Bank A sold the share from Bank B yesterday for 100 Dollars it buys it back today for 150 Dollars. Bank B made a profit of 50 Dollars and can revalue all other Arcelor shares it holds 50% higher. If Bank B holds 1000 of these the profit on paper would be 50,000 Dollars.

Miraculously richer Bank B buys same shares from Bank A for 250 Dollars leaving 100 Dollars of net profit with Bank A. If Bank A also held 1000 of those shares the profit on paper would be 100,000 Dollars. This game between the two banks can go on in perpetuity and will make both banks bigger, more powerful, pay bonuses to their managers and make their shareholders richer although nothing is being produced and no service being provided.

It is not only that some virtual funds are being moved from one bank to the other, it is that income is being generated which is last but not least be recorded in statistics as "growth". If one got a money-printing machine in one's basement one can of course pay out huge dividends and bonuses especially if one doesn't have to fear that the police once comes to raid the premises. In today's reality the EU Commission's and member states government's civil servants only show up at the money-printers in order to repair their machines in case of a paper jam as we have seen during the ongoing financial crisis. But, the most crazy monetary theory nowadays seems to be the quantity theory of money which mainstream economists and central banker still uphold although it is obsolete given the facts we all see in front of us.

According to the theory the value of a unit of money on paper (in other words those currencies that do not derive their value from precious metals such as gold or silver) stands in relation to the amount of goods available for purchase. Let's assume that all that is on the market are 1000 loafs of bread and the people who can buy nothing but these loafs altogether have 1000 Dollars. The quantity theory would assume that one bread would cost 1 Dollar. And, let's assume that a helicopter throws another 1000 Dollars from sky down to the people who would now have 2000 Dollars. If there are still only 1000 loafs of bread on the market, the quantity theory assumes that the price of bread will double.

The model only works because one can only buy bread with the money, but if there was also a financial market the people could buy from the money thrown down onto them from the helicopter stocks from the bakery which is an extremely likely scenario if the money thrown from the helicopter is caught by only one person. According to the logic of the quantity theory he would have to buy alone 500 loafs but what would he want with such an amount of bread? Instead, if the stocks of the bakery are rising because he bought those stocks this could lead more people to purchase stocks of the bread company instead of the bread. In that case the stocks will further rise but the bread-price now has to fall despite the double amount of money being available should all 1000 loafs still find a buyer. In essence this is the development of the past decades. Banks are flooding as "money-helicopters" the market but as these funds predominantly reach those people who already have more than enough, the goods markets are only marginally affected.

As long as these virtual funds do not rain down on the good's market of the real economy, no inflation will affect the man in the street. Instead, this money is used for buying stocks and shares or financial "products" and in this field really creates inflation but on financial markets one doesn't use this term. Here one refers to "gains" that are said to reflect a positive economic development. But, in real terms these trillions of monetary wealth are the results of a snowball system that will ultimately collapse when the money-helicopter doesn't come anymore.

Really splendid, indeed!

British Prime Minister David Cameron literally shot himself into his own knee when demanding to be allowed to continue spinning the virtual reality casino's wheel in "the City". The European partners may reconsider returning British gold reserves at a favourable rate of let's say 1,600 US Dollars should Mr Cameron wish to repatriate the assets the government of Anthony Blair had lodged with the European Central Bank (ECB) in 1998 at the rate of 288 Dollars in an attempt to have a foot in the door. About Two Thirds of British gold reserves where brought to Frankfurt at a much lower rate than what it would be worth today.

But, if Great-Britain is going to continue to cause huge economic damage to other EU member state's economy by upholding an unsustainable 'business model' one may think in other capital cities that one should return the gold at the rate of 1998 and not at today's rate and by this compensate the loss of economic capacity created by the financial excesses of "The City"

As the Anglo-Saxon model is based on the so called Hedge Funds Industry that generates money out of hot air and uses such funds to buy-up real economy enterprises across the world, one may understand that some countries do not like to see their industries become subject to takeovers financed by virtual money

Germany only very late, under Social Democratic Chancellor Gerhard Schröder, allowed British and American Hedge Funds to operate in it's territory.

France has always been guided by protectionism.

Especially in the UK this money – spinning "industry" has advanced to the major business and has successively replaced the manufacturing and innovative industries in Great-Britain.

Instead of producing industries, physical labour and manufacturing entities nowadays 'smart, young, urban, professionals' generate money without working or without any relevant manufacturing being involved. No sweat, no blood.

It is comfortable for a nation to lay back and print money while others still work and produce the goods one can import, but it is not a model for the future. In fact, since the Roman Empire, no such system survived in history for long. The decline comes along with a rising brutality, barbarism and degeneration

Hedge Funds existed in various forms in history but in 1966 they were given their name. Until the end of 2007, the year when the final collapse of our financial system became irreversible, all 9,000 Hedge Funds gambled with about 2.7 trillion Dollars.

The top 100 of these betting offices flip over some 1.8 trillion Dollars every day. Most of the Hedge Funds only exist for a few years, more than 60% of them disappear within 3 years.

Among the biggest and most well-known are the British MAN Group, JP Morgan Asset Management and Goldman Sachs Asset Management and are directly linked to the broker houses of the same name. The underlying idea of the hedging is to buy undervalued commercial paper and to simultaneously borrow overvalued and to sell those after a certain time.

These transactions can be reversed after a specific time-span making it possible for the Hedge Fund to generate profit entirely independently from the development at the stock market.

Over the decades since 1949 when the first of these transactions had been observed by Fortune Magazine this method has been refined and became ever more sophisticated. But, the speculation is still kind of the same. The classical sense of the term "Hedging" doesn't really apply anymore as it used to be a securitized transaction in which the currency exchange risk was eliminated by buying a certain currency at a fixed price in the future

Today's Hedge Funds don't securitize or insure anything but speculate at the very edge. The effects are usually enhanced by enormous amounts of capital from outside the company, in most cases borrowed funds. In 1998, the Long Term Capital Management (LTCM) Hedge Fund collapsed as the relation between capital stock and loans has been 1:20. In reality LTCM controlled 5 billion Dollars but traded for 125 billion. When a miss-speculation hit the fund the entire global finance system suddenly was at risk

The two Hedge Funds which sank the Investment Bank Bear Stearns worked with a ratio of 1:30 meaning that for every Dollar of own capital an additional 30 Dollars of external funds were raised. By employing this tool smallest changes in rates could make huge profits. LTCM indeed managed to realize 40% annual return on investment at the beginning. Usually, Hedge Funds have a certain preference which they speculate in, like so called 'Global Macro Funds' which are betting on changes in the macro-economic field, such as rising or falling exchange rates or the development of interest rates or Hausse or Baisse at the stock market, or even a crash.

Even with the latter a lot of money can be earned as we could observe in Summer 2007 when the "Lahnde Capital" hedge fund which had speculated on a devaluation of the sub-prime mortgage papers, so called "Asset Backed Securities" (ABS) that ruined many other Hedge Funds, made miraculously 1000% in profit. It is vitally important to bet on something unpredictable, go against the tide and by this maximize the profit. Or loose, phenomenally, too. It is like on a black jack or Roulette table. Betting on horses is safer as one could at least observe the previous races and conclude from the performance of horse and jockey what the possible result could be.

But to conclude that after a rally at the stock markets a period of slower growth would follow could be fatally wrong. It could be the opposite which we have observed during the dotcom bubbles of the Clinton-Gore years and the real estate hype that absorbed a lot of the liquidity when the Clinton-Gore bubbles burst in the wake of September 11.

The next bubble that has been created was the alternative energy hype for which the Climate Change talk of EU Commission and member state governments provided for the perfect backdrop. Of course Climate Change is a real threat but one should also look at who benefits from a hype. It is remarkable for UK Independence Party leader Nigel Farage, once a boy of "The City" himself, to advocate British independence and one may ask what it shall be based on as apart from investment banking there is not much left in Great-Britain which could feed it's citizens.

The British government under Prime Minister David Cameron is now confronted with the fall out of Thatcherism and it will be interesting to watch how the Tories and Liberal Democrats will solve their crisis.

Nothing really changed

When the Polish EU presidency and the European Parliament in October 2011 clinched a deal on the regulation beefing up standards and requirements for the practices of short selling and trading in credit default swaps (CDS), a financial product insuring against default, the sky was lit with hope that our leaders had understood and something would finally change.

But, the rules that are said to impose much more transparency, increase the powers of the EU's financial watchdog and virtually ban certain CDS trades, thereby making speculation on a country's default more difficult won't become effective before November 2012.

Immediately, conservative British politicians, also those of UK Independence Party (UKIP) cited an attack on "The City" that they claim is vital to the British economy.

It seems, EU Commission, EU Council, member state governments and the majority of MEPs are either too weak, not competent or not willing to apply radical changes in order to avert the worst.

It is hard to believe, that these people think that we got all the time of the world to solve the problems we got trapped in by investment banks, hedge funds and speculators who managed to make it look as if it was not their fault but the (de-) fault of the nation state.

It is not good enough to regulate CDS trading a little bit. One should rather rethink the legality of such financial instruments other than for guaranteeing import-export transactions, which today account for less than 2% of all CDS – trade volume.

And, on top of that, some transactions do not require a minimum capital, such as those credit-lines handed out to OECD – states and those guaranteed by a CDS. When in 2007 the German Hypo Real Estate (HRE), that later cost the German taxpayer an exorbitant amount of money, took over the Dublin based German-owned financier DEPFA whose 'speciality' had been to hand out loans to governments, the Activa position on the balance sheet of HRE got blown up by 240 billion Euros, but the risk-weighted Activa only increased by 34 billion Euros.

It has proven to be illusory to believe that an AAA rated guarantor is able to have the required cash deposit to cover the risk of his "Swap".

When two banks guarantee each other commercial papers they are in the end better off in terms of capital requirements although the risk that they hold has not vanished at all. These 'Cross transactions' are for that reason the favourite business for banks and consequently led to the blowing up of the CDS-market.

It also happened many times that a bank had inadvertently insured it's own guarantees at another bank, in other words obliged itself in case of default to compensate the other bank for the loss. "It is", the American author Nassim Taleb wrote in October 2009 in the Financial Times "as if one bought an insurance policy for the Titanic from someone on the Titanic."

In real terms there is no other market but the global financial market that has virtually nothing in common with the traditional understanding of what a "market" is. Mainstream economic theory defines a market as being a place for trading goods and services and where prices are built by competition bearing an impact on production output and demand.

Key to a functioning market is that no actor or participant, also not a buyer can have a dominating position granting him the sole discretion to determine prices or conditions of a certain good. But, exactly the opposite is the case on the world's financial "markets". Almost every major investment decision by the investment banking oligopolies is being dictated by a dozen players.

Only less than 20 financial institutions are allowed to gamble on the golden floors of the primary markets where the trillion-fold volumes of financial "vehicles" are being engineered prior to their release to the secondary market and the ordinary investors. This privileged 'pole' position of the investment bankers is guaranteed by law and also these so called 'primary dealers' are exempt from many regulations that apply to all other market participants.

Whoever wishes to emit a large amount of stocks or corporate bonds anywhere on the world inevitably requires the service of a financial institution of which only a few are allowed to provide such.

Likewise is the sovereign debt, as long as it is being financed by bonds, Dollar by Dollar or Euro by Euro through the hands of this cartel that also invented any financial "innovation" like derivatives and other useless money-spinning tools that today cause such a headache.

On top of that, the actors of the primary market are able to manipulate the placements in such a way that most of the risk rests with the investors while they have a guaranteed profit. Seven major banks are sharing between them 90% of the derivative's market with an estimated volume of 200 trillion Dollars while the CDS-market that before the crisis accounted for 60 trillion Dollars is only controlled by 5 giants: J.P. Morgan, Goldman Sachs, Morgan Stanley, Barclays Group and Deutsche Bank.

The latter became the market-leader among those majors that also dominate the futures, swaps, options and credit derivates market by their oligopoly and enjoy also a privileged position in obtaining information which is crucial as we have seen in case of the toxic American mortgage assets. While the "stupid money" of the outsiders still bought those papers the investment bankers already knew what they had wrapped there and started to bet on the collapse of the market.

Rating agencies in conspiracy with the oligopoly contribute in market manipulations that for the wealthiest clients of the investment banks are advantageous but leave the ordinary citizen who put his life time savings into jeopardy at risk.

At present, one observes a stereo-type debate between the UK and Continental Europe. Typically for the discussion related to the financial transaction tax both sides miss the point, the EU Commission in believing that this would change anything by making transactions less risky when 57 billion out of 8,000 billion are collected and the defenders of financial capitalism in trying to make their opponents believe that it was impossible for 'first world' countries to shut down tax havens in banana republics

The question who will feed Britain once the financial bubbles created by "The City" burst is yet to be answered as Prime Ministers Thatcher and Blair both did their part in de-industrialising Great-Britain and putting everything behind an "industry" that produces nothing but hot air leaving the agricultural sector have less than 1% share in British GDP.

With 67% of the UK's GNP being indirectly dependent on 'The City' and it's money spinning wheels of fortune, the nervousness at the Conservatives is understandable. Their system is at stake. Having shifted their manufacturing base to China and the IT business to India, the British have hardly anything to revert to should the financial casino shut down.

But since the G 20 summit of 2009 nothing really threatened the Anglo-Saxon – model.

Too big to jail

While in Greece German flags are burning as many citizens there believe that it was solely the German banks and government's fault that the country drowned in debts closer scrutiny reveals that in fact also German banks (except for Deutsche Bank AG, of course) got fooled by so called "investment banks" mainly situated in New York.

That's why Occupy Frankfurt activists and Occupy Wall Street protesters expressed their solidarity with each other in video messages and simultaneous demonstrations held over the past weekend.

It will probably never be possible to fully establish how much of the trash papers on the balance sheet of public banks in Germany, such as IKB and the Landesbanken, a bill the taxpayer has to foot, has passed through the hands of a smart investment banker of Deutsche Bank AG. But, it is evident that it had been huge amounts.

"Along with Goldman, Deutsche Bank was the leading market maker in abstruse mortgage derivatives"[2], writes the former investment banker Michael Lewis in his book "The Big Short",

"Abstruse mortgage derivatives" had been the papers based on American mortgage CDOs and ABS that plummeted since the beginning of the crisis on 11th August 2007.

Back to Wall Street where everything begun: the head of Deutsche Bank AG's Asset Backed Securities (ABS) division, a very young man by the name of Greg Lippmann generated a profit of one billion Euros for Deutsche Bank AG in 2007, the year the crisis began.

Greg Lippmann had, as the German financial paper Handelsblatt asserted, as early as in 2005 been handed an analysis that predicted the collapse of the US's mortgage bonds market but that had not been reason enough for Deutsche Bank AG to at least reduce the acceleration of their engagement in that market segment. Even worse, Mr. Lippmann had the chuzpe to at

---

2   Michael Lewis, The Big Short, Inside the Doomsday Machine, New York 2010, S. 78

the same time orchestrate the billion-fold bets anticipating the upcoming crash that later made him become a star at Wall Street.

That makes it clear that "Deutsche Bank AG didn't even bother bundling dubious American mortgage papers and selling these to their clients as long as their own portfolio remained clean", the conservative German Handelsblatt wrote assuming that "exorbitant commissions had been paid".[3]

Interestingly, Michael Lewis describes in his book how a meeting arranged for by Mr Lippmann with Hedge Fund managers proceeded during which he convinced the latter to bet against the Deutsche Bank AG – supported Mortgage Backed Securities (MBS).

Deutsche Bank AG obviously wanted to become a mediator between the 'Long' and 'Short' side of this transaction so in other words Deutsche Bank AG wanted to earn a commission on selling on trash papers.

As it was clear that these papers had been construed in a way that a default was imminent one of the hedge fund managers asked Mr Lippmann in disbelief who was "the idiot on the other side?"

The answer of Greg Lippmann had been remarkably simple: *"Düsseldorf. Stupid Germans. They take rating agencies seriously. The believe in the rules."*[4]

One of the participating investors noted later: "However corrupt you think this industry is, it's worse."[5]

But, who where those stupid Germans from Düsseldorf? IKB and WestLB have their seats there. A lot is speaking for them being the major buyers for the toxic assets Deutsche Bank AG created by betting on the default of papers that at the same time was praising in front of IKB and WestLB.

One should always become suspicious when a German Landesbank is trying to jump onto the bandwagon.

Several transaction between IKB and Deutsche Bank AG are evident and it can only be seen as cynical that Deutsche Bank AG betted against the same paper it had just sold onto IKB and the Landesbanken. Later, it transpired, that Deutsche Bank AG was behind the EU Commissions drive

3   Handelsblatt 8.2.2008
4   Lewis, a.a.O. S. 93
5   Lewis, a.a.O. S. 103

to privatise the German Landesbanken so any conspiracy theory is at hand in such a case.

The fact that Deutsche Bank AG was behind several transactions with IKB is evident as Deutsche also acted as trustee in some of the transactions utilising the infamous Rhineland-Funding-Conduits to which it extended the credit-lines without which IKB never had been put into a position to by the toxic assets. At that time Deutsche Bank - CEO Josef Ackermann recently admitted that "it is true that we at some occasions had a different understanding of the market than IKB".

The last act in the IKB tragedy went as follows: Deutsche Bank AG – CEO Josef Ackermann, whose office was raided a few days ago by German criminal police, cut the credit-line for IKB and rang the president of the German federal agency for financial supervision (BaFin), Jochen Sanio. He told him that the small bank soon would be bankrupt and also had bundles of dubious commercial paper in their books.

After putting down the receiver Mr Ackermann reportedly quickly orchestrated the short-selling of a bundle of IKB stocks so Deutsche Bank AG still made a bit of money on the final decline of IKB.

In total, the German taxpayer had to pay 10 billion Euros.

The highly reputable German Professor Walter Perron, an expert in criminal law and economics, asserted the behaviour of Deutsche Bank AG – employees and management in regards to the IKB case as outright fraud.

Also a former federal judge, Axel Boetticher, demanded in 2008 that federal prosecutors should investigate the case. Same should also apply to the Landesbanken who also got mislead by Deutsche Bank AG and their Wall Street – partners in crime, some of them reputable "investment" banks.

II

BUTLER TO PAY FOR PARTY?!

**Not leftist, conservative governments pile up debts,
but the latter make it look vice versa**

Banks managed to put blame onto governments

Now that we see the 3%-er rescue the 30%-er, the question arises whose debts we are talking about?! A study by McKinsey (Mapping Global Financial Markets) proves that today's public debts aren't primary the result of a classical Keynesian stimulus cycle that had countered an economic downturn.

The primary deficit of industrialised nations between 1975 and 1997 has been constantly negative. Only for the time after 1997 an up and down of the state indebtedness can be noticed that would match the classical Keynesian theory of stirring growth by state interventions. But, a closer scrutiny reveals that the debts were hardly used for public investments or for stimulation of the economy by an increased consumption. Not leftist, "socialist" governments piled up these debts by generously distributing social benefits, but it is conservative or right wing governments that behave like Santa Claus – to the rich. That's where debts on the one side of the balance sheet and wealth on the other come from.

Truth is that states got indebted because of tax evasion of major corporations and banks who used every legal loophole provided by the political class. In Germany, especially, the corporate tax reforms of the Red-Green coalition government under Gerhard Schröder forced public households into debt in order to make good on what had been paid by companies.

At times a tax dumping competition between all EU member states was well and alive in granting tax incentives to rich multinational corporations or offering ever more favourable tax breaks and low corporate tax schemes. Funnily, it was not Ireland but Germany which had the lowest corporate tax in the EU although German media always branded Ireland to be a tax haven. But, as there was no stimulation coming from the state in form of any Keynesian enhancement this resulted in private consumer credits skyrocketing. This kind of privatized Keynesianism brought the US down.

In Europe, all of the Eastern European member states engaged in the same unhealthy economic policy of getting their citizens indebted in order to finance private consumption that showed double digit growth rates in retail business. Retail business was the only sector that grew in Eastern Europe and it grew by consuming Western European, mostly German and French, goods. Germany produces and exports mainly capital goods (technology) while France provided for consumer goods (cheese and wine). Both countries had a good share in the Eastern European markets while the UK was left out, partly because their retailers were refinancing themselves outside the Euro-zone and suffered from an exchange rate disadvantage but also because British industries, like the US American, hardly produce anything.

Most of British GDP is directly and indirectly dependent on "The City", i.e. the ruthless 'investment' banks, private equity firms and hedge funds that brought down the economy in many countries by trading virtual reality tokens called derivates and commercial debt obligations (CDOs) which could hardly be backed up by any real production output.

It has become obvious now that the bulk of private loans are bad and will never be repaid. To the contrary it would be economically disastrous if these debts were to be paid back as tightening the belt over a long period will diminish consumption on a worldwide level.

On top of that it is clear that the majority of families who got into the mortgage - "house-trap" will never be able to pay back these debts anyhow while it also doesn't help to take away the houses from them as they are already in negative equity. It would just be extraordinarily cruel and inhumane to confiscate a house, auction it under negative equity principle and leave the family with all those debts. This applies to US American households as well as Spanish, Portuguese, Irish and Eastern Europeans. These debts that are to a large degree owned by banks, insurance and finance companies can only be written off. Logically, on the other side, wealth that has been created out of those debts also needs to be declared null and void.

Based on the Ameco database, the development function of the public debt shows beyond doubt that national debt is not a primary result of a classical Keyenesian stirring of the economy during times of economic downturns. Instead the primary deficit of industrialised nations between 1975 and 1997 had been constantly negative. Only after that time a constant up and down in government debt can be noticed which speaks for the theory of stirring the economy but with steadily increasing total government debt.

So who are the beneficiaries who suck taxpayer's blood? The Merrill Lynch World Wealth report 2010 speaks of 10 million high net-worth individuals (HNWI) world wide whose wealth has grown in 2009 by 18.9% to now 39 trillion US Dollars despite the financial crisis.

For the first time ever in the Asia-Pacific region there are as many HNWI as in Europe. 53.5% of them live in USA, Germany and Japan

Wealth of all European dollar millionaires in 2009 alone rose by 14.2% to 9.4 trillion US Dollars. In the US a plus of 17.8% let it rise to 10.7 trillion but the biggest ever growth could be noticed in the Asia-Pacific region: plus 30.9% or in absolute numbers 9.7 trillion US Dollars.

A side effect of the Tsunami and the following nuclear catastrophe in Japan will be that the Dollar will decline further once the Japanese rich will have to sell their Dollar obligations as the funds will be needed for reconstruction.

But, such depreciation of the Dollar is in the interest of the US: instead of quantitative easing that was to end in June 2011 will gently let the air out of the bubble. The Federal Reserve (FED) would have had it much easier to prolong the QE2 phase and buy up treasury bonds at a much lower rate and by his get out of the claws of the dragon.

A depreciation if not decline of the Dollar, as much as it may be in the interest of the US, will be a film the Chinese don't want to watch. Interestingly in this context is the fact that two weeks prior to the disaster in Japan, Pimco, a daughter of German insurance giant Allianz AG, one of the largest hedge funds had already shifted it's assets out of the US Dollar and by this rescued some 300 billion, as if their management had known what was to happen.

While East Asia will be licking it's wounds, the US might recover and win back some of it's financial sovereignty, if, for instance, a few more natural disasters play into their hands.

The Greek Patient

In the meantime, the EURO-zone is dissolving and it is also because the German taxpayer's reluctance to shoulder all debts is understandable.

German Chancellor Angela Merkel's political future had been in jeopardy as she had considerable difficulty to win the German Bundestag's approval for the enhanced European rescue mechanism (EFSF) by her own majority. She was so desperate to get it pushed through against a growing number of dissidents from her own party that she accepted to rely on votes from the oppositional Social Democrats and Greens, the smallest fraction in the German parliament. In the end, Mrs Merkel managed to have all but 15 votes of her governing coalition behind her covering up the dissent and unease of liberal-conservative members of the lower house of the German parliament.

Social Democrats and Greens were demonstrating their pro-EU stance as both parties are eager to regain power in 2013 for which they might need support from Socialist party DIE LINKE which opposed the bank-shareholder - rescuing mechanism known as "EFSF" citing unfair burdens for taxpayers as well as brutal social cuts that go hand in hand with stringent austerity imposed by the Troika.

When talking about the Greek debts causing the first state-bankruptcy in Europe after WWII one hardly hears anything about those who benefited from the accumulation of said debt. It is a known fact that Deutsche Bank AG, Goldman Sachs, Nathan Meyer Rothschild, HSBC, Lazard Freres SAS and others had made billions by speculating with Greek bonds and Credit Default Swaps (CDS) and later were employed by the Greek government as "advisors" to select the raisins in the pie that need to be privatised in order to fulfil the Troika's demands.

Then, ALPHA BANK A.E., N M Rothschild & Sons Ltd. and UBS Ltd. got appointed by the Greek government to sell off all table silver. Of course, all these banks have rich clients who might want to buy the profitable pieces of Greece's assets.

As corrupt as all this already sounds, this is not the bottom of the barrel, yet. One may wonder where all these debts came from and why Greece's population was not incredibly rich (except for their upper class). Closer scrutiny reveals that Greece chronically suffered from a negative trade balance. That is not a big surprise either. Greece imported more than it exported. Not new. And, like almost all Eastern and South – Eastern EU member states Greece piled up debts because of an enormous trade imbalance resulting from consumer goods.

All EU member states (except for Czech Republic) who joined in 2004 were forced to import top-shelf products from the West while their own industries ran out of business or were taken over by Western companies. But, in case of Greece all this wouldn't add up. Greece did not notice such a rise in consumption than the newcomers from Eastern Europe did. Greece imported something else that was far more expensive and that could hardly be 'consumed': arms.

At the same time when Greece's debts skyrocketed, Germany under the Social-Democratic-Green government of Gerhard Schröder and Joseph ("Joschka") Fischer, doubled it's arms export. Most of the weapons were exported to Greece. One may fear that some of these arms the government in Athens might find useful in fighting off the citizen's revolt against the Troika's torture-tools.

So it has not been the average Greek citizen who indulged in consumption of luxury goods and by this created the tremendous debts that EU and IMF pretend had to be bailed out for which a harsh austerity program is to be imposed leading to brutal wage cuts and barbaric social cuts. But although hundreds of billions are being pumped into the system, through the means of the EFSF, Greece's, Ireland's, Portugal's and Spain's debts are not shrinking but still growing. Since it become subject to being "rescued" Greece added some 20 billion Euros in debts to it's balance sheet.

Instead of dumping ever more billions on the graveyard of the financial markets one should grant governments direct access to loans from the European Central Bank (ECB) at low interest rates by this finishing with the perversion of the system in which private banks get a credit line for next to nothing from the ECB handing out loans to states for an exorbitant interest that is artificially fuelled by speculation and a conspiracy between banks, speculators and rating agencies. Instead, the programs presented by the Troika are not aid but killer-programs. Greece will never be able to pay back it's debts. Everyone knows this, so why, one may wonder, are our elected leaders so eager to prolong the death of the Greek patient?

The answer is easy: the political leadership wants to put the entire burden of Greece's inevitable insolvency onto taxpayer's shoulders. The later Greek will be declared bankrupt, the better for institutional investors, banks, hedge funds and speculators and the more expensive for the taxpayer. On 8th February 2012 German news had it that Germany was well prepared for a greek default, meaning that Deutsche Bank AG probably got rid off it's last toxic assets by selling it to the European Central Bank (ECB).

Already in autumn of 2011 a 50% cut of the Greek debts cost the German taxpayers 14 billion Euros, but German banks, insurance companies and other speculators would "loose" only 6 billion Euros, reason why the majority of German citizens reject to dump more money in that black hole of the financial market. One and a half years ago this relation would have been reversed.

It is clear that the international banking federation under Deutsche Bank AG – CEO Josef Ackermann had been the mastermind behind the Euro-Group's plan for exchanging Greek bonds when releasing the next tranche for Greece in October 2011 because that plan makes sure that when in future the Greek taxpayers can't service the new bonds any longer, the international financial mafia will sit on dry land already and won't be forced to write off not a single Euro.

There is no such thing as a rescue mechanism for the EURO, but for the banksters and speculators who brought about the trouble. The financial mafia pockets every Euro that Greece receives from the EFSF and IMF. It is, of course, understandable that people like Mr Ackermann have an interest in keeping the public billion-Euro-pipelines afloat, but EU Commission, Euro-Group and Council obviously forgot whose interests they ought to represent.

But, what usually gets forgotten about when talking about the debts of the "PIGS" (Brussels-vocabulary for Portugal, Ireland, Greece & Spain), is the wealth that is standing on the other side of the balance sheet. Not only public debts exploded over the past few years, also privately accumulated wealth did so, and both for the same reasons, firstly because of the EU-wide tax-dumping competition that EU Commission and every member state government entered into and secondly because of the bank-rescuing.

Public hands needed to increase their debt while corporate taxes were lowered by every single deregulation and harmonisation wave that came from Brussels over the years. The bonds EU member states issued for covering their budgets after major corporations were given legal ways for tax evasion were bought by institutional and private investors. This is why the debts of the states are the wealth of the ultra-rich-high-net-worth individuals (UHNWIs as Merrill Lynch calls them) in our society who own banks and hedge funds.

Not only Warren Buffett and George Sorros, legendary speculators, advocate what no democratically elected government or parliament ever dared to call for: a wealth tax for the UHNWIs. That, indeed, would be the only way how capitalism could be rescued and that this is in the interest of the upper class could hardly be doubted. At that time Italian minister-president Silvio Berlusconi is not the only one who did not understand that. That's why he had to go.

This does not speak against a radical debt-cut but against a system in which a few investment bankers, hedge fund – junkies and insane rating – analysts who had already provoked the crash in September 2008 by their chronically erroneous conclusions dictate to sovereign, democratically elected governments their profit maximization conditions.

When Socialism collapsed 23 years ago, it accepted to be dictated the conditions by the winners. Now, that Capitalism finds itself in a similar position, it's protagonists still believe they can dictate how they shall be rescued. That is absurd as it not only leads to the bankruptcy of entire states, but also to the end of democracy.

Athena's head on the block

At that time European Parliament President Jerzy Buzek had his own way to comment on the Greek crisis. "Sometimes there is no choice, and only painful reforms allow the state to go through a difficult period. As the Prime Minister of Poland, I had to carry out to such reforms. Sometimes the political price to pay is huge. I know that the Greek government needs support to carry out the reforms." And, typical fro a right –wing politician like the former Polish prime minister who can be blamed for most privatisations in Poland after the Socialist time, he increased the pressure on the government in Athens in a particular arrogant way: "Today, in the case of Greece, there is one pre-condition. Greece needs to show responsibility and to achieve the announced reforms. There is no solidarity without responsibility." And, from today's position Mr Buzek's mantra sounds like cabaret:

"The crisis proves that we need to strengthen economic governance in the EU. Only in this way will EU economic and monetary policy work properly. The present crisis shows clearly that the Stability and Growth Pact is necessary. It should be strictly respected. We need to maintain the stability of the euro. It is important for the euro-zone, also for countries that are outside and want to join, but also for those who do not intend to do so. The euro is a symbol of our European success."

Mr. Buzek has been one of the founders of the Solidarnosc movement in Poland and later a key figure when negotiating structural reforms in Poland under the government of Lech Walesa, a Nobel Peace laureate who became immensely unpopular after breaking with the unions which once were his power base and introducing capitalism. And, Mr. Buzek, as prime minister of Poland, once negotiated widely criticised privatisations of major industries de-facto de-industrialising Poland leading to mass-unemployment. Among the official advisors of the Solidarnosc movement has been Jeffrey Sachs, a senior IMF negotiator and later associate of billionaire George Soros.

Likewise did German Chancellor Angela Merkel not get tired of demanding 'structural reforms' from the "socialist" government of at that time Greek Prime Minister Papandreou. But, many of the other EU - leaders made Germany indirectly responsible for the Greek disaster as it had been the aggressive export strategy of German industries that created huge deficits in Southern and Eastern Europe member states. Such export strategy came along with a wage dumping spiral that led to the collapse of the German domestic demand due to declining purchasing power in the aftermath of drastic social cuts and a labour market reform known as "Hartz IV" introduced by the Red-Green coalition government of Social Democratic Chancellor Gerhard Schröder, Mrs. Merkel's predecessor.

Parallel to this, market dominating Deutsche Bank AG put fuel to the fire by guaranteeing Greek state bonds and speculating with so called Credit Default Swaps (CDS). The fact that troubled Hypo Real Estate (HRE) kept billions of such toxic assets in it's books forced Deutsche Bank AG CEO Josef Ackermann to demand a bail out by the German government in September 2008 as otherwise Deutsche Bank AG's huge profit margins had suffered.

The reason why Chancellor Angela Merkel sternly resisted any calls for rescuing Greece by funds from within the European Union has to be seen in this light. It is more comfortable for the German government to have international institutions such as the IMF to organize the bail out. Mrs. Merkel is keenly aware of the delicacy of further bail-outs in the Greek tragedy no matter how insistent Mr. Ackermann may be.

While Chancellor Angela Merkel demands from Greece to crack down on social subsistence the German government behind the scenes urges the Greek government to spend billions on buying arms from Germany's weapon's industry.

Germany's weapon's export has doubled in the past five years. Greece is the second largest importer of German arms technology.

The 11.3% profit-increase of 'Rheinmetall', a major German weapons manufacturer in Düsseldorf, is seen as symptomatic for an economic crisis that coincides with an upswing in arms trade. Although debts are piling up in all countries forcing governments to cut down on social expenditure, public subsistence, education, health care and environmental agendas, many states spend ever more money on arms, partly because the Lisbon Treaty calls for successive increases in arms – spending of all EU member states.

Export-junky Germany is accused by many leaders more or less directly of living off it's fellow EU member states and neighbours. Even the OECD demanded moderation in this aspect.

Germany is currently holding Position 3 in the world arms exports.

Greece got a distasteful history when it comes to military processes and one can only hope that all these new weapons will not be used once the government of Prime Minister Papandreou has been replaced by first an extreme right wing and maybe later even military government amid social unrest and clashes between demonstrators and the state's authorities.

What a disgrace how Mr Papandreou had been treated at the summit in Cannes after he had pledged to take the cause to the country and have a referendum about the reform package be held. Once this most democratic move became known Mrs Merkel and Mr Sarkozy ordered him to report and told him to either resign or withdraw his proposed referendum - plans. How ridiculous to speak of democracy in Europe in that moment. It couldn't become more obvious that the EU is not living up to any of the standards it so proudly holds up when forcing the government of the country where all democratic ideas had once been born down to it's knees. What a shame!

The Greek economy is in ruins, drastic cuts the "Socialist" government had been dictated by EU and IMF inevitably led to a further decline in Greece's GDP while social cuts provoke fierce resistance among citizens.

According to the data available for the state budget for the seven months of 2010 (January - July), on a fiscal basis, the deficit amounted to 12,100 million euro against 20,050 million euro during the same period in 2009.

This represents a 39.7% year-over-year decline, against a targeted 39.5% annual decline foreseen in the Government's economic policy programme. The question, however, arises whether such a minimal effect justifies a harsh regime of fiscal austerity that brings every wheel to a halt.

The fiscal consolidation of the first six months of 2010 is due both to expenditure restrictions and revenues increases. Furthermore, these data do not yet fully reflect all fiscal measures included in the Government's programme for 2010, such as the second increase in VAT rate by 2 percentage points applied since July 1, 2010.

Increasing VAT that is paid by every consumer and so to speak the general public while the rich upper class as well as international financial institutions such as Deutsche Bank AG and Goldman Sachs who caused the Greek crisis by speculating with Credit Default Swaps (CDS) were left unharmed.

The decline in the percentage reduction in the deficit from 45.4% in the first six months of 2010, to 39.7% for the seven months (January-July 2010) can be traced to a substantial increase of interest expenditures in July as well as to revenue increases lagging behind the target.

In particular, net revenues of the ordinary budget increased by 4.1% year-over-year.

This reflects an increase in receipts from the revenue increasing measures adopted by the Government, including the first increase of the VAT rates, and receipts from excise tax and corresponding VAT on fuel, tobacco and alcoholic beverages due to the adjustment of their tax rates.

It also reflects receipts of 805 million euro from the imposition of an extraordinary tax on profits of large companies, receipts of 327 million euro from the banks' liquidity support scheme, as well as a 116 million euro year-over-year reduction in tax refunds.

However, the government avoided to introduce a wealth tax that would affect "Ultra High Net Worth Individuals" (UHNWI's) as investment house Merril Lynch calls billionaires of which Greece is full of and who are still gambling in the financial virtual reality casino.

The real disaster of the Greek crack down on social expenditure becomes visible in schools, hospitals and universities. Ordinary budget expenditures declined by 10.0% year-over-year against a targeted 5.5% annual decrease.

Primary expenditures declined by 13.2% against a targeted 5.8% annual reduction and interest expenditures decreased by 0.2% against a projected 5.6% annual increase.

The decrease of primary expenditures is mainly due to the restriction of expenditure in health and social security (lower grants to the Social Security Funds by 1,326 million euro compared to the respective period of 2009), a 890 million euro reduction in grants and consumption expenditures, a 700 million euro reduction in the allocation of earmarked revenues and reduced expenditure for salaries and pensions (decreased by 775 million Euro).

Apart from international financial institutions which used Greek bonds for a snowball system on the playground of the financial markets another factor can be made responsible for Hella's decline: the trade deficit.

Public Investment Budget (PIB) expenditures declined by 36.3% and PIB revenues increased by 23.8%, compared to the respective period of 2009.

The budget cuts, so far, have not affected the military expenditure. So with executing such strict budget discipline and fiscal austerity along with brutal social cuts the Greek government was able to save 1 billion Euros in half a year. Given the fact that when Greece got into trouble almost 2 years ago in 2010, the total debts were about 148 billion Euros one could say that in 74 years the state would be out of the woods!

Celtic Tiger ended as bedroom carpet

The Irish government became a master in perverting the system as the Irish state borrowed money from it's own banks which it had rescued in 2010 at a higher rate than the ECB's base rate.

The desperate attempt by the Irish government at the beginning of 2011 to attract capital by it's newly issued bonds has been partly successful but not because the international financial markets have any confidence in the Republic of Ireland (which at that time has still been rated "A", although "C" would by far have been more realistic) to ever grow out of debt but because some lucrative privatisation deals are coming up at the horizon once the IMF has taken over. At this stage it won't matter anymore whether Ireland is governed by a drunkard or any other pale bureaucrat. Charismatic politicians would hardly want to have their name be attached to the disastrous final decline of modern Ireland, the "success model" of the EU.

Throughout the "Celtic Tiger" scam-based economic boom that left Emerald Island with stock of real estate valued at about 700 billion while annual GDP was at around 170 billion to a large degree generated by an insane building boom far beyond actual demand giving an average of 2 houses per family to the population of 4.5 million also motorways were built. These will soon be privatised and sold as a bargain to ironically probably the same crowd that by their Ponzi - scheme had brought down the public finances.

The Irish government had already buried some 25 billion Euros in infamous Anglo-Irish Bank and just recently had to increase it's engagement to make it an incredible 500,000 Euros per capita that are dumped with criminal structures that led the bank and their shareholders.

These people were "Ultra High Net-worth Individuals" (UHNWIs) who are friendly with former *Taosieach* (minister-president) Bertie Ahern who stepped down over a slush funds scandal in which he was accused of having engaged in some kind of creative accounting as the bookkeeper of the governing party Fionna Fail and legendary *Taosieach* Charles Haughey who led a life-style like only kings do in other countries.

Mr. Ahern and his Finance Minister Charlie McGreevy, later Internal Market Commissioner, had invented the "Celtic Tiger" that now ended as bedroom carpet. Mr. McGreevy, by profession an accountant, never worried, he told me just a few months before 11th August 2007, about the fact that Ireland's GDP for more than 10 years has been by some 30% much higher than it's GNP meaning that the Irish Republic was exploited at an even bigger scale than the English ever did it over 800 years.

As long as states seek to refinance themselves through private banks that themselves are refinancing through a publicly owned bank, i.e. the European Central Bank (ECB), they will never grow out of debt as the interest rate private banks will charge the state will always be higher than the rate they borrow themselves from the central bank.

The question arises why any state should aliment the private banks in this manner and not simply get refinanced directly by the central bank?

The banks that the Irish state guarantees for all had engaged in the "Celtic Tiger" scam and reported 20-30% profits each of the ten years of shareholder-indulgence, so they made approximately 300% over 10 years.

Now, that the markets turn sour the banks revert to the state to bail them out rather than requesting their shareholders who pocketed these unreal returns year after year to contribute as well.

On the downside of the scam the real economy is crippled by a credit crunch as well as a dramatically declining social purchasing power, while the Lisbon Treaty forces the government in Dublin to execute a harsh regime of fiscal austerity that closes hospitals, cut's through the social net by a chainsaw and threatens to bring public life to a halt.

Instead of bailing out shareholders who miss-speculated and by this prolonging the painful decline one could also hand a life-line to the people by increasing social purchasing power, a massive public investment creating sustainable growth in the real economy and by eradicating a debt that in any case will never be paid back. This would be the time to get rid off old fashioned corrupt structures and by going counter-cyclical create the future for a really modern Ireland.

For some time in 2009 it looked that Ireland might be the first EU member state to default and declare state bankruptcy, but then it all looked like a race between two other building-bubble economies, Spain, and Portugal both Euro-zone members, and only in 2010 it became clear that Greece would be the first one to call the shots.

In Madrid, on 17th October 2009, it took more than a million people to the street in protest against the government's plan to liberalise abortion legislation. Although it certainly is the case that this is an issue high on the agenda as the Lisbon treaty will probably be in effect but shortly, one can also say that in a crisis as severe the displayed outrage of a people in sociological terms can be interpreted as a ventilate function. The masses want to protest the "cruel killing of embryos" as the Catholic church brands the new law, but would the turn-out be that high if there was no depression? The people wanted to let steam off and found a reason in those laws as there was a general sentiment that things went wrong although nobody could point at which part of public life it was, yet.

And, how will the demonstrations look like when Ireland had to adopt Lisbon treaty liberalisations? In it's second referendum the Irish overwhelmingly voted 'Yes', but that has probably been due to the fear to be left out in the cold as payback time nears.

Indeed, tough decisions will be on the agenda for the years to come. The scam-like building boom of the 'Celtic Tiger' years has led to mass unemployment in the building industry affecting other sectors of the economy as well.

In a classical Ponzi-scheme run by building – banking syndicates aligned to at that time Taoiseach Bertie Ahern and his Fianna Fail party, over-valued property has been over-financed.

The Irish Sunday Times pointed out that of the 1.6 million households in Ireland 40% (= 645,000 families) of which have mortgages totalling 148 billion will result in 30% of negative equity for these families by the end of the year as house prices are dwindling down rapidly.

Tragically, 76% of those in negative equity are first time buyers, in other words young families, as they see the value of their homes fall between 2007 and today by 30%.

If prices fall by 50%, the Irish Sunday Times wrote, 350,000 families will be in negative equity. In 2007 and 2008 25% of loans to first time buyers were 100% mortgages. Most of the mortgages exceed the 25 year term and run up to 35 years.

A young family can easily be ruined, unless the state protects them.

But, the at that time Irish government under Fianna Fail - Taoiseach Brian Cowen had issued a flat-rate – like guarantee for the small country's banks that let strong sentiment go around that the bailout package will become a bill only the taxpayer can foot. No legislation has been proposed yet that addresses the more pressing issue of how to protect the citizen rather than the bank's shareholders by taxpayer's money.

At the same time said taxpayer is confronted with the likelihood of brutal decisions when it comes to government spending and social expenditure.

Many citizens feel that they had been betrayed by their government's indulgence about presumable "economic good times" as EU Internal market Commissioner Charlie McGreevy, a former finance minister and inventor of the 'Celtic Tiger' - yarn, called it.

It has not only been true over the past 2 decades that Ireland has been a net-receiver of EU funds that bought the country new schools, hospitals, a few motorways and better roads, but it is also a fact that especially during the 'Celtic Tiger' boom period Ireland's GDP was constantly 30% higher than it's GNP, meaning that 30% more of the in Ireland accumulated wealth has left the island than stayed. The colleagues of the Irish Sunday Times neglect this fact persistently as it would raise the fundamental question of distribution of wealth on Emerald Island. It would also shed some light on the Irish media's bias stance in the Lisbon treaty referendum. Well, private media is owned by someone who may have other business interests, too and one may ask how free a government that pays some 60 billion Euros out to shareholders of a bank that speculated in the name of their owners, like it was in the Anglo-Irish – case.

Banks should write it off, many citizens said as these multinational players and their shareholders weren't paying high taxes but had skyrocketing profits. For such a brave act the Lisbon Treaty would be a tremendous obstacle as the Irish government would have to dismantle the entire system. That indeed would be equal to a revolution as declaring debt void means to nullify wealth on the other side of the equation.

It speaks for itself but not for the EU's crisis policy that Ireland has been pushed aggressively to accept the "rescue" mission of EU and IMF. It becomes obvious that as soon as public funds are made available for the rescue of banks stocks and shares rise to never seen highs.

The Irish example proves explicitly what the EU rescue packages in reality are about: the securing of the profits of banks engaged in Ireland, foremost British and German banks the latter who are said to have some 150 billion at stake. Their rescue will be financed by tax payer's money.

This is also the reason for at that time ECB president Jean-Claude Trichet's demand to reinforce the "Stability and Growth Pact" although he knows that Ireland has never violated the Maastricht accord in the past by exceeding deficits. Mr. Trichet's becoming pushy is directed against the taxpayer who shall pay for the rescue package and for this has to accept a brutal austerity that will bring every wheel to a halt in the Irish economy.

The Irish disaster is not a result of lax deficit rules but rather a failed tax and finance policy which allowed speculation bubbles to be created by a corrupt political leadership that conspired with a criminal business community.

What would have been needed by EU institutions are completely different measurements. The ECB should have extended credit lines directly to the governments and stop immediately to subsidise bank – profits by public money. It also becomes evident that dealing with state-bankruptcies on a case basis is not sustainable. One rather should think about an overall strategy to get rid off the debts piled up by private banks and speculators. The EU should not have become a bank-rescuing mechanism but should rather rescue it's citizens and honest businesses.

HOUSE OF CARDS

US of A, the country that once ruled the world

It's only logic that Pimco, one of the largest hedge funds of the world and daughter of German insurance giant Allianz AG, sold all it's US tresuary bonds two weeks prior to the Tsunami and subsequent nuclear disaster in Japan as then the US Dollar reserves from Japan would be repatriated in order to finance reconstruction which will let the Dollar plummet so that the FED had to buy back all foreign debt leaving the Chinese with their mouths wide open as they see their 3 trillion USD worthless toilet paper flush down in radioactively contaminated water. A masterpiece seen from US perspective as they can relatively controlled let the air out of the bubble they created with printing US treasury bonds trillion fold by their scam artists.

It became evident that the US's economic model was a house of cards. Nothing is real in the US-economy, not the growth rate, not the savings rate, not the national income and productivity tables. Nothing.

It is the consequences of the wrong economic model applied. In order to understand this one has to look at the underlying factors:

The 'S'- curve

That our present system is as rotten as the past socialism becomes obvious when one scrutinises the supply – demand relation. Never before did industries produce such an incredible amount of low quality goods, useless or superfluous products and trash.

It has become obvious in the 1930ies that the mixture of free markets and unlimited capital accumulation had been explosive. Its apologists for the next 40 years had a hard stance. Keynesianism has been the logic conclusion drawn from WWII.

It suggested that the state created a regulatory framework and if necessary also the necessary domestic demand. This seemed to work quite well in the 50ies and 60ies of last century. But, it has been the capitalistic investment dynamic that enhanced the post-war prosperity, driven by the need of reconstruction, distribution of new mass-manufactured goods as well as a general consumption desire.

Continuous wage increases, a pre-requirement for rising consumption shares, under the above conditions had been no threat to increasing profit rates because the rapid rise of productivity due to automated production lines gave room for a generous distribution of wealth.

In economic theory the development of the demand curve is often referred to as the 'S' curve. At the beginning only a few people bought washing machines and refrigerators but as soon as wages increased more and more households could afford the new luxury. The curve steeply leads upwards. Finally, washing machines and refrigerators are part of a general standard.

Now, mostly young people or people whose fridge got broken buy one. The demand curve is almost flat. Then, with new variations and improved versions of already successfully introduced products such as washing machines with 10 instead of 5 programs and centrifuges or mobile phones with internet connectivity the curve lets the curve go up again.

The 'S' curve is *the* dominant analogy of demand driven economies. The rapid growth of demand along the steeper parts of the curve stimulates above average investments in order to create the required capacities. Because one concludes from the present demand what the future holds in store it is quite common that an investment – overkill creates overcapacities.

A market cleansing due to overcapacities kicks those who came too late out of business.

During the post WWII era an extraordinary amount of products all of a sudden became mass-manufactured goods which required huge investments for creating the necessary production capacities. A company which intends to double its car manufactory's output requires to have considerable more investment goods than a company which wants to supply the double amount of mobile phones.

The expansion of capacities of European companies in the post war era by this had also been an important stimulant for the US as the American companies at the beginning had been the only ones who could provide investment goods. However, in the due course, the European companies seeking investment goods inadvertently became rivals of the American corporations supplying same kind of goods.

Simultaneously, the upper end of the 'S' curve of standard goods of the industrialised societies had been reached in the late sixties. The worldwide created capacities under profit share and return-on-investment aspects had been much too big. The competition on the world market sharpened up and profit rates declined.

Much too much capital had been invested in creating these capacities which yet had to amortise before the corporations could change the field of business. The investments declined sharply and for a while could no longer pose as a well for profitable demand.

This constellation, and not currency turbulences and the oil price shock, had been the deeper rooted reason for the first worldwide economic crisis after WWII.

In the western free world this challenge was met by a dreadful financial deregulation binding capital in useless speculations along with mass production of junk products and trash. In the Socialistic east the attempt to keep pace with capitalistic production output choked the command economy.

Whereas Socialism promised that one will get all one needed Capitalism until today seems to promise that we will need all we are getting.

Barroso – Commission copied US model of hedonic pricing

An alternative way of making markets and investors believe that there are growth rates when in fact there is stagnation or even recession has been brought to perfection by the US and copied by the EU under the Barroso-Commission.

The so called hedonic pricing allows in statistics to apply 'quality adjustments' to miraculously show growth rates for instance in the car industry by assuming that because cars built nowadays contain features and improvements which are recorded as growth although today less cars than in the 1950ies are sold.

Since its beginning modern economic statistics would record prices on nominal basis on the one hand and in deflated manner on the other hand. This is the only way to be able to compare prices realistically.

If, for instance, an economy grows by 10% in a year it may stand for a magnificent boom or a deep depression. The only question is whether 10% more goods are sold or whether everything simply got 10% more expensive.

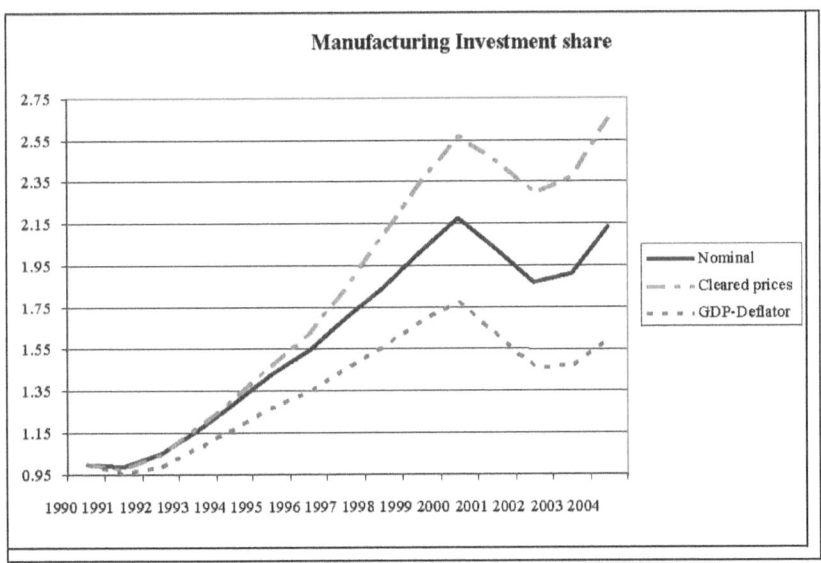

Source of data used for Graphic: NIPA (National Income & Product Account)

And, if inflation is around 2% but economic growth around 10% the overall economy is in perfect shape. But, if prices rose by 15% said nominal growth of 10% stands for a disastrous recession. Also wage increases of 10% in times of stable prices would be something different than during times of galloping inflation.

Since the early 1990ies an ever greater disparity between nominal and cleared prices can be noticed leaving the GDP deflator well behind. Hedonic pricing in the US showed growth rates during the Clinton-Gore administration although not more PCs were sold during the dotcom-boom but technology with better processors.

As most products over time improve their quality this system quite elegantly let's inflated prices disappear. Because increasing prices go in line with an increase of turn-over the latter appears as if there was an increase in consumption whereas in reality there is none.

It is a methodological question and it should be solved immediately as all those growth rates and inflation statistics are useless and even dangerous as no economist can verify what kind of development our economies in reality are taking.

Real change would start right here. One should not forget that the Eastern European Socialism collapsed 23 years ago because the system was no longer sustainable despite state controlled propaganda throwing sand into the eyes of the citizens.

The credibility of the advocates of the present system in decline is minimal. Sarkozy and Merkel until recently stood (and Cameron still stands) on the other side calling for deregulation, liberalisation, and privatisation. And, by employing former Clinton-aides President Barack Obama made clear that he was not in for real change. It takes more than one brave president to clean out Augur's stable.

Holy Cows that don't give milk anymore

Why the US' decline affects us all:

The US managed to let their growth and productivity statistics shine as if it was the biblical star above Bethlehem. International investors, banks and sovereign wealth funds sent billions over Atlantic and Pacific and were given trash-paper in exchange for that.

There has been a lot of talk about the "booming 1990ies" in the US. Not only, defenders of Clinton and Gore maintain, have there been dotcom-bubbles but also real investment. Truth be told there was no such thing as any significant real economic growth.

The trick employed by the Clinton-Gore administration had been the hedonic pricing which due to quality adjustments allow improved goods be recorded as economic growth although only the consumption expenditure rose but not the number of sold cars, electronic goods and houses.

Problem with hedonic pricing is that although quality improvements increase the standard of living these can not be measured or quantified. But, on paper it looks good to say that consumption has increased by 5% even though this was only because of price increases.

By this method one can also eliminate inflation while the real economy's growth appears to be stunning. This led many people to believe the legend of a new technology investment-boom in the 1990ies. The figures showed a five times higher investment in that sector than 10 years earlier. But, if one scrutinises the nominal figure it shrinks to less than half of it.

The boom in the new technology sector solely stems from an increased quality standard of processors as well as software which have been fictitiously been added to the real investment expenditure.

Without hedonic price-clearance the investments made in manufacturing industries all those marvellous growth figures of the 1990ies look rather modest. However, the faked investment dynamics the US showed to the rest of the world and making everyone believe it was 1.5 times higher than in real terms it has been attracted huge foreign investment.

The American 'consumption boom' of the past 15 years also stems from the book of the fairies. Long lasting capital goods such as electronics, household items and furniture have not been purchased excessively as the Bureau of Economic Analysis (BEA) in Washington tries to make people believe.

According to the official BEA macro statistic the real expenditure for capital goods has between 1990 and 2004 exploded by the factor 2.5 which would be a phenomenal annual growth rate of 17%!

To suggest that the upper quintile of American society had doubled its consumption every year is hard to believe. On the other hand, wages for the vast majority of Americans stagnated and even fell drastically for the bottom 20%, so where should all this magnificent demand come from?

The truth is that the nominal expenditure of the Americans in the same time period has merely doubled. But, to assume that cars, DVD players or refrigerators were not subject to price increases in the US would be naïve.

If we look at the official consumer price index a modest annual increase of 3.5% remains from the celebrated "boom" of the Clinton-Gore – years.

And, also the much admired growth of productivity of more than 4% per annum in the second half of the 1990ies is owed to the creative accounting of the US government.

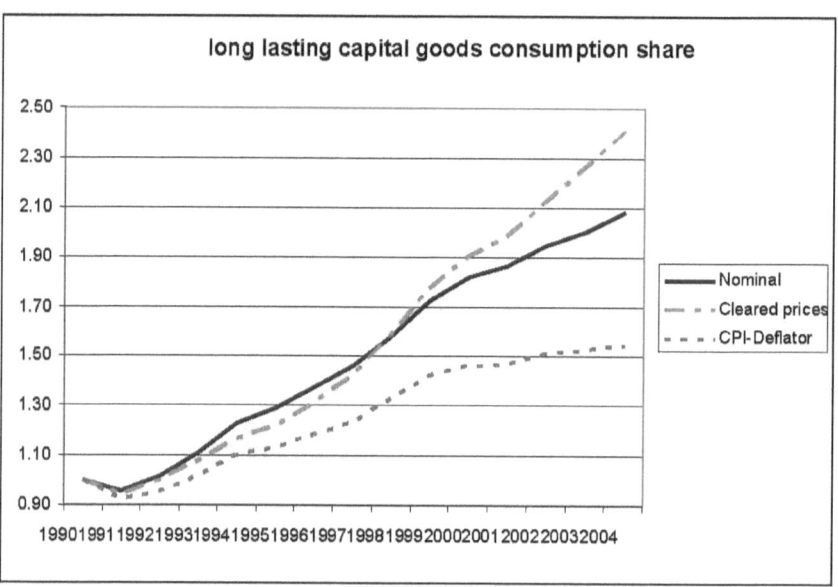

The only miracle Clinton and Gore were able to create was to attract by such manipulated economic data foreign investment which by building bubbles financed the ever growing current account deficit of the US economy.

One of the caprioles of the hedonic pricing fetishists has been the announcement that the US economy grew in the second quarter of 2008 by unbelievable 3.3% while the rest of the world already took bracing position for a sharp recession. Sole purpose of this news was to keep the show on the road. German car makers, for instance, trusted the American data and are now surprised to see the demand for Porsche, Mercedes, BMW and Audi automobiles decline by double digit figures.

Again and again, the American stock markets closed positive, stocks and shares of American as well as international exporters suddenly could notice increased demand again. Not for long, though. It transpired that the US economy was hit by record unemployment, a sharp (-11%) decline in the housing sector and the collapse of the car industry which recorded a decline by 25%.

It would be time for a heart-to-heart talk between the international community and the US administration. Those manipulations ought to be banned. And, EU Commission and member-state governments have to abide by this ban, too, as the virtual economy's holy cows won't give milk anymore.

US economy produces nothing anyone really wants to buy

But, the failed strategy is not the only reason for the U.S.' desperate attempts for further expansion. Other than oil, weapons and more or less useful IT devices (and, of course financial products which let the world get strangled) there is not much the U.S. economy produces these days so the financial bubbles in search for a good return of investment wobble into the energy sector.

The U.S. doesn't really produce anything but a few cars which are hard to sell, military 'goods' that shouldn't be bought and Microsoft software which only dominates the market because of a classical monopoly situation. Even the "iPADs" and other "Apple – technology" were produced under scandalous conditions in Chinese child-labour camps. If exploitation of minors who are held like slaves is the price that is to be paid for having such technology, one should think about it and not laud and applaud an "iGod", also not post-hum.

Largely, anything else that comes out of the U.S. is dubious financial products which cause a lot of problems for the rest of the world.

The U.S.' production lines were already destroyed in the Reagan years by an interest rate policy that let not only the US industries and their production lines cripple but as these astronomical high interest rates of almost 17% had been imposed on so called "Third World" countries it also caused a disaster globally.

After the Bretton Woods system collapsed in 1971 the Dollar all of a sudden was subject to gravitation laws as there has been no international treaty in place anymore that obliged anybody to store the U.S. currency. Since the U.S. economy had become weaker and weaker, it had not been a natural law anymore that the US Dollar would remain the leading currency in the world. The Dollar was *kaputt* after the last bit of Keynesianism that had been exercised during the Carter administration which had been unsustainable as production had declined significantly and inflation peaked at 10%. This shows that Keynesian distribution of wealth only works when it is matched by economic output. These have been very bad prospects for the US Dollar. President Ronald Reagan tried to make the US Dollar attractive again by increasing the interest rate and by this fighting inflation. It came down from 10% in 1980 to 8, 5, finally 4%. The real interest rate which during the 1970ies had been negative reached the highest level of 7% in 1982.

Consequently, the effective interest rate culminated at 16.4% in late 1981. With a nominal interest rate of 16% Ronald Reagan inadvertently laid the basis for an ever greater trade deficit which was off-set by an influx of foreign capital by foreign entities and states who found it attractive again to hold US Dollar reserves, be it US treasuary bonds or any kind of financial instruments, commercial paper, asset backed securities however hollow these prove to be today, or T-bills. The Dollar rebounded under Reagan and became strong again. By his interest policy, President Reagan indirectly supported the financial industry which started to create bubbles. The astronomic inflation of the 1970ies was brought down, the Dollar strong, but by this Reaganomics artificially created a recession which as a side effect let the right-wing government of Ronald Reagan crack down on the unions which until then had been strong in the United States. Production declined, a de-industrialisation wave swept through Pennsylvania and other traditional blue collar – states. The crisis of 1987 brought all wheels to a halt. Reagan was finished. His successor, his former Vice-President George Herbert Walker Bush, a lame duck throughout his presidency, couldn't manage and as the result baby-boomer Clinton as president created bubbles which were just following the mere logic of a classical Ponzi-scheme to make the rich become richer.

Profit over profit, but someone got to work for it

The rule always has been that only wealth that has been created can be distributed but some people in Wall Street have misunderstood this logic and thought that it was enough to accumulate wealth, not produce it. They are now being taught the lesson the hard way. To have others work for the wealth one wishes to consume has always been a dream of mankind. It has never worked for long. It may work for a while on the basis that one goes stealing, first some of the achievements of society, culture, education, social security, then, if it is not possible to deprive the own people of ever more rights one may try to go abroad and exploit other people, but this usually creates resistance. Some people must have thought that they could do it anyway as they thought of themselves as superior.

Today, the Americans want to consume which by failing to produce goods in sufficient quantity inevitably led to an ever greater trade deficit which in parasitic manner is off-set by selling useless paper to the rest of the world which culminates in the impertinence to impose dreadful, unrealistic, profit maximization dictates on other people's economy. The tragedy lays in the fact that in most countries the perfect economic givens were at hand: economic output of the real economy was matching demand. But, some financial crisis suddenly led to an imbalance. Because of the excesses of the financial junkies the real economy suffers. The truth is that only now will we see high oil prices because of speculation. Once the worldwide economic crisis becomes a real depression, even the oil price will fall.

It has not been the oil industry's hunger for exploring new wells alone that let Bush open the hunting season. It has rather been a combination of the creation of extreme deficits known as *Reaganomics* as well as an unhealthy – virtual - excessive growth of the *Clintonmania* that didn't leave the American economy any oxygen to breath.

Something got to change in the US

So who would be so insane to invest even ten cents in an economy which evidently wasn't worth the paper it's protagonists were attesting each other viability on? After the E-business and Dotcom bubbles had burst a new playground had been found. This time, the same scam artists announced, everything would be safe. Instead of hot air in tin cans one would now only emit commercial papers which had an underlying security of a real estate collateral. That sounded solid and even experienced investment bankers may have thought that nothing could go wrong. But, nobody wanted to check on the validity of the valuation of such real estate collateral. What should have raised concern, however, was the fact that the US all of a sudden had an endless amount of highly valued property which served as security and this although nothing like a building boom was seen anywhere in the US, so how come that real estate growth rates allowed for such a capital accumulation? The trick employed by the US' scam artists was to pretend that an increase of investment in real estate had been condoned by simply applying so called "quality adjustments". Houses were let for a higher rent because of quality adjustments. The National Income and Product Accounts (NIPA) – tables of the US' Bureau of Economic Affairs show that imputed rents did not go up but consumption expenditure in terms of housing has increased meaning that because of the assumption that houses were better in the 1990ies than in the 1970ies had experienced an increase of investment although these figures were simply adjusted because of inflation.

Under this scheme known in statistics as hedonic pricing, the assumption that a good being produced nowadays is better than it was ten or more years ago. Then, the mere quality adjustment may appear in the eyes of the beholder as an increase of value.

Under these paradigms even Uncle Tom's Cabin would have been valued at the range of a middle class bungalow. It can only be hoped that President Obama has understood that a little bit of Keynesianism alone won't cure the American economy as the lack of production output can't be compensated by faking growth figures like it had been done during the past decades and that America's friends would be disappointed once more if such manipulation was to continue.

State subject to Moody's Mood – Standard Poor, Granny poorer

Another issue are the so called "bad banks". The rating agencies have yet not decided whether to gout the bad bank construct or not. But, the fundamental question whether the banks may treat the state guaranteed credit line as state bonds or whether they would still be required to hold the equivalent as capital on stock. This problem illustrates once more how bizarre it is to make legal requirements dependent on the mood of rating agencies such as Moody's, Fitch's and Standard & Poor. More significant, in fact, may be at the moment that the suffering in the bank's board rooms has not been great enough, yet. At the moment the market value of many of those toxic assets are pointing upwards which does not mean that these obligations aren't as toxic as they were thought to be. Whoever has a closer look at the US' statistics knows about the over-indebtedness of American households that has compensated shrinking wages over much more than a decade by ever higher consumer credits and mortgages. As a result debts have been piled up which can never be paid back, even if prosperous times came back in a few years.

There is also no reason to believe in that fairy tale that companies whose capital stock had been too tiny for surviving in economic more stabile times and that have been forced into over-indebtedness by Private Equity sharks will survive the current crisis. To think that commercial debt obligations (CDO's) and other papers that bundled such bad credits are yet to make headwind is a result of the institutionalised insanity of the financial markets. On those speculative markets not a fundamental value is traded but anything that looks promising to be sold for more than it has been bought for. This expectation is well and alive at present because the US government prints enormous amounts of cash in order to reanimate the market for structured credit obligations. For 18 months a program of the American Central Bank, the Federal Reserve, buys up and by this takes off the market mortgage backed securities and commercial obligations totalling 750 billion US Dollars, most of which are stemming from troubled Freddy Mac and Fannie Mae. On top of that, US treasury secretary Timothy Geithner tries to motivate vulture funds and private equity firms by state-backed guarantees to buy the toxic trash off the banks. By this method, the banks shall get rid off toxic assets of up to one trillion US Dollars. These are not the papers held by Fannie & Freddie but the real Sub-prime mortgage trash. This program de-facto can be seen as a state-run 'Bad Bank' and has created in October 2009 alone an additional demand of some 40 billion US Dollars which may not sound too much in relation to the market volume of several thousand billions but on a speculative market the mere indication that a certain product sees an increase in demand is usually enough encouragement to other speculators to jump onto the band wagon.

This way once more a self enhancing effect creates artificial demand and let's prices go up. There are many examples for such absurd theatre: When, for instance, more than 40 years ago US President Richard Nixon launches his appeasement policy towards China, some financial junkies in London started an intensive trade with ancient Chinese state obligations from Emperor's times and although none of these papers had ever made a single cent in profit for decades the prices paid for that trash skyrocketed.

Of course, nobody expected at that time that the People's Republic of China would ever resume interest payment on these antiques. But, everybody in the market calculated with an increased demand because of the nearing of the US and China and solely because of such sentiment the prices increased. Those who managed to get out of the market in time made a fortune on these worthless and useless obligations. It will be similar with the present hype about the worthless toxic papers or those bank stocks which have created a sheer rally of a thousand per cent in the past 18 months although none of the problems that have caused the financial crash had been solved.

Not even half of the toxic depots have been written off so far, and the world economic crisis continues at pace rate. But, the financial- and stock markets are booming again. Is it Goldman Sachs, JP Morgan or Deutsche Bank AG, one stands tall again. And, while most of the engineering and manufacturing companies in Manchester or Stuttgart have to worry about their re-financing as credit lines are cut, private equity sharks can bath in cheap money keeping them afloat.

If the goal had been to re-install a system of ever lasting growth and speculation in the virtual reality casino, than the 'bad banks' and the bailing out of banks as well as the supply with cheap money has been the right order of battle.

Of course, the bank's new profits are of same quality as have been those before the crash. Virtual reality gains resulting from a gigantic snowball system in which more or less dubious commercial papers are sold at ever higher prices that are pushed up by exceeding credit lines - until the next crash comes. It is only logic that bankers and investment fund managers aren't too much concerned about the next crash as their task is to produce short term results for the next quarter of a year. The short term success is the goal. And, another reason why bankers and fund managers look into the future rather relaxed can be found in the reassurance by the state that they won't be let down. 'Too big to fail' has been the credo in even relatively small cases such as the German SME - bank 'IKB' or the completely useless Hypo Real Estate (HRE) in which the German government buried totally unnecessarily 160 billion Euros that swiftly ended up in the pockets of rich Deutsche Bank AG shareholders. In light of this it becomes understandable that German banks are not very interested in the "bad bank" or the 480 billion Euros worth of state guarantees by the German government body "Soffin" from which only less than half were drawn so far. Commerzbank AG for instance just returned two thirds of the state guarantees as these cost money, just like when making use of the "bad bank". The de facto reassurance by the state, instead, doesn't cost a single cent.

In a way, the vulture funds doped by the US taxpayer's funds function like a "bad bank" as they take on all the financial trash that currently floats around. In fact, the rescue mission by the US government in hopeless cases such as the insurance conglomerate AIG which had re-insured toxic assets worth 441 billion Dollars, or the equally questionable rescuing of mortgage giants Fannie Mae and Freddie Mac has swept billions of taxpayer's money into the pockets of the hot society of the financial world. In case of AIG it has been 93.2 billion US Dollars of which 11.9 billion Dollars were paid to Deutsche Bank AG, almost as much as Investment Bank Goldman Sachs which received 12.9 billion Dollars in compensation for failed credit derivatives. If the state had not jumped in, the banks had to write it off. Instead, they are paying dividends to shareholders and bonuses to their fund managers and investment bankers.

But, not only in the US and Germany are there generous state-organized money spinners. Seen from banker's- and shareholder's point of view an incredibly lucrative "Bad Bank" – model has been implemented in Ireland. NAMA, a state body designed to buy up all problematic loans and mortgages, will pay more than 77 billion Euros for loans of which more than 50% are not serviced anymore. Nevertheless, the Irish state will give the banks state obligations in exchange for that at face value without any deductions. The Irish taxpayer will have to pay these state obligations and it's interest day by day until the state is bankrupt. Before that, of course, any social spending and public investment will be cut back to the bare minimum. The stock markets reacted enthusiastically and the stocks of the two major banks on Emerald Island, Allied Irish Bank and Bank of Ireland, skyrocketed by 30%. On the other side financial institutions and banks are still on strike when it comes to supplying the economy with badly needed liquidity. This is the main tool in the fight between banks and the state and it is not since yesterday that major banks are not fulfilling their obligations in advancing loans and credit lines to industry and SMEs but since a couple of years. Especially since it has become more lucrative to gamble in the casinos of NASDAQ, DAX and 'The City' in London than following the core business of traditional banking, all major institutions have become investment banks who wish to see their commercial risk being covered by the state and their losses be taken over by the taxpayer. An alternative scenario would, indeed, be possible. The state could, for instance, force the banks to increase their capital stock. Those banks which are unable to do so, should be forced to place their toxic assets in a "Bad Bank" without compensation and write it off. Instead of guaranteeing the toxic papers the state could then go and supply the 'good banks' which by then might have burnt all their cash, with fresh funds and combine this with the obligation for the banks to issue credit lines and loans to industries, SMEs and private households. The advantage of this scenario for the taxpayer would be that he is not only left with the trash but also has a grip on the profitable active positions of the banks balance sheets. By this method, public interest and the taxpayer are protected as every Euro or Dollar being invested into those banks will result in ownership rights any other investor would always seek in a free market economy. The dreadful privatisation of profits and simultaneous socialisation of the losses would once and for all be brought to an end. A good one for state and taxpayer. Sweden has exercised exactly that after it's banking crisis in 1994. Nordbanken and Götabanken had been nationalised without compensation for the shareholders and the taxpayer owned not only a dump full of trash paper, but also the good part of these banks which indeed did produce some revenue. Unfortunately, after successful reanimation of the banks these have been returned into private ownership again. It took only a short while until the private owners and their bankers started the same insanity all over again. It has to be clear that public ownership without accompanying regulations that eliminate such speculative transactions that had led to the previous disaster wouldn't make sense. On the other hand, if such financial craziness was banned, would there be such an interest in private ownership of banks? Probably much less. So far there has been no progress in terms of better regulation that would protect us in the future.

Debts, not Wage increases

President Barack Obama still owes tough decisions concerning the American economic model of the past decades, but it seems he had to cut a deal with Wall Street in order to win re-election. I would not entirely give up on him to become a more radical anti-capitalist president in his second term but he would risk his life. On the other hand, does this man be a lame duck from the very beginning of his second term? He doesn't look like that. On the other hand, he has certainly been shown Oliver Stone's "JFK" from a perspective we all haven't ever seen it.

The consequences will be felt in Europe and throughout the world. With worst economic figures coming to light these days European manufacturers suffer from the American decline heavily.

The more the state's ability to stabilise profit share and demand reached its natural limitation the consumer indebtedness entered centre stage. This kind of privatised Keynesianism totally lay in the neo-liberal trend of privatisations.

Not the state is building up deficits in order to help the economy with creating profitable demand but the vast majority of citizens take out loans and mortgages in order to finance consumption the level of wages would not suggest they could afford.

Commonly, wage-dumping would strangle domestic demand and lead the economy into agony which we have witnessed in Germany over the past ten years. But, in the US wages were brutally brought down in the 1980ies. For 70% of all American employees the real wage in 1989 has been below the level of 1979. For the bottom 40% in those 10 years wages decreased by 10% while the 1990ies only brought stagnation.

In December 2000 the real net wages in the private US economy (except for management positions) has been 5% lower than in 1979. The reaction has been longer working hours and second and third jobs.

Also after 2000 the median family income did not increase significantly although it was said that there has been an incredible economic boom. Nevertheless, the US reported a steadily growing consumption share of 3% between 1985 and 1995 and by 4.3% thereafter. Rapidly increasing consumption let the US economy but because of huge imports also throughout the world grow at pace rate.

It has not only been the American upper class but also the family of 'Joe the Plumber' did not tighten their belt despite shrinking wages.

The growing disparity between income and spending at first was bridged by knocking the piggy bank and later by taking out loans and mortgages. The indebtedness of American households had reached unbelievable 80% of the available income in the 1980ies, in the year 2000 it was almost 100%. The ultimate kick then came after 2001 when low interest mortgages amid increasing real estate prices created the perfect environment for average households to accept ridiculous loan proposals.

This helped the US economy get out of the recession after the dotcom – bubble of the Clinton-Gore administration burst. The bulk of the mortgages hasn't been used for building or buying houses but financing consumption. That's how an artificial building boom became the lifeline of an otherwise ailing economic system.

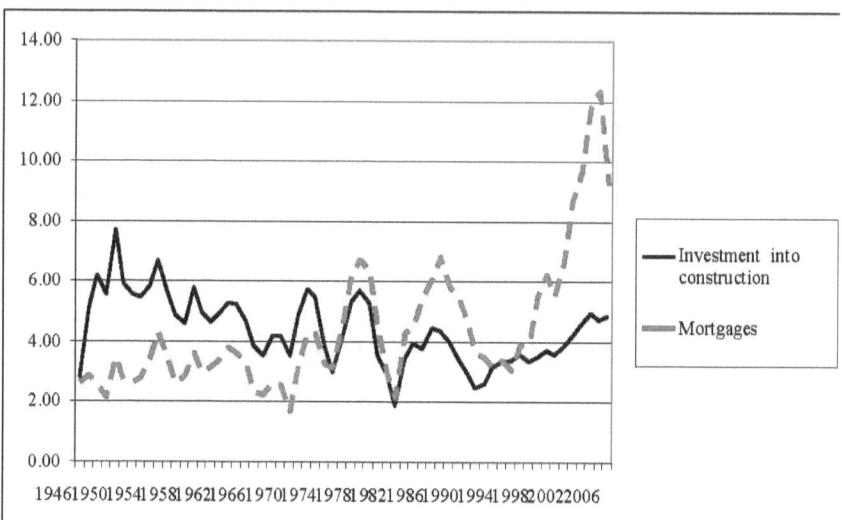

The real estate – hype resulted in an over-indebtedness of the American consumers by 125% of the disposable income at the end of 2006.

These loans were not used for luxury goods but increasingly often for financing relatively banal issues such as paying school fees or hospital bills. Because of the shrinking wages the standard of living of middle class families could only be maintained by furnishing mortgage loans to bolster their spending power.

The Consumption Expenditure Survey (CEX) which doesn't include the richest parts of society shows that the share of luxury clothes, jewellery, travel, fun parks, entertainment electronics and holiday homes in relation to the disposable income since the 1980ies is constantly declining.

On the other hand, the CEX share of education and health care has drastically increased mostly because of the inflation in those fields of public subsistence where the state has pulled out.

In other words: in order to bring America back on track, the Obama administration will have to make sure that life becomes affordable again for the ordinary citizens. Privatised Keynesianism doesn't work. Private healthcare and education lead to inflation and become unaffordable for those who really need it while they appear to be advantageous for those who are better off.

Mr. Obama has a lot of work to do and he can't do it the Clinton-way as there is no room for manoeuvring unless he creates bubbles as well. But, the American middle class has already eaten up their savings and houses a long time ago.

How to tame a monster

In the meantime the European Parliament once more missed out on a chance to radically overhaul the financial system and by this rescue the European economy. The new regulation will be insufficient as the capital requirements will simply be priced in. From now on, hedge funds and private equity firms will have some more paperwork to do in order to register but then they will get the official blessing to continue spinning the wheel of fortune. It is as if the financial crisis had not happened.

Never before in the history of mankind has there been such a profitability as in the financial merry-go-round of the Casino Capitalism. In 1945 interest policy was strictly governed and movement of capital regulated the share of the financial "industry" in the total corporate profits in the US was around 10%.

Between 1973 and 1985 American banks, funds and insurance companies never accounted for more than 16% of all corporate profits.

But, then in the 1990ies under President William Clinton who together with his Vice President Albert Gore created the dot.com bubble this profit share doubled. Just before the peak of the financial bubble building was reached on 11th August 2007, the share of financial company's in the US's total corporate profits reached 41%.

Yet, today, three years after the financial crisis took off, the share is still around 30%. A lot of the criticism President Obama is confronted with has to do with this fact even though many citizens might not be able to voice it

And, in Great-Britain under Prime Minister Margaret Thatcher a similar shift from manufacturing to gambling had happened. After the "Big Bang" the deregulation of The City has led to a de-industrialisation of the British economy. The manufacturing base had literally been moved to China, the IT business to India. Under "New Labour" of Prime Ministers Anthony Blair and Gordon Brown this development intensified radically. Today 67% of British GNP is directly resulting from financial gambling in The City. Agricultural production is accounting for less than 1% of the GDP. I asked Mr. Brown 2 years ago what would happen if The City was to go down. He uttered that it would "always be there". But, what if nobody buys these toxic assets any longer?

The Euro-zone is by no means any better. The total financial product of all banks had risen from 220% of GNP in 1998 to 360% in 2007 meaning that banks were moving three times more money that all combined manufacturing as well as service industries of the real economy produce in goods and services. Still, it is 350% today as the hot air has yet not been let out of the bubble. Rescue packages still feed the rich shareholders by pumping ever more liquidity into the arteries of a monster that will never have enough.

Other than in US and UK the Euro-zone, foremost Germany, still produce capital goods such as cars and machines and not only financial "products" but especially after the Social Democratic – Green government which liberalised the financial market and rolled out the red carpet for hedge funds and private equity firms the share of the latter in GNP rose to 18.5% in 2008 notwithstanding the additional gains of already existing insurance companies, funds and investment firms.

The monsters created are not only controlling artificially created trillions that easily out-number the actual goods and services of the real economy but are also far bigger than any amount our democratically elected leaders direct.

32 trillion Euros were accumulated in the balance sheets of the banks of the Euro-zone. The global financial capacity is estimated to be 170 trillion US-Dollars, 8 time of the World's GDP. Since September 11, 2001, the US financial industry sold obligations and financial instruments in the amount of 27 trillion Dollars to the rest of the world.

But, America's export of industrial goods is only a fraction of that amount. Even worse is the trading of Derivates and Credit Default Swaps (CDS) that constituted a volume of 32 trillion Dollars in 2009. At peak times in 2007 these artificial financial instruments and guarantees reached 60 trillion Dollars. The entire volume of the derivate's market was 600 trillion Dollars before the crash and now still amounts to 350 trillion. In addition to this, futures and options have to be added. These amount to more than double of what is traded outside the stock markets.

The European Parliament's initiative therefore can only be seen as symbolic. Effectively, the EU issued a gambling license to the Jedi Riders.

The Conspirators

Closer scrutiny of the US' National Income and Productivity (NIPA) tables as well as the Savings Rate prove that normal income from work is not sufficient to accumulate any relevant wealth. Also in Europe it is neither hard work nor innovative entrepreneurship that is the base for most of the wealth that is being moved from one playground of the financial market to the next, but it is the bloodline principle that makes people investment house Merrill Lynch refers to as Ultra-High-Net-Worth-Individuals (U-HNWIs) rich: The US economists Kotlikoff and Summers[6] prove in their study "The Role of Intergenerational Transfers in Aggregate Capital Accumulation" that at least 80% of all American wealth results from inheritance.

This includes the capital accumulation that further increases the bubble-building by multiplying numbers and zeros in the virtual reality casino of our times which is likewise not an achievement as it is based on shear economic power and a portion of luck for the gambling heir and/or his managers.

Other studies at different times and in different parts of the world come to similar conclusions[7] such as E.N. Wolff in "Wealth Accumulation by Age Cohort in the U.S., 1962-1992: The Role of Savings, Capital Gains and Intergenerational Transfers", or the "Geneva Papers on Risk and Insurance" by A. Atkinson, or "The distribution of Wealth and the Individual Life-Cycle", published by Oxford Econ. Papers, and by N. Oulton, "Inheritance and the Distribution of Wealth", also published in Oxford Econ. Papers.

---

6   Kotlikoff, L. J., Summers, L. H., The Role of Intergenerational Transfers in Aggregate Capital Accumulation, (Journal of political economy, 1981, vol. 89, no. 4)
7   Wolff, E. N., 'Wealth Accumulation by Age Cohort in the U.S., 1962-1992: The Role of Savings, Capital Gains and Intergenerational Transfers', Geneva Papers on Risk and Insurance: Issues and Practice 24., Atkinson, A., The distribution of Wealth and the Individual Life-Cycle, Oxford Econ. Papers, n.s. 23, July 1971, 239 - 54, Oulton, N., Inheritance and the Distribution of Wealth, Oxford Econ. Papers, n.s. 28, March 1976, 86 – 101

The reason for the present crisis is not only the dreadful speculation and gambling in the financial merry-go-round at Wall Street, The City of London, some offshore banking centre under palm trees, British tax havens on Isle of Man, Guernsey, Jersey or in 'boom-cities' such as Dublin where a quarter of the world's GDP was laundered in the black holes of the 'free market'.

The collapse of the present system foremost is owed to a dreadful disparity of income that led to a re-distribution of wealth from bottom and middle of society to it's top.

In the US the level of wages today is at the level of 1977, clear of inflation, leaving four fifth of Americans 35 years behind while the upper class was able to multiple it's wealth which it passes on from generation to generation.

But, Europe is not much better off in this regard. Level of wages (clear of inflation) in most of the old (Western) EU member states these days is somewhere in the mid 1980ies. The capital coefficient shows that despite an ever rising productivity of around 2.5% per annum, which would mean a plus of 42% over the past 25 years, the vast majority of Europeans did not benefit at all.

But, the heirs have an ever greater amount to play with. Not only, that they have never worked for their wealth which raises the question why one calls a capitalistic western free market system a 'society of achievers', but the golden cage in which they grew up in most cases has been built upon by brutal exploitation, or outright criminal behaviour over centuries.

In Germany, presently the EU's economic powerhouse and potentially richest member state, the accumulated wealth has an even more distasteful smell: two thirds of all industrial enterprises, trade companies and private banks in West-Germany are owned by some 500 families that very often are interlinked by marriages and ancestry and who almost exclusively stem from the German aristocracy.

A famous book by Bernt Engelmann in the 1970ies under the title "The Reich vanished, the Rich remained" proved that these families in 1913 had a similar power base as they had 60 years later and which they even expanded, especially during the Third Reich. Forced labour, torture in concentration camps and two brutal world wars, although military-wise lost, made this class and the heirs of this class incredibly wealthy.[8]

---

8   Bernd Engelmann, Das Reich zerfiel, die Reichen blieben, München, 1975, S. 299

Even today, in a formally free and democratic Germany, these circles have full control of what is going on in Germany and in Europe. In the so called 'Düsseldorfer Industrie Club' and similar exclusive circles the owners conspire against the democratic will of the majority of citizens.

Their banks are being rescued by the taxpayer whenever their top managers like Deutsche Bank AG CEO Josef Ackermann picks up the telephone and calls Chancellor Angela Merkel. On European level, the 'European Round Table of Industrialists' (ERT) conspires to undermine EU institutions. The Lisbon Strategy of 'Stability & Growth' is one of the results of this.

The funds moved by hedge funds, private equity firms and so called 'investment' banks to wherever profit can be maximized are owned by dynasties. Our present economic system produces for profit and not for actual demand consequently forcing the heirs and their managers only to invest into what promises ever greater return and not what might be more sustainable. That's why the declining financial capitalism is anti-economical.

The question of ownership of capital is the key to the social divide in our society. This key is handed from one generation to the next one while it is virtually almost impossible to penetrate the concrete wall between the social classes, at least not by hard work and good entrepreneurship.

Only a few cases every now and then that pose as an exception actually prove the fact that it is by far more important who one's parents are than how intelligent, clever, innovative and hard working one is. If above was not true, wealth statistics, savings rate and income tables looked completely different and our economic system would not collapse for the fifth time in 400 years.

Deja-Vu

To make it short: Socialism got crippled by Centralisation, Capitalism by Concentration.

Number of Americans in poverty at highest in 50 years", the Financial Times headlined on 14 September 2011. In 2010, 46.2 million (15.1%) people fell below the poverty line. It is probably the highest percentage ever as 50 years ago the collection of data only commenced.

Empirical studies have proven beyond doubt that there is a strong connection between self – sustaining investment dynamism and "creative destruction" in unregulated markets. Such destruction of already invested capital through innovation provides the basis for ever new investment.

But, the more capital intensive an investment in machinery had been, the bigger is the resistance to devalue such which also gives the ever small amount of players more and more power to make it impossible. Stagnation is the consequence.

This problem for the first time occurred at the beginning of the 20th Century. Out of hundreds of small competitors a few market-dominating major corporations that linked the capital – typical unsaturated demand for profit maximization to the power to direct investment decisions and also political power.

Markets now were dominated by a few dozens of major suppliers who behind closed doors fixed prices and secured their market shares leaving out any newcomers with innovative products. Under these circumstances capital becomes very conservative and no "creative destruction" is happening anymore. New technologies are only entering the market if the majors take them over which they of course only do once the old ones are written off.

But, in all fairness, one has to say that this dreadful oligopoly-development could hardly be stopped politically or by an advanced merger-control constantly unbundling conglomerates because at the beginning of the 20th Century it had been technological requirements itself that especially in the field of heavy industry as well as electronics or chemicals needed a capital minimum to enhance the development. Technically, it had to be either big or it wouldn't have been possible at all.

A market, however, that requires a high capital minimum to participate is not an open market as any newcomer had no chance at all.

Already at the beginning of the 20th Century the growing market concentrations of ever fewer suppliers resulted in exactly the same reactions we know from the recent years in which investment dynamism and the process of technological innovation is slowing down dramatically.

Instead more and more capital streamed onto the financial- and stock markets. Market value of American stocks multiplied many times between 1924 and 1929 while the ordinary capital goods stock grew only modestly. Growth and profits that could not be increased by the real economy any longer were simulated by speculative gains. The profit piece in the cake got bubbles.

But because, unlike today, in the back-then-days banks had no money-printing machine in their basements by which they could create endlessly liquidity out of nothing the snowball system reached it's limits pretty soon. In 1929 the mega-blasé burst and the profit piece collapsed like an 'Apfelstrudel' in the microwave, resulting in the worst economic crisis ever, regimes of repression, fascism and ultimately WWII.

Already from 1914 onwards until the middle of last century Capitalism didn't make mankind richer but poorer. The destruction that began during the Great Depression and that ended with the mass bombardment of the allies in 1945 has been anything but ‚creative'. It has been brutal, bloody and absolutely senseless. It brought hunger and misery back to industrialised nations. It made society become barbaric and threw back the economic development by many decades.

After WWII Capitalism managed in industrialised countries to regain for 2 decades it's old dynamism because the demand for investment kept up for an unusual and historically unprecedented long phase allowing profits to constantly be re-invested.

One reason for this has been that WWII destroyed literally all economic capacity in Europe which resulted in a huge demand for reconstruction. The second factor that played a significant role was the fact that because of it's dark history Capitalism was completely discredited and in order to be able to continue to exist Capitalism was willing to compromise a bit and allowed for some social regulations such as wages that were in line with the rise of productivity, a social security network and by this a stabilising purchasing power.

Steadily increasing wages and social expenditure could only contribute to the economic dynamism because a third factor came into play: the "S-curve" as the suddenly rising consumption industry is referred to. Mass products such as fridges, dish washers, TV sets, and cars became the standard even for working class people. The rapidly growing demand required huge investments and carried the economy for over 2 decades.

But, once all production sites were built and all households had fridge, dishwasher, car and TV the curve that had pointed straight upwards bowed a bit and by this the requirement for investment leaving over-capacities behind. Profitable investment opportunities became rare and by this also the profit rates.

This situation, and not the oil price shock, had been the reason for the world wide economic downturn in the 1970ies. Following this, in most countries neo-liberal concepts were applied whose diagnose of the reasons for the crisis culminated in the assumption that the profit share in the income – cake had gotten too little.

Only goal of the neo-liberal doctrine was to increase the profit share again which led to a dreadful cycle of de-industrialisation while rich became richer and ordinary citizens poorer.

But, to have social democratic governments like the one of Gerhard Schröder and Anthony Blair go with a chainsaw in their hands through the social net was not enough. The shareholders and owners of major corporations wanted the profit share to ever grow bigger.

That's why the average wage share had to decline further along with ever poorer social benefits.

Although the 'Basic Law', West-Germany's post WWII constitution that had been adopted by the united Germany in 1990, guarantees a social principle the social contrasts in today's Germany are larger than during the German Kaiser-Reich before WW I.

The share in the income-cake for the bottom 50% of population in 1913 had been 24% but today only 14.9% of all income is shared by bottom half of German society. While in 1913 the richest 10% of Germans accounted for 40% of income it is today only 1% that owns 23% of all income. In the US a similar development can be observed: of every Dollar by which the income in the US had grown between 1976 and 2007, 58 cents ended in the pockets of the ultra-rich 1% top of society. The bottom 60% in the US account for only 21% of income.

But, not only in a relative way, also in absolute figures the general standard of living declines for the vast majority of citizens. The average real net wage of an employee in Germany in 2006 was tumbling at around the level of 1986. In other words, 20 years of economic development have bypassed the majority of people.

Actually, they lost it, because in the bottom quintile of the income statistics wages are being paid that relate to the 1950ies in West-Germany. This is ridiculous for an industrialised country, and a rich nation like Germany, especially, so.

Communities and city councils are forced to close theatres, public libraries, fail to renovate schools, hospitals and universities while Germany's upper-class accumulated 4,000 billion Euros, foremost by gambling with 'financial instruments', in particular also with derivatives and credit default swaps of states such as Greece, Portugal, Ireland, Spain and Italy.

Europe-wide wages, pensions, social benefits, education & health care expenditure are being axed in order to bring things back on track but it is the life-quality of the vast majority of citizens that suffers under this insanity.

In the US more than 30 million people require food vouchers. Average wages are tumbling at around the level of the 1950ies (clear of inflation).

In the real economy a constant de-industrialisation can be asserted. The share of manufacturing business in the general economic data in the US had been in 1989 some 17%, in 2009 it was only 9% of people who were employed by industrial companies.

Not much better is the United Kingdom. In 1997, when "New Labour" under Anthony Blair took over from the Tories the British industries still contributed 20% to the UK's GDP. At the end of 2009 this share has fallen to 11%.

Instead, the financial sector was booming. These shifts are not primarily owed to automated production and technological progress but are the result of the wrong economic priorities and a lack of industrial investment. This could have been stimulated by politics. But, if wages decline, the consumption share also points downwards and by this leaves over-capacities at industries from which shareholders withdraw their capital and put it where it can accumulate with skyrocketing profits: the financial markets.

This last chapter of the history of capitalism proves that the industrialisation that made it rise and become overwhelmingly strong is destructing itself at pace rate. The more unregulated the profit maximisation is being pursued the quicker the present economic system declines. Although the Anglo-Saxon countries have advanced on this road of no-return much more than the continental European economies, the direction is the same.

It could be worthwhile not only to study the military and political history of the 20th Century but also the underlying economic conditions.

IV

IN THE CLAWS OF THE DRAGON

Privare (latin= to rob)

Before turning to China & The West, we should look for a brief moment at an outrageous conspiracy against one of the West's chief economic officers, Mr Dominique Strauss-Kahn ('DSK') who as finance minister once played a dubious role when trying to privatise French state assets but had opposed to show the torture tools to the Greek government when being president of the IMF and for that he should be lauded no matter what kind of stupid other behaviour he can be accused of. The crocodile's tears Euro-Group-chief Jean-Claude Juncker had seemed to be crying over his "close friend" Dominique Strauss-Kahn appear to have been a bit fake one may think when listening to the Luxembourgoise Minister-president speaking about Greece suggesting an ever more brutal privatization wave that would be pursued by a model West-Germany imposed once over the former German Democratic Republic.

Mr Juncker proposed to install a '*Treuhand*', a trust agency that should accelerate the privatization campaign of the Greek silver table cutlery for which rich clients of banks such as Deutsche Bank AG, HSBC, Frere Lassard SA, Goldman Sachs, Nathan Meyer Rothschild and others that had brought about the trouble by trading Credit Default Swaps on Greek state bonds are standing by in order to turn it into gold. It is clear that only the profitable state entreprises are subjet for privatization which raises the question why, if these were profitable, should not remain in public ownership enabling the state to derive some income badly needed to retire debt ?! No private investor ever would be interested to take over a non-profitable state company unless it is deemed to become « lean » and eventually produces profits on the back of the employees who usually have to sacrifice their social benefits in order to keep their jobs.

Mr Strauss-Kahn, although he had won his merits as a brutal privatisation-fetishist as a minister in the Socialist government of Lionel Jospin, had clearly opposed Mr Juncker's ideas. Maybe he remembered how the German Treuhand de-industrialised East-Germany. Or he got reminded of the mysterious assassination of it's boss, Detlev Karsten Rohwedder in 1991, who got replaced by an even more strict privatization hardliner. The kind of 'hostile takeover' of the East German centralised planning economy by the West German trust agency 'Treuhand', an itself centralised planning authority, had a lot in common with the early stages of capitalism but here the only market mechanisms that came into play were the fraudulent behaviour of the bidders. Unfortunately, the sellers of the 'Treuhand' had been less good capitalists than the buyers were.

The system of the 'Treuhand' had been, as Germans would jokingly would call it – 'bribingly easy' and vice versa. In most cases it worked out as follows : The buyer (usually from the West) were bribed by promising subsidies from Bonn and Brussels as well as cheap loans from Banks in Frankfurt to buy a factory while the land was given as a free incentive. The buyer took a mortgage secured against the land, let the company go bankrupt and founded a new company back at home in the West. Those bribes which had not been paid in the transaction got knicked by some of the employees of the bankrupt company as an incentive for not having been bribed.

In Germany, today, only 20 years on, the so trustworthy sounding word 'Treuhand' has the same hollow sounds as the word of the 'good death', 'Euthanasia'. On unification day, 3rd of October 1990, the (West-) German Bundesbank asserted that the entire industries of the GDR were worth one thousand billions of (West) Deutsche Mark. A year later the so called government trustee 'Treuhand' had accumulated 258 billion in debts by selling-off property previously owned by the East German public. Where have all those billions gone ? Today we know that the transfer was from the East to the West like it is in our society now from the bottom to the top.

Jean Ziegler, at that time UN special rapporteur on the right to food, said in 2008 that "the privatization of the world weakens the normative capacity of governments." And, he continued, "it reduces governments and parliaments to a subordinate role of dependence. It empties of meaning most elections and almost all voting by the people. It deprives public institutions of their regulatory power. It kills the law. In the republic, such as we have inherited it from the French Revolution, it subsists now only as a shadow of itself." Nevertheless, EU Commission and IMF pursue a model that has already forced many developing countries but also industrialised nations like Yugoslavia or even a super-power, the Soviet Union, into bankruptcy with all the terrible consequences for the citizens.

The promises made by the protagonists of privatization are always exactly as big as the profits of major corporations and banks that get engaged. It is usually promised to have a free market instead of state regulation, efficiency instead of bureaucracy, competition instead of monopolies, smart and motivated employees instead of lazy state officials. Instead of boring bureaucracies lean and flexible private enterprises were to supply us with electricity, water, heating, transport our parcels, teach our children, dispose our garbage, lock up our criminals, treat us when we are sick, take care of us when we are old, bring us from A to B and be more service-orientated and efficient while competition was said to bring down prices, increase employment and let the GDP grow faster than ever before.

Great-Britain under Prime Minister Margaret Thatcher pioneered the development in the 1980ies when British rail, telecom as well as energy and water had been turned into profitable objects for private investment. It ended in disaster but nevertheless became the model the EU Commission copied in each and every liberalisation – regulation that found many friends on the continent after the collapse of the Easter European Socialism that discredited public ownership completely. But, whereas Socialism got crippled by centralisation, Capitalism choked by concentration.

There is no really free market and almost no competition. Like the entire economy nowadays public subsistence is dominated by a few major corporations which turned the formerly public services into profitable business models.

The French water companies Suez and Veolia have conquered first the European and by now the trillions heavy world water market. German energy conglomerates EON and RWE have turned into global players after yet another liberalisation- and deregulation – wave. "Unbundling" as the EU Commission promised became a paper tiger because whoever owns and controls a network is sitting on a classical monopoly.

Virtually all major multinationals are nowadays specialised to provide service that once used to be the elementary responsibility of the state:

water, energy, transport, health care, education and social security, but also administrative, policing and even judicial services.

Structure and Quality of the formerly public services have been changed fundamentally by the private basic subsistence industry in Europe in the past 21 years and these changes differ in a way that is often diametrically opposed to what had been promised.

CHINA & Deutsche Börse AG run the show

Does the turbo-capitalistic Chinese communism has to rescue the ailing communistic Capitalism of the US?

Despite of two decades of privatisation hysteria and anti-étatistic propaganda the state in general still plays a major role in the European industrial sector. But not only in Europe the state and by this the taxpayer had to come to the rescue of major corporations such as GM and Chrysler.

In many countries the state still plays an active role as industrial entrepreneur and it may one make think why the industrially successful nations have not been those in which the state had surrendered it's industrial policy to the neo-liberal dogma.

In this regard it is worth mentioning that the US got shocked recently by the prediction of IMF and World Bank that in less than 5 years the People's Republic of China will become the number one world economy.

Deutsche Börse AG got the license to print money despite the failed merger with the New York Stock Exchange's EURONEXT. to Frankfurt, Germany's export leaning economy is getting ever deeper into the claws of the dragon as the Chinese state capitalistic economy is absorbing resources and innovation in a way Germany won't be able to compete with. So far, Germany has been able to generate huge trade surpluses because of wage- and tax-dumping that won it's manufacturers huge advantages over other EU member states.

With the collapse of more and more Southern and South-Eastern European economies also because of Germany's aggressive export strategy and the decline of the US, the biggest importer of German capital goods, Germany now increasingly relies on Chinese demand of it's goods.

But, to compete with China will be difficult for Germany as wages are already on the level of the early 1980ies (clear of inflation) and the other cost factors such as raw materials and energy resources will lead to an extremely dangerous rivalry.

German shareholders will have to tighten their belts when dealing with China as in addition to being profitable a privately owned enterprise traded at the stock market needs to produce a shareholder value. This is a clear disadvantage for capitalistic companies. State owned companies only need to be sustainable in their production as they don't need to feed shareholders which is a clear advantage for the Chinese model.

Indeed, in China most of the enterprises are still owned and controlled by the state. One doesn't have to accept the form of worker's exploitation in Chinese companies to admit that these are extremely successful.

In the last four months of 2010 the Chinese state owned industries accumulated a net profit of 85 billion US Dollars which to a large degree is available for the public hand and does not unlike in Western World corporations disappears in private shareholder's pockets.

In this sense China is a good example for state owned companies that are managed in a similar way as capitalistic corporations and which also offer incentives and structures for bonuses but are free from pressure to create short term gains for pleasing shareholders. Instead, the accumulated wealth is being re-invested, something most of our major multinational privately owned corporations are missing these days.

Although Chinese companies are certainly not a good reference for an utmost of socialism but rather brutal exploitation of their workers the fairy tale of supposedly inefficient state owned industries is led ad absurdum. Likewise do privately owned major corporations not live up to what a free market economy would demand from a modern, innovative and sustainable production.

This is also true for many other South East Asian companies such as the major state-owned steel industries in Southern Korea and Taiwan which for many years already produce more efficiently than any privately owned steel factory in other parts of the world.

In Sweden many state-owned companies were made efficient and profitable by the introduction of an incentive scheme that let these companies operate equally good or better than any private competitor.

Until the mid 1990ies the quota of state-ownership in the EU has been at around 17%. Then, a liberalisation- and privatization Tsunami pushed it to under 10% resulting in the destruction of industrial capacity that in the US as well as Great-Britain led to de facto de-industrialisation.

The French Caisse Deparnage (CDC) founded under Louis XVIII is still state owned and a shareholder in about 250 French corporations including most of the CAC 40 listed industry – leading companies. These assets are frequently used in order to fend-off hostile takeovers or transfer of jobs to cheaper production sites abroad.

In reality there is no country that doesn't have the state fulfil certain economic functions, especially when it comes to subsidies for research and innovation. IT business is the fastest growing industry of the past decades and until today the area of the economy most dependent on subsidies and tax shelter schemes.

In Southern Korea, Taiwan, India and China up to 100% of the investment in that sector are financed by the state the Financial Times noted.

But, also outside the IT business many private major corporations are only profitable thanks to the state-interventions. In Germany the government comes up with 30% of all costs for research and innovation that is conducted by major corporations such as BASF or Merck und Philips.

If the state subsidies for research lead to a patent, then, of course, the revenue derived from that patent will be enjoyed solely by the company's shareholders. Most SMEs can only dream of such comfortable state-aid.

Also the banks in all OECD countries, foremost the US and EU member states are enjoying a de-facto state guarantee – for free and when Greece, Ireland, Portugal and other states are being "rescued" it is foremost the shareholder value of the banks that is at stake.

In case of the nuclear industry it is also the state which carries all the risk. Electricity from nuclear energy would be far too expensive if the industry had to insure their reactors against meltdowns like in Fukushima. And, the alternative energy market is as well funded by the state.

Agricultural production is heavily subsidised and in Germany it is the state which regulates the tariffs for medicine and by this makes sure that the pharmaceutical industry can pay 30-40% dividends every year.

Nobel economic laureate Joseph E. Stiglitz once asserted that one of the biggest successes of the US were the results of the public financed research at universities especially in the field of IT and biotechnology. He is right, 'the market' is not the great inventor anymore as many innovative products are often side products from military research. The internet for instance got developed in the nuclear research facility CERN.

One thing is clear, though, research and innovation require a long breath, especially in terms of finance, and the hungry private shareholder can not wait that long. That's why the state steps in.

In other words, the talk about a state-free economy is a neo-liberal myth. The state plays an important economic role in all countries and the only substantial difference between China and the non-communistic world is that the engagement by the state does not to such an extent benefit rich private shareholders and instead allows for profits to be re-invested.

That's why China is on the road to success and the Western Free Democracies are doomed if they don't change fundamentally and rapidly. The hostile takeover by China is in full swing.

Better red than dead?!

It is easy for a leader that stands tall to wipe away doubts on his human rights record by admitting that one still has some work to do in this respect. After that, one can talk business. China wouldn't want to watch that film in which the US totally collapsed, foremost because it holds almost 3 trillion Dollars in US treasury bonds and wouldn't want these assets go off in flames of the volcano American investment bankers are dancing on. That's why China buys about 4 billion Dollars in T-bills every day.

At the same time it sells about 6 billion per day 'under the table' to every little dictator in Africa. As longs as China buys, even at lower rate than it sells, the financial merry-go-round can go on.

It is a stabilizing momentum for the US but not a selfless act of generosity on the Chinese part. China needs Dollars for two reasons: first of all China is far from being autonomous. It has to bridge a food gap and an energy gap.

Secondly, China has learnt from Western free democracies quick: the introduction of Western lifestyle lead to the creation of a class of society living off the work of others. A rather un-communistic approach that might let Mao turn in his grave.

The Financial Times (FT) had announced 18 months ago that the world economy was on the road to recovery citing the sudden demand of steel by the Chinese who the colleagues of the FT said were buying a lot of steel because of an increased demand. But, they forgot that Chinese GDP is mostly dependent on export.

Given the Yuan's artificial low exchange rate would mean that China was committing suicide by paying for steel imports in Dollars for it's domestic consumption. A ridiculously naïve thought by our colleagues.

What had happened instead was that China bought steel contracts, futures etc, but never imported that steel. Like in a perfect Ponzi-scheme those futures were sold on to whoever believed that the steel prices would further go up. China has learnt quicker than most analysts in the West had thought. Chinese state-capitalists now know how to build bubbles. Real estate bubbles, and steel bubbles.

China could, of course, by the sheer size of it's domestic demand jump-start the world economy by using it's Dollar reserves for satisfying demand of it's 1.4 billion population that is longing to consume the way they were taught we Westerners were doing it. But, that would mean that China was at least socialistic if not communistic.

The US were hoping for that to happen as this would eventually also ignite industrial production in the US. But, although the wage-level in the US has continuously declined and today is on the level of 1977, it will not lead to a re-industrialisation of the US any time soon.

Fighting high inflation resulting from the Keynesian strategy President James Carter pursued, President Ronald Reagan de facto de-industrialised the US by high interest rates that crippled any development and suffocated SMEs. Instead, the virtual reality casino got started and spun ever faster under President William Clinton. Soon, the industrial base was exported to China. At the same time the IT business only celebrated hypes in the unreal internet dimension while it's power base shifted to India.

President Barack Obama nowadays is confronted with the consequences of mal-governing by his predecessors Reagan and Clinton. His administration is eager to cover up what is inevitably going to see the light of truth: not only is the US bankrupt but it also has lost it's ability to self-heal it's wounds.

Probably because the Obama-administration understood this the Bureau of Labour started to manipulate statistics. Officially 103,000 new jobs were created in December 2010 making the unemployment rate decline (officially) by 0.4% to 9.4%. However, at least 175,000 new jobs have to be created on a monthly basis in order to absorb the new workforce that is entering the job's market in order not to increase the unemployment rate.

Funnily, the so called U-6 table of the Bureau of Labour fell by 0.3% to 16.7%. This is obviously owed to a 'reform' after which only those persons are being considered unemployed who receive benefits which usually terminates after half a year and throws these people out of any statistics. President Obama only increased the minimal basic payment to 99 weeks.

The real unemployment rate of the US is 22.4%. In order to reach pre-crisis levels until 2015 that officially had been 5% in December 2007, the US would have to create 10.5 million jobs plus 175,000 per month in order to honour population growth.

It is clear now that the US are completely in the hands of China as another manipulation of US statistics had been discovered by EU chronicle some time ago: the Bureau of Economic Affairs (BEA) had to admit that it's growth statistics contained hedonic pricing methods that allowed for quality adjustments. Let's say a car being built in the 1990ies was x-times better than a car built in the 1970ies. But, in 2010 less cars were being sold than in the 1950ies although population doubled.

Only a lunatic would speak of real growth, but hey, it let the virtual reality casino spin ever faster the better the Clinton-Bush-Obama growth rates were presented. The bad news: Europe is not doing much better since the Barroso-Commission decided to adhere to same statistical principals. We can only take brace position and let the Chinese take over even though their 'Communism' sounds hollow as well.

EU: Germany hung itself

While Financial Weapons of Mass Destruction once more are in the process of destroying an existing world order by leading to over-indebtedness which the citizen is forced to tighten their belts for, owners of big capital become acquainted with the idea of a haircut.

It becomes easier for them to agree to writing off since it transpired that most of the toxic assets are held by the ECB anyways while they had transferred their illegitimately accumulated wealth to Switzerland in the shadow of every publicly celebrated round of "rescue mission" for Greece, Ireland, Portugal and Spain.

The trade imbalances between Germany that accumulated 326 billion Euros of surpluses by it's aggressive export strategy and other EU member states of which the "PIGS" (Portugal, Ireland, Greece and Spain) piled up 344 billion Euros inevitably will lead to hyper-inflation also in Germany.

Cashless transactions between the EMU states are dealt with by their national central banks through the inter-bank payment system "Target2". The German Bundesbank thus finances via Target2 the bulk of bank loans in those countries that have a trade deficit with Germany.

In other words: Germany hands the countries it exports to the credit-line required to buy it's goods. And, in order to be more competitive with it's products than anybody else the German industry over the past 20 years let wages stagnate and decline while social subsistence was sacrificed on the altar of a neo-liberal ideology that exploited workers as well as SMEs to squeeze ever more profit out of 4/5th of Germans.

With no money in the pockets of German consumers Germany's domestic market took a dive.

The absurdity of the "rescue" missions for Greece become clear when one realises that there is no limitation for the imbalances in the Euro-zone. Only limit is the willingness of the surplus - states, foremost Germany but also France, the Netherlands and Italy, to finance the net-import of their goods as well as the net exports of capital of the deficit - states.

A correction of these deficits would only be possible if domestic goods and services in the PIGS would become much cheaper in comparison to the substitutes of such goods from abroad.

That would mean a drastically lower production cost, shrinking wages, axed social benefits and ultimately a tightening of the belt for the vast majority of citizens unless the rich upper class would be forced to return their illegitimately accumulated wealth.

To assume that the contradictions of our economic model will be resolved without a harsh confrontation that most likely will lead to violence would be naïve as the rich class doesn't understand yet that their speculation-hypes in the PIGS has been irresponsible and led to a death spiral.

The willingness of the surplus – states to finance the deficits by their national central banks will abruptly come to an end in exactly that moment when the rich class of the deficit-states followed by ordinary citizens will transfer their savings to the surplus-states.

This logic step would dramatically make it clear that the population in the deficit – states doesn't want to be held liable for dubious loans by EZB and IMF to the private sector as well as the state but want to socialise the losses with the rest of the Euro-zone.

The end of the European Monetary Union (EMU) and by this the Euro will materialise in the minute that banks in the surplus-states reject deposits from citizens of the deficit-states.

The decisions of end of July 2012 open the curtain for the final act as none of the half-hearted measurements will rescue the Euro but will prolong it's decline.

German Chancellor Angela Merkel would be well advised to study the financial history of the 20th century. While Great-Britain had financed it's WWI - costs by taxes, Germany did same by bonds in combination with recklessly printing money. Between 1914 and 1918 the external value of the Reichsmark had halved.

After unification in 1990 West-Germany's manufacturers and retailers celebrated a boom but soon got into an expansion crisis. 17 million new consumers were not enough to absorb the overcapacities that West-Germany's industry had built.

With the introduction of the Euro as single currency Germany finally seemed to have achieved by economic means what Adolf Hitler failed to achieve by military terrorism and torture: the economic dominance over continental Europe.

In 1918, the German Reichsbank under Rudolf Havenstein stoically believed that the amount of money (M3) had nothing to do with the level of prices and the exchange rate. Result was the exorbitant inflation of the Reichsmark that at the same time rapidly devalued.

The analogy between "Eurobonds" that many seem to believe could rescue the single currency project today and the behaviour of the Reichsbank in

1918 financially does make sense even though other factors such as the lost first world war and the Versailles-treaty played a role for the rise of NAZI dictatorship.

Unless a radical move is being made by our leaders immediately towards confiscating the illegitimately accumulated funds rather than continuing to crack down on citizens and taxpayers by inflating the amount of money by supposedly "rescuing" states not only the Euro will be in jeopardy.

V

Placebos don't cure cancer

The EU's half hearted reforms won't be good enough

"Six Pack", Eurobonds, improved consumer protection, mortgage market stabilisation mechanisms which the Economic Affairs committee had called for in mid 2011, harsh austerity measurements and any of the typical neo-classical torture tools will only amount to fighting the symptoms and not the cause unless the fundamentals of our present economic system are re-defined.

As long as the profit maximization dogma forces the real economy to produce only for profit and not for actual demand it will lead to bubble-building effects that inevitably will create hyper-inflation as the growing demand by shareholders for ever more interest and dividends will concentrate income earned outside the real economy in the hands of a tiny upper class of society.

The moment that these bubbles burst an incredible amount of superfluous cash-Tsunami will flood the goods markets of the real economy and devalue the work, income and savings of real people.

In order to avoid this from happening the state once set forth strict rules for the banking "industry" that limited the credit potential. Banks themselves were interested to hold sufficient reserves in order not to fall bankrupt or to be forced to take expensive loans themselves from another bank or the central bank. Banks used to build reserves which they parked with the central bank and which they could access easily if needed. This only changed when the inter-bank market was developed. "Investment banks" sprung up like mushrooms that were able to turn any obligation and even toxic assets into liquidity.

In the old days, before the "masters of the universe" invented financial monsters and financial weapons of mass destruction the credit cycle in a bank functioned as follows: A deposit was taken and led by a pipe to the loan department of the bank. Said pipe had a reserve canister that did not supply all the liquids to the credit section but kept a certain reserve which would only continue to be transported once more liquidity came after it, in other words, only when the central bank opened the taps.

Under these conditions central banks had control over the amount of credit obligations being issued by banks and an explosion like in the last 15 years had been impossible.

It has been a political decision to liberalise and de-regulate the financial markets and by this to let the banks off the hook in allowing them to generate liquidity by whatever dubious method of trading virtual funds and "financial instruments" that were "so sophisticated that is hard to understand" as ECB President Jean-Claude Trichet said in January 2007 in Davos months before the crisis began on 11th August 2007.

In the UK this development began under Prime Minister Margaret Thatcher who broke the neck of the unions after the Falklands war and put everything behind "The City" by this de-industrialising Great-Britain. 'New Labour' under Prime Minister Anthony Blair and Chancellor of the Exchequer Gordon Brown spun an ever bigger wheel of Private Equity – fraud schemes and Hedge-Fund - scams and even placed two thirds of the UK's gold reserve with the Frankfurt based European Central Bank in order to have a foot in the door for eventually joining the EMU and Euro. Nowadays 67% of British GNP (agricultural sector accounts for less than 1%) is directly or indirectly linked to "The City". While in industries all wheels stand still, the wheel of fortune is spinning ever faster in London. Great-Britain has abolished the minimum reserve requirement for banks completely.

In Germany, it has been the "Red-Green" coalition government of Gerhard Schröder who rolled out the red carpet for hedge funds and private equity sharks that used their artificially created funds to engage in a gigantic buy-it-strip-it-sell-it – poker game while on the Euromarkets suddenly foreign currencies following the deregulation-wave from Brussels. Nominally, the ECB still asks for a anyhow minimal 2% reserve but first of all this only for certain kind of deposits and secondly can this be circumvented by creative accounting. In any case, the reserve requirement becomes ridiculous in comparison to the volume of the trade balances of these mega Frankenstein banking institutions.

Most of the financial 'innovative products' had only one task anyhow: to reduce the required liquidity for huge transactions to the bare minimum in other words, to accelerate the circulation of the liquidity in the pipes by multiple force making it possible to finance ever more debts with less and less liquidity from the central bank. On the other side of the balance sheet, of course, opposite to these debts accumulates a huge wealth. The legal requirements for minimum reserves are no longer a tool for any central banker to control the amount of debts handed out by commercial banks and likewise has it become impossible to control the amount of circulating money, M3. The uncontrolled creation of virtual funds outside of the central banks has led to the crisis and it will be impossible to tame the monsters that have been created over the past 15 years by the political leaders who wilfully assisted a corrupt scam.

One can not blame the "investment" bankers or hedge fund managers for using every loophole our democratically elected leaders provide for their dirty business. If they don't do this they will be fired by the shareholders and owners of the institutions they manage.

It becomes clear why the real economy has been hit that bad because of this insane mechanism when one realises that BASEL I had ruled that credit lines handed out to companies had to be valued at 100% risk-level making such less lucrative and more expensive for banks. This is why all private banks reduced their engagement in the classical core business task any bank should have: to supply the real economy with liquidity.

Germany is envied by all other EU member states these days for it's sudden recovery letting it appear to get stronger out of the crisis than any other country. That's at least the official reading the German government presented today in Berlin. But, is that really true and can Germany rescue the rest of the EU by granting a seat in it's life rafts?

The reality check reveals that the development is anything but positive. Yes, Germany celebrates an 'Aufschwung' (up-swing) unseen in it's post WWII history. This is clever propaganda based on deliberate misinterpretation of the facts.

Low wages that were owed to Germany's aggressive export strategy let domestic demand implode for many years already. Most of Germany's GDP is owed to export to US and EU members, especially in Southern and Eastern Europe. The trade imbalances ruined the finances of Greece, Portugal, Spain, Hungary, Baltic Republics and Slovenia.

The US is bankrupt and won't be able to purchase many more German goods and the German - masterminded austerity programs imposed on member states by EU and IMF will only develop it's destructive power to the full in the second half of 2011.

Within two years 366,000 industrial workplaces vanished, in 2010 alone 136,000. Nevertheless, Chancellor Angela Merkel's government speaks of a 'job-miracle', but only recruitment agencies can show an increase. These low paid jobs in many cases replace proper employment that is governed by tariffs and regulation.

It is hard to understand why the German government thinks it is a moment of celebration when the capital goods sector shows 17% less industrial production in 2010 than what it has been before the crisis in 2007.

And, last but not least, one may wonder what Mrs Merkel's Christian Conservative-Liberal coalition wants to make voters believe the 'positive effects' will be when in May the labour market liberalisation opens the borders for Eastern Europeans to find work in a country that does not know a minimum wage and brought down the level of wages to pre-€uro times.

Truth is that the German economy recovers on the wings of a wage- and standard dumping that will become a death spiral pointing downwards when at the cost of xenophobia cheap labour influxes further bringing down wages to below of what it was in 2000.

Attention Continent: Take Brace Position!

EURO-bonds add fuel to the fire, while EU institutions have given up, it seems.

One thing becomes clearer every day: the debts won't be paid back. Neither those debts Goldman Sachs, Deutsche Bank AG, Nathan Meyer Rothschild, HSBC and others had imposed onto Greece, Portugal, Spain, Ireland and Italy nor those the Eastern European member states accumulated in order to finance their negative trade balance towards Germany.

The only sustainable method to reverse this fatally wrong development of the past two decades is the politically controlled devaluation of the wealth- and debt-bubble by nullification of all old state debts in a concerted action across all of the Euro-zone. It would better to force the entire EU under this procedure.

Instead, the MEPs in the European Parliament's 'Crisis Committee' stress that both EMU and the single market needed a stronger co-ordination of national tax policies, which sounds hollow as in recent years only VAT but not corporate taxes got somewhat harmonised. On top of that MEPs call on the Commission "to carry out an investigation into a future system of Eurobonds".

The fact that this is being discussed behind closed doors at ECOFIN meetings for quite some time already is evident since it transpired that an international bankruptcy law for states was considered an option. But, our leaders still haven't learnt, it seems, as they had the wealth of the rich on their mind when they proposed Eurobonds carrying a special risk which shall bear higher interests that will ultimately lead to yet another spiral of interest hikes.

It speaks for itself but not for her that German Chancellor Angela Merkel had actively pursued the Eurobond-solution as the more risky the bonds of other states are becoming the more investment in German 'Bundesschatzbriefe' will be attracted which will result in lower interests to be paid by the German government.

On a short term Germany would benefit from this solution but the rising interest rates in troublesome countries will accelerate their decline. It will prove illusory to be able to avoid a significant haircut, especially when the German taxpayers will have to rescue German banks by taking over the bad debt obligations from Greece, Ireland, Portugal, Spain, Italy.

The history of debt crisis teaches us that haircuts are not an isolated, single act of a desperate government but rather the probably most common method to get rid of the debts of predecessors.

One of the latest haircuts had happened in the aftermath of the neo-liberal era of Menem in Argentina in 2002 when the governments of Eduardo Duhalde and Nestor Kirchner pushed through a 75% cut that let the country's economy recover.

In history there are many good examples for nullifications of debt. In it's early years as a sovereign state France had been in trouble over late payments for eight times. Spain has not been able to cover it's foreign debt before 1800 for six times and in the 19th century for 7 times. In the past 300 years there have been 250 foreign debt crisis that resulted in at least partial nullifications and write-offs of debt.

Last but not least the United States' decision in 1971 to lift the gold standard in order not to be obliged to pay France in gold as President de Gaulle had demanded it has been nothing less than a cold bankruptcy of the US since this has been the unilateral decision to break an agreement over such a sensitive issue as debt and it usually would result in a war.

Neither the US nor Argentina or any other state needed a "state bankruptcy law" for their haircuts. The EU also wouldn't require this if in a rather concerted action it decided to declare 75% or 100% of it's old debts null and void. But, one should protect small deposits of up to 500,000 € as these are genuine savings accounts of the average citizens.

In Germany this would mean that 'Bundesschatzbriefe' that are almost entirely being held by small investors, employees be exempt while the 'Bundesanleihen' held by institutional investors such as private banks and insurance companies as well as ultra-rich high net worth individuals ("UHNWIs" as Merrill Lynch calls them) should be written off.

All old debts of the Euro-zone in 2010 reached 7.7 trillion Euros. Altogether, the EU member states account for 9.6 trillion Euros of debts. If most of these debts were declared null and void most of the private banks in Europe probably would become insolvent. In order to avoid a dreadful chain-reaction and by this the devaluation of the ordinary savings one would have to nationalise, recapitalise and restructure these banks. This would be very easy if one made the wealth accumulated through the irrational speculation of the past decades become liable for the nullified debts.

This would only hit the ultra rich multi millionaires and billionaires. According to the world wealth report of "investment" bank Merrill Lynch in 2009 these privateers owned and controlled a financial bubble of 9.4 trillion Euros – almost exactly the amount owed by all EU member states.

These funds had quadrupled in the past 10 years and even in the crisis year 2009 had skyrocketed by double digit figures. That is the wealth bubble that stands on the other side of the balance sheet.

Much is being said about public debt, not only in Greece and Ireland but also countries like Germany but mainstream media always tends to sketch the problem as a result from over-spending and a too generous welfare system that supposedly leftist governments had created.

That is wrong. The state quota did not rise during the past 4 decades because of some kind of socialistic Keynesianism. It is a myth that under social democratic or socialist governments the welfare state expanded. It usually is the opposite.

Today's public debts aren't primary the result of a classical Keynesian stimulus cycle that had countered an economic downturn.

According to the AMECO database the primary deficit of industrialised nations between 1975 and 1997 has been constantly negative. Only for the time after 1997 an up and down of the state indebtedness can be noticed that would match the classical Keynesian theory of stirring growth by state interventions.

But, a closer scrutiny reveals that the debts were hardly used for public investments or for stimulation of the economy by an increased consumption. Not leftist, "socialist" governments piled up these debts by generously distributing social benefits, but it is conservative or right wing governments that behave like Santa Claus – to the rich. That's where debts on the one side of the balance sheet and wealth on the other come from.

In order to revive our economy and protect the average citizens we have to let the air out of both, the wealth- and debt-bubble, in a controlled way. Our states would be able to function again and provide for public subsistence, health care, social benefits, education and cultural life again. And, our SMEs would be enabled to refinance themselves again while the financial casino would permanently be closed.

This controlled nullification of debt and the wealth that stands against such would not affect the real economy and the average citizen but only ultra rich who either inherited millions or gambled and speculated.

But, to the contrary, by seeking a solution in Eurobonds along with a relatively small amount of only 100,000 € to be guaranteed in banks the EU is bracing itself for an uncontrolled crash in which most citizens and SMEs will lose all their savings while their social existence will be in jeopardy.

VI

THE GREAT DEPRESSION – NOW IN TECHNICOLOR

The Big Bluff

European industries across the board are in a sharp decline. The worldwide economic crisis once more took it's beginning in the US. But, why are German, British, South Korean and Japanese carmakers and other manufacturers so terribly hit? And, is it really as bad as 80 years ago? The most significant difference may be that in 1929, the US had been the largest creditor, today it is the largest debtor; however, the outcome may be the same due to structural flaws of the economic system. Americans and Europeans are sitting in the same boat, not the same life-raft, though. And, the disaster is a result from mismanagement by those who think that when being bailed out by governments that it only requires a bit of fine-tuning in order to bring things back on track and keep on trucking. This, basically, is the approach EU Commission and EU Council are taking.

History doesn't repeat itself, but there are always periods which show similarities, some of these frightening, some encouraging ones. History develops like a spiral and we have it in our hands to make it point either upwards or downwards. The explosive mixture of the crisis of 1929 which resulted in the Great Depression bringing bitter poverty and hunger back into industrialised nations which led to World War II consisted of 5 major components which may ring a bell for us, too:

In the pretext of 1929 there has been a huge imbalance of income distribution. The concentration of income at the top of society crippled domestic demand.

This re-distribution of wealth from bottom to top of society resulted from the gains of an increased productivity. US productivity per employee rose by 43% between 1919 and 1929 but it had only been transferred to the profit share while wages stagnated.

Secondly, this effect got enhanced by generous tax breaks by which the US government, like in recent years, had pampered the upper class. Domestic demand foremost increased by the consumption of luxury goods while GDP growth solely consisted of investment in the investment goods industry which in the 20ies still grew annually by some 6.5%.

The investment in the capital goods sector had been much less significant which led to a shrinking consumption share. When in 1929 investment into capital goods due to overcapacities lost its dynamism the crash that followed *stante pede* spoilt the party for the upper class.

The third reason for the Great Depression to spread ever faster in the 1930ies was the swindles and bluffs by holding companies and investment trusts which orchestrated a firework of mergers and takeovers. Although superfluous capital got absorbed and by this increased the return on investment, mega corporations - being producing- and financial conglomerates under the same roof counting endless layers - dominated the markets.

These monsters naturally had no interest in innovation and development as speculation promised a higher return. On top of that, the impenetrable structure of such 'Russian puppet'- corporations made manipulations of the balance sheets, by which profits could fictionally be pushed upwards, extremely easy.

Much more severe in fact was that the Enron's, WorldCom's, Lehman Brothers, Merrill Lynch's and Goldman Sachs' of that period created financial pyramids which because they included the producing industry in their structures took these with them into the grave when collapsing.

Investment-Trusts back then, like Hedge Funds today, posed as the fourth evil requiring high returns from the companies they owned in order to finance the interest payments for the credits they took for their speculation. But, ever higher returns are only achievable by one-time – effects such as cutting down on wages, social expenditure as well as investments, the latter which once more strangles the economic dynamism.

Lastly, the fifth major reason for the collapse of the economic system of that time is to be seen in the fact that after WWI the US had posed as the largest creditor on the world's financial markets. Today it is the largest debtor. Other than nowadays, in the 1920ies the US exported much more than it imported. The surpluses were financed by an influx of gold and silver. In addition, German bonds were greatly appreciated by the American upper class to have otherwise superfluous liquidity being absorbed.

With a bit of sarcasm one can say that these American bonds served to a large degree the reparations payment of the German government. The money Americans invested in German bonds only virtually travelled to Germany. De facto – as WWI reparation payment – it ended up in Uncle Sam's deep pockets. The US government badly needed those funds for paying interests for its own bonds, which, and this is quite amusing, benefited exactly those people who had signed for German government bonds as well.

One may not find it tragic that the American upper class by this absurd cycle paid itself interest but the problem was that this huge imbalance of vagabonding funds seeking investment opportunities on the one hand and the enormous debt on the other became a self enhancing mechanism.

Like in any other chain-letter or Ponzi-financing scheme it has been clear that the debt will never be paid back. We are today in a similar situation, although diametrically reversed as this time it is the US which is the debtor, but the huge imbalances are of same magnitude and the crashes inevitable no matter how much bailout-packages are put on the table.

It is not a specifically American problem. The fatal consequences of an economic system which' manufacturing industries are dying a silent death while weapons and derivatives have become the main export goods are not a mere coincidence. They are the result of the wrong path of development also we in Europe are marching down since the late 1990ies.

We are not better than the Americans, we only started later and for that reason our economies haven't degenerated as much, yet. The advantage we Europeans could benefit from is that we still have the chance to reverse history's course.

A closer scrutiny of the development of global financial wealth reveals that in the past 25 years the volume of financial wealth has grown much faster than nominal GDP. Between 1980 and 2005 the investment in any kind of financial instruments, be it Commercial Debt Obligations (CDOs) or bonds of privately owned companies has multiplied by the factor 20.

This newly accumulated wealth has been used to finance the purchase of ever more obligations and stocks.

Largest beneficiary of this development have been owners and shareholders of US companies. But, also public debt has, after a longer period of stagnation in the 1990ies, exploded.

The US' financial markets created a constant influx of foreign capital. This off-set their massive imports. The trade deficit is enormous. Main US exports in the past three decades have been dubious financial instruments and treasury bonds by which domestic consumption and standard of living were financed.

Even if President Barack Obama wanted to depart from this sick economic model, the question would remain how would he maintain the standard of living for the great majority of American households? He should re-industrialise the US, but that will take time. Other than debts there is not much left over from the dotcom hype of the Clinton-Gore years.

When speaking of a financial bubble one should not only mention the stock markets, financial markets and hedge funds which got into trouble but also the excessive public and private indebtedness. The latter has grown in the past 25 years many times bigger than the real economy's growth.

The debt-bubble which started to build up during the 80ies and 90ies had reached an unimaginable volume. It has been the direct consequence of an ever increased profit maximisation and capital amortisation.

This is especially so because the neo-liberal agenda of wage-dumping, cracking down on social standards and granting tax relief to ultra rich and major corporations only reduces the costs of production but can hardly solve the problem of creating profitable demand since the declining purchasing power makes any self-sustaining investment dynamism impossible.

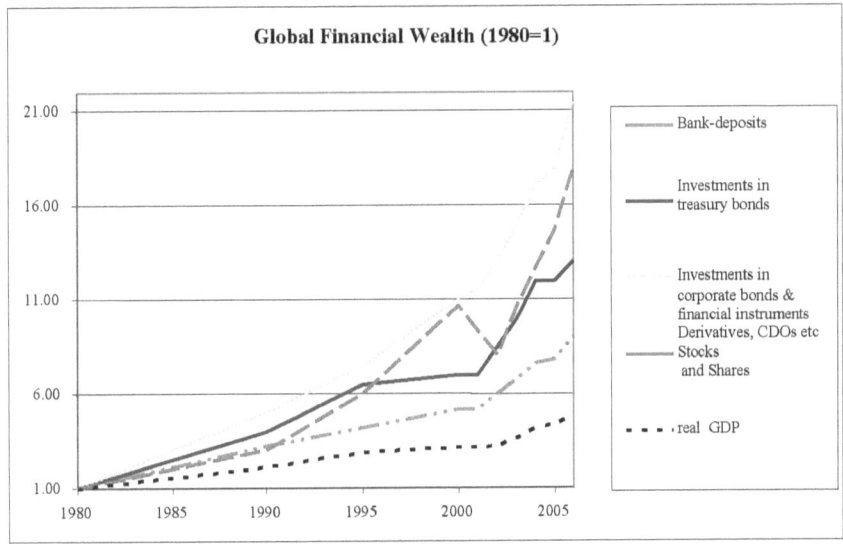

Any economic policy which seriously is inclined to increase the return on investment and capital amortisation needs to provide the frame for an ever-lasting growth of demand from either one of the four potential wells: upper-class consumption, credit financed state expenditure, consumer indebtedness or export.

Different countries were granting different priority status to these four components but whatever has been the highest priority all of the aforementioned forms to increase demand produced and always will produce this financial foam that surmounts the real (producing) economy.

It is because every credit issued to state or consumers inadvertently leads to a pyramid of debts on the one side and a bubble of financial wealth - even if it is only on paper or stored electronically - on the other side. This follows the same logic like lasting export surpluses of one state require to have deficits by other countries on the opposite side.

Also, the subsidizing of luxury consumption in the US has been based primarily on speculative capital gains which the companies had financed by an ever increasing indebtedness.

The US had lived quite well by that scheme. It allowed the US to pay for their imports by worthless paper. Once this system is led ad absurdum supply won't match demand in any way anymore. US citizens will have to tighten their belts.

Logic, that the owners of Wall Street who had to a large degree supported Mr. Obama's campaigns four years ago as well as now in 2012, won't agree with him changing the rules of the game completely by letting international institutions regulate and control what used to work so damned well for so long.

The infamous term "credit crunch" takes a different meaning as it is not only the financial crisis which is responsible for the breaking down of the inter-bank lending market. The problem is much deeper rooted. It is the constant struggle of finding a balance between supply and demand, credit and debts, import and export, haves and have-not's. The French right-wing "Socialistic" approach will only be populism as the real issues aren't dealt with.

Who stole the raisins from the pie?

German state debt in % of GDP

While the public as well as private debts exploded during the past three decades there can also be an incredible multiplication of accumulated wealth noticed. Like on a balance sheet of a company there is a 'minus' on one side and a 'plus' on the other.

But, one could hardly operate a company successfully if the debts are exploding and are kept on the balance sheet while at the same time the profits are hidden from the shareholders by parking them in an offshore account without appearing on the balance sheet.

Literally speaking, this is what the planet's elite has been doing with us. In 1970 the entire wealth bubble accounted for 12 trillion Dollars but until 2005 it has been 12 times of that figure, more than 140 trillion.

The world GDP was totally decoupled from the wealth explosion and while developing countries in the so called "third world" had to starve their populations to death in order to make room for yet another bubble that followed each and every privatisation and opening of the various markets, the workers, employees and SMEs in the industrialized countries were given credit cards instead of wage increases and over-priced mortgages and expensive loans in order to finance consumption and production.

Although some of the accumulated wealth also vanished each time when one of the smaller or even bigger bubbles burst, there has been no such crash (yet) that interrupted the constant growth of the financial wealth. On the contrary: financial wealth grew ever faster and now amounts to ridiculous four times of the World's GDP meaning that if all these owners of the virtual funds all of a sudden wanted to withdraw their money and buy goods, such as designer clothes, furniture, high-tech and whatever valuable, it would not be there in sufficient volume. A dramatic devaluation would kick in. In other words: the worldwide financial wealth market is kept alive by dodgy cheques.

But, what makes piles of virtual money so attractive is not the hypothetical possibility to consume such excessive wealth but rather the fact that it guarantees it's owners further income without forcing them to work at all. Dividends, interests and capital gains since the 1970ies have experienced a steep increase in it's share of GDP in all OECD countries. This increase has been the result as well as the cause of the exploding monetary wealth. Result because greater wealth results in bigger income and cause because the vast majority of such income is not consumed but re-invested.

This self-enhancing effect allowed the owners of big capital to concentrate more and more economic power in their hands. Even though this concentration may only be nominal and couldn't be realized the entire mechanism does have a tremendous impact on the real economy. The increases in stock and share prices and ever higher payouts create immense pressure for the management to at least keep the level of the payouts at whatever costs otherwise the share prices may drop. The sword of Damocles of a capital withdrawal is hanging over each and every management decision.

That's why redundancies are becoming an option even in economic good times. If the only way the level of payouts can be maintained is by cutting down on labour- and production costs, the management will go for such even though it is a one-time effect and even though it may damage the company's future performance because of such cuts. Many companies which had profitable operations had reduced staff and were winding down business if less than 8% profit were made over a year. This results in a vicious cycle in which the management is forced to put aside ever more capital for the shareholders in order to keep the return on investment high enough to attract further capital which again is not invested in any sensible way but to a large degree dedicated to pleasing the shareholders in the next round. A dreadful disparity between shareholder income and production growth is becoming a gulf.

In the end these huge amounts of virtual funds are increasing the power and influence of the financial industry, the banks, hedge funds and investment funds which direct decisions in the real economy as well as in our societies of which the recent rescue missions for the ailing financial house of cards by our political leaders is a clear proof. Billions and soon trillions of taxpayer's money are dumped on the graveyard of the bubbles the owners of big capital created over decades who still profit from the debts we all have to shoulder and for which we are told to tighten our belts.

So is it true that we all simply had to save a little bit more money in order to be on the sunny side of life? Well, the most important predicament for a happy saving are high incomes. But, the average citizen will never be able to save enough money in order to be allowed into the millionaire's and billionaire's clubs. In all countries at all times the saving's rate grows in line with increasing income.

Extraordinary high incomes are achieved in our present economic system by those who do not work but let others work for them. That's the reason why only a marginal portion of the world's wealth results from savings made from work-income. The vast majority of the real big capital results from inheritances and re-investment of already existing wealth. A study on capital wealth in the US concludes that 80% of the total American financial wealth results from inheritances[9]. That's probably not different

---

9   Kotlikoff, L. J., Summers, L. H., The Role of Intergenerational Transfers in Aggregate
     Capital Accumulation, (Journal of political economy, 1981, vol. 89, no. 4)

in Europe. The fact that big capital creates big income and by this poses as a self-enhancing model is the reason why financial wealth is even less equally distributed than income. Below is an overview of the distribution of financial wealth in the various income percentiles in the US between 1998 and 2001.

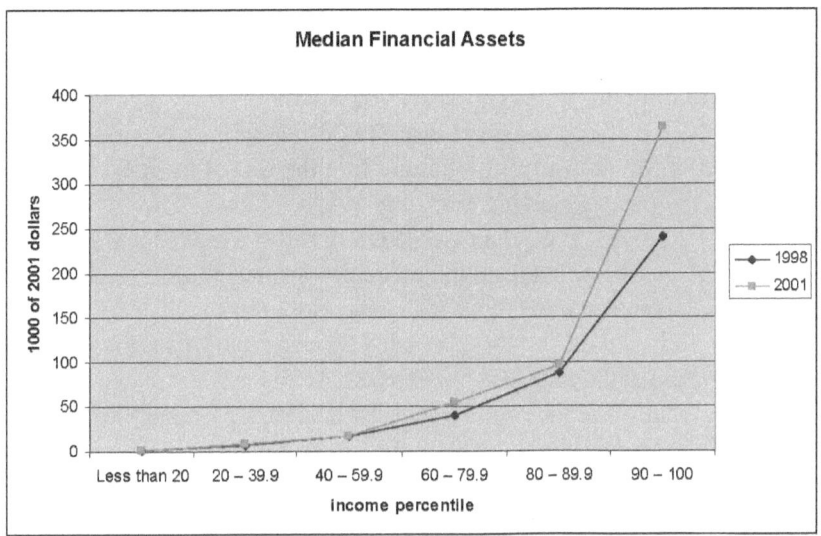

SCF 2001; gross wealth of all families with income

The two curves indicate the over-proportional concentration of wealth at the top 10 % as well as the over-proportional growth of wealth of the richest group of society in the years between 1998 and 2001. Interesting is the fact that the bursting of the dotcom bubble obviously not only didn't harm the rich class but even benefited them while small and medium investors who had been led into the market too late lost most of their assets in the Clinton-Gore internet-hype.

In OECD countries wealth generally is concentrated in a few hands. More than 50% of families in industrialized countries do not account for any wealth at all while the richest 1% own and control more than half of all financial wealth. These are the people the broker house Merrill Lynch in it's *World Wealth Report* refers to as 'High Net Worth Individuals (HNWI) and who own more than a million Dollars in cash. In Germany for instance there were just 800,000 persons who had a million Euros on cash deposits. According to Merrill Lynch there were 10 million HNWIs worldwide in 2007 who owned all together some 40.7 billion Dollars, half of all privately held cash deposits.

In industrialized countries typically the HNWIs are the top 1% of society. By this, one can say, wealth today is much stronger concentrated than in 1929 which for a long time has been referred to as the most perverse wealth concentration. 80 years ago, 1 % of the richest in the US had owned 40% of the total cash deposits.

These millionaires and multi-millionaires for who every bank roles out the red carpet are also the main beneficiaries of any hype, be it driven by stocks and shares or obligations. In Germany 70% of all privately held stocks are owned by the top 1% of society. Only 8% of the German population own stocks, so in a way it is a funny thought that the rest of us, the 92%, have to listen to the news reporting from the DAX-, Nikkei-, Dow Jones- and NASDAQ – 'Casinos' every day. In the US the stocks held in private hands is about 20% but the concentration is equally insane. Within the HNWI – group there is another even more exclusive club: the so called Ultra High Net Worth Individuals (UHNWIs) who by definition account for more than 30 million Dollars in cash deposits. At present there are 100,000 UHNWIs globally and they can be seen as the global monetary aristocracy and main beneficiaries of today's financial capitalism. They were able to let their income and wealth explode over the past 30 years as they profited more than anybody else from the privatizations, profit maximizations and bubble buildings. The head of the global wealth management of JP Morgan Private Bank said that these UHNWIs account for 30-40% of all financial assets.[10]

Generally, one can conclude from all statistics that the bigger the portfolio, the greater is the growth in that sector. The income and wealth of the UHNWIs grow much quicker than any other household's portfolio. Whereas the HNWIs saw their global wealth grow by 9.4% in 2007, the UHNWIs could witness their wealth explode by 14.5%.

But, even within the UHNWI-group of the ultra rich there are still distinctions been made: the Crème de la Crème of the global monetary aristocracy are 1,000 billionaires which are listed by the Forbes Magazine.

These billionaires are topping the UHNWI wealth explosion by skyrocketing 35% annually like in 2007, the year in which the present worldwide crisis had it's beginning on 11th August. Interesting, that in contrast to the public finances which got into severe trouble by the financial turmoil of August 2007 the wealth of the richest did not suffer at all from the crisis it has caused by it's excesses.

---

10   Financial Times 07th July 2004

The fact that wealth grows the faster the bigger it is has been proven by the Forbes data in 1995-1998. The wealth of the richest 400 Americans had grown by 95% from 379 billion Dollars to 740 billion Dollars clear of inflation within those three years. But, even that have been peanuts in comparison to the wealth explosion of the richest 10 multi-billionaires who could multiply their wealth by 270%.[11]

One can also see in the real economy who benefits from the financial capitalism: stagnation and recession of mass products are countered by an ever greater prosperity of the luxury goods sector. In 2006 alone 159 billion dollars of luxury goods were sold, 9% more than in 2005 and 50% more than in 2000. In the last three months of 2007 Richemont, a typical provider for luxury goods who recruits his clients from the UHNWI list, increased his turnover by 14% although the financial crisis had just begun and the British bank Northern Rock had experienced a bank-run by it's smaller clients.

The hunger of the ultra rich to maximize their profit requires an ever more ruthless re-distribution of wealth. The so called Gini coefficient which reflects the income distribution and by this indicates the disparity between lower and higher incomes has risen since the early 1980ies dramatically, especially in the Western industrialized nations[12].

The following graphic shows explicitly who benefited from the development of the past 20 years:

It is, of course, totally irrelevant for the standard of living of an UHNWI whether his wealth grows by 2, 5 or 20% per annum or whether it stagnates. He or she will always be able to shop at Richemont and only use a marginal amount of his money for purchasing goods of the real economy.

Nevertheless will said Ultra-High-Net-Worth-Individual always make sure that his money be multiplied by the best possible investment which his bankers, hedge fund managers and brokers may find. In the centre of the financial capitalism has been the task to maximize the profit for the richest families and to make those richer who own already more than they themselves, their children, grandchildren and great grandchildren can consume in the next one hundred years to come.

11   Arthur B. Cernickel, An Examination of Changes in the Distribution of Wealth. From 1989 to 1998: Evidence from the Survey of Consumer Finances, 2000
12   Galbraith, J.K., Kum, H., Estimating the Inequality of Hs. Incomes: A Statistical Approach to the Creation of a Dense and Consistent Global Data Set; Review of Income and Wealth, Series 51, Number 1, March 2005

Tools in this bizarre game of such insane profit maximization are wage dumping, social cuts, tax avoidance schemes, redundancies, closing down of profitable production sites, reduced investments, neglected innovations and minimized research, but also economic and military blackmailing of entire countries and wars of aggression including occupation of sovereign nations, dictatorships and torture regimes.

The result of this wealth and income distribution are slowing down productivity and growth figures, a declining standard of living for billions of people, destroyed economic capacity, social injustices and growing poverty. The present system is a methodological insanity that results from the logic of an economic system that only driving force is the creation of private profit. During certain periods and under specific conditions this driving force has contributed to making the economy more productive and society in it's entirety richer, even though said richness has always been distributed unequally. Today's financial capitalism instead has replaced the creative and productive destruction in Schumpeter's[13] understanding by the destruction of creativity, productivity and wealth.

Deutsche Bank conspiracy

German SPIEGEL Magazine's "Greek Oracle" undermines democracy.

German magazine DER SPIEGEL is known for it's sometimes manipulating way of reporting in a style of self-fulfilling prophesies. But when it's editors wrote in Mid 2011 about a likely exit by Greece out of the European Monetary Union and a re-introduction of the Drachme as legal tender it was overstepping itself.

The Greek government was fuming as the devious appearing reporting by DER SPIEGEL resulted in yet another downgrading of Greek Government debt by Standard and Poor's that comes at a time when there have been no new negative developments or decisions since the last rating action by the agency just over a month ago and therefore was branded by the Greek finance minister as "not justified". In a statement the Greek finance ministry wrote that "Credit rating decisions should be based on objective data, policy-makers' announcements and realistic assessments of the conditions facing an economy, not on market rumors and press reports." The conspiracy that obviously exists between mainstream media, rating agencies and banks becomes evident when one looks at who is benefiting from these rumors,

---

13   Joseph Schumpeter, Austrian economist

namely those banks, foremost Deutsche Bank AG who brought about the Greek debt crisis by issuing and trading Credit Default Swaps on state bonds.

Same banks and a willfully assisting media who were quick to assert 'overspending' by the state when it comes to social security and pensions have no problem with calling for the public hand, the EU Commission, IMF, European Central Bank and ultimately the taxpayer to rescue them. Although the "Socialist" government in Athens has agreed to a harsh regime of fiscal austerity and the sell-off of all the state's assets, among them some really lucrative public subsistence privatization deals, the slaughtering of the holy cows by those who once fed them is not quick and far reaching enough for Deutsche Bank AG's London Branch, HSBC Bank PLC and Lazard Freres SAS (who have become "advisors" to the Greek government last year).

One may understand the Greek government's frustration had they thought to do everything right by following the rules dictated to them appointing ALPHA BANK A.E., Nathan Meyer Rothschild & Sons Ltd. and UBS Ltd. to sell off the table silver. Like in Portugal, where early elections are being held after the collapse of the "Socialist" government there the financial dictate undermines democracy leaving the citizens only with the choice of voting in protest for a right wing populist or even fascist party. The neo-liberal agenda of brutal social cuts is being portrayed by mainstreams media as being without alternative and any kind of protest against exploitation of citizens and the killing of public life is being crushed by same media letting it appear without any chance to succeed.

But, there would be an alternative which would only hurt ultra rich who had previously benefited immensely by the speculation boom: a hair cut along with the introduction of an EU-wide wealth tax on deposits above 1 million Euros.

Instead, in yet another conspiracy the Euro-zone finance ministers and banks have developed a sick business model that is neither sustainable nor democratically legitimated. The rescue mechanism that is said to 'help' Greece, Ireland, Portugal, and soon Spain and Italy in reality is not designed to rescue those countries but the speculators who had invested in those countries because they expected exorbitant interest to be paid.

Greece, Ireland and Portugal account for a total debt of 620 billion Euros. Although this cripples the economy and public life in those states, it can be seen as peanuts as "investment bank" Lehman Brothers alone had lost some 500 billion Dollars.

Once more, on Swiss bank accounts some 4,000 billion (or 4 trillion) Euros of tax evaded funds are lodged, that also exclusively resulted from speculation with government bonds from Greece, Ireland and Portugal, so there would be a way to find a democratically legitimate solution to the debt crisis by either a simple confiscation of those illegally accumulated funds or by imposing a 50% tax on the gains resulting from such speculation.

The owners of those Greek, Portuguese and Irish obligations would lose only 7.75% of their wealth, a marginal amount given the fact that in a normal year one can earn exactly that easily on the financial markets.

Public finances in all countries would immediately be brought in order and the confidence in the European Monetary Union be restored.

But, instead of going to repatriate the money owed to the public hand the German government among others and the EU Commission debate a bank levy to make the causers of the financial crisis 'contribute' to solving it.

Especially in Germany taxpayers are outraged by the plans of Chancellor Angela Merkel's coalition government to collect the ridiculous amount of 1 billion Euros every year for the so called 'restructuring fund'. Even that figure seems to be doubtful as Deutsche Bank AG already announced that it elected only to pay 70 million instead of the 500 million Euros Mrs Merkel had hoped for.

Up to now the German state debt has risen because of the present financial crisis and the rescue mechanisms for banks by 315 billion Euros. This may illustrate in what kind of long-term perspective our leaders are thinking: in about 300 years the German government will be able to inject the equal amount into the ailing banking system.

And, the Greek government managed to 'save' 1 billion Euros within half a year of implementing the social cuts demanded imposed by EU Commission, European Central Bank and IMF. Given the fact that roughly 140 billion are needed one can predict that it will take Greece only 70 years to be out of the woods, but the price to be paid will be a complete shut-down of public life, social subsistence, health care, education and culture.

Moving the deck chairs on the titanic

EU Commission President José Manuel Barroso commented in January 2011 at the occasion of the presentation of the annual growth survey that the top priorities were to create macro-economic stability through fiscal consolidation, structural reforms at the labour markets and growth enhancing measures in single market trade and common energy policy.

"We need a plan to balance the books", Mr Barroso said emphasizing that "many Member States also need to tackle large and persistent macroeconomic imbalances. At the same time, bank restructuring must be speeded up to bring stability to the financial sector. Only then will we create the conditions for confidence." EU Commissioner for Employment, Social Affairs and Inclusion László Andor repeated his call for more flexibility and social cuts which he of course didn't call that way but "moderation". He was also repeating the point that society was ageing and because of that reforms to pension systems were inevitable.

"Reforms are needed to ensure that they continue providing adequate protection, play their role in preserving and improving skills and employability and creating incentives to work in order to preserve human capital and take full advantage of recovery. (…)Such reforms can sometimes be painful, but I am convinced that they are crucial. It is essential that we take swift action to reform our labour markets to raise employment, people's skills, create job opportunities and enhance social inclusion", László Andor, EU Commissioner for Employment, Social Affairs and Inclusion, told us. However, this position totally neglects the fact that productivity is rising constantly allowing for more wealth to be accumulated. Per capita Europeans are richer and richer and it shouldn't matter whether a person is 8, 18 or 80 years old as there is an ever bigger cake being baked meaning that it is a mere question of distribution of wealth.

Nevertheless, the EU Commission repeats it's mantra of social cuts as being the only way forward.

I asked EU Commission President José Manuel Barroso and EU Economic Affairs Commissioner Olli Rehn at the occasion of the presentation of the Economic Growth Survey on Wedenesday, 12th January 2011, why their 10 steps did not contain some kind of burden sharing for the banks, i.e. a hair cut in order to consolidate finances but Mr Barroso said he didn't want to discuss this. Mr Rehn then said clearly that it was not in the interest of the Commission to make the banks suffer but to recapitalize them.

The economic growth survey the EU Commission presented along with it's ten steps to economic governance only contain the same old tools of further labour market flexibility and fiscal consolidation, in other words a continuation of the austerity policy that results in drastic social cuts, wage dumping and tremendous reduction of public subsistence and services.

Let's follow the Money

Greens and Liberals in the European Parliament opposed the introduction of an EU - wide Wealth Tax.

Asked whether the EU – wide "own sources tax" Commission President José Manuel Barroso proposed could also be a European wealth tax rather than another VAT – like levy Greens and Liberals only want a financial transaction tax, not an EU wide wealth tax although it is clear that unless one takes away the illegitimately accumulated funds from ultra-rich high net worth individuals as Merrill Lynch calls them, the bubble-building will continue and the debt crisis will become ever more severe. Chairwoman Rebecca Harms of the Greens, a German, argued that rich Greek billionaires should contribute to the rescuing of their country but she did not support the idea of a EU wide wealth tax. Likewise, Chairman Guy Verhofstadt of ALDE, former Prime Minister of Belgium, said he would only support a financial transaction tax.

It is clear, however, that such tax would simply be priced in by the investment bankers but would hardly change anything in the financial casino. The rescue mechanism that is said to 'help' Greece, Ireland, Portugal, and soon Spain and Italy in reality is not designed to rescue those countries but the speculators who had invested in those countries because they expected exorbitant interest to be paid.

Greece, Ireland and Portugal account for a total debt of 620 billion Euros. Although this cripples the economy and public life in those states, it can be seen as peanuts as "investment bank" Lehman Brothers alone had lost some 500 billion Dollars. The funds stand against those huge debts are to a large degree no longer in the books of the banks who caused the crisis but on private bank accounts of the bank's shareholders. The worthless paper Greek, Irish, Portuguese and Spanish bonds are printed on got dumped in the European Central Bank (ECB). In other words, the European taxpayer owns now the debts while the profits went to Switzerland and various offshore locations around the world.

Proof that this is true can be found in the Financial Direct Investment – streams (FDI) from outside the EU. Funds being invested in the EU from other parts of the world have quadrupled over the past 10 years meaning that the offshore banks under palm trees serve as a money laundering machine for the EU's upper class as well as major corporations helping them to repatriate funds having prior to this more or less legally evaded taxes. But, not only the "PIGS states" as bankers cynically call Portugal, Ireland, Greece and Spain are in trouble but also Germany that presently appears to stand tall and strong. The reality check reveals that the German government debt had increased by 300 billion Euros because of rescue missions for banks. That is almost the amount of Germany's budget for one year.

But, why is the taxpayer always helping out these banks and their owners who got it wrong when speculating? In a free market economy every entrepreneur and also every private person is liable for his doings. Those who benefit should also carry the risk, is a fundamental aspect of a free economy. At times where the citizen is being told to tighten his belt, member state governments as well as EU and IMF invite the rich upper class to an open bar. Instead of collecting a tax from those who pocketed 4 trillion Euros by speculating with all kinds of financial instruments, also government bonds, the German government imposes a special baking levy of roughly 1 billion Euros per year. This one billion shall be lodged in a fund that shall prevent future crisis.

Given the fact that Germany already took over debts for 300 billion Euros one can speak of quite a long term strategy of the government. In 300 years one would be able to afford another financial crisis. And, further cuts are also not an option as the Greek disaster shows. Over one year of drastic cuts the government in Athens was able to "save" 2 billion. But, the total debt is 148 billion Euros and is steadily growing because of exorbitant interests the government elected to pay to private banks who themselves refinance at the European Central Bank at 1.25%. Greece would need "only" 70 years to get out of the woods but that still sounds like a joke.

Deutsche Bank AG, one of the main beneficiaries of the speculation in the "PIGS" states had indirectly, through it's stake-holding in Hypo Real Estate (HRE) and involvement with UniCredit received 20 billion Euros from the German taxpayer but only offered to pay 70 million into the government fund. At the same time, Deutsche Bank AG CEO Josef Ackermann paid out 10 billion Euros in dividends to shareholders.

Even in the United States of America the government is getting tougher on the causers of the crisis. Bank of America was forced to agree to pay back 8.5 billion US Dollars as it was seen selling toxic papers in the amount of 16.5 billion.

On Swiss bank accounts some 4,000 billion (or 4 trillion) Euros of mostly tax evaded funds are lodged, that also exclusively resulted from speculation with government bonds from Greece, Ireland and Portugal, so there would be a way to find a democratically legitimate solution to the debt crisis by either a simple confiscation of those illegally accumulated funds or by imposing a 50% tax on the gains resulting from such speculation

The owners of those Greek, Portuguese and Irish obligations would lose only 7.75% of their wealth, a marginal amount given the fact that in a normal year one can earn exactly that easily on the financial markets.

Public finances in all countries would immediately be brought in order and the confidence in the European Monetary Union be restored. But, instead of going to repatriate the money owed to the public hand the German government among others and the EU Commission debate a bank levy to make the causers of the financial crisis 'contribute' to solving it.

Seen from the German Green party's position it is only logic that their MEPs do not favour taxing the ultra rich as it was them who when in government with Social Democratic Chancellor Gerhard Schröder liberalised the financial markets and rolled out the red carpet for hedge funds and investment banks in Germany. How would they be looked at by their clientele if they told them now that they had to take away a bit of their huge profits?

EU legitimizes Casino

The EU Commission which for years pushed for ruthless de-regulation, liberalization and privatization on 2nd of January 2011 lauded what it says will supervise the financial markets it. Forgotten is the fact that the Barroso - Commission persistently did the opposite over many years and rolled out the red carpet for hedge funds and 'investment' banks.

"The date of 1st January 2011 marks a turning point for the European financial sector", Internal Market Commissioner Michel Barnier announced. "Today, three new European Authorities for the supervision of financial activities – for banks, markets and insurances and pensions respectively - start their work a few days after the launch of the European Systemic Risk Board."

From now on the dangerous dealing and wheeling of the masters of the universe will be watched closely but not banned. Many experts are doubtful about the placebo effect they say the new rules will have on the risk management of investment banks and hedge funds as the new capital requirements are simply priced in while an ever bigger wheel is being spinned.

Nevertheless, Commissioner Barnier reiterated that "the crisis highlighted only too clearly the limits and sometimes the failings of our supervision system in Europe. The accumulation of excessive risk was not detected. Surveillance and supervision were not effective in time. When trans-national financial institutions faced problems, the coordination between national authorities was far from optimal, and this even though these institutions are more and more numerous."

In other words: the fire brigades are standing by and will pump taxpayer's liquidity into the arteries of an ailing economic system whenever the 'investment' banker's Ponzi schemes have reached it's limits again.

But, Mr Barnier repeats his mantra that "Europe is learning the lessons from the crisis and that is why today, it is giving itself a new apparatus of surveillance and supervision. To detect problems early and to act in time – in a coordinated and efficient way. This new structure are the control tower and the radar screens that the financial sector needs. The European Systemic Risk Board will monitor the entire financial sector, to identify potential problems which could contribute to a crisis in the future."

For as long as the artificially created wealth is rescued by taxpayer's money the new regulations might only have cosmetic effects as the current crisis is the result of hyper-inflation in the financial markets of toxic assets and not a lack of liquidity. Once the liquidity bomb that is 8 times bigger than the World's GDP bursts it will flood the good's markets and cause tremendous inflation. Unless money in the financial markets are replaced by tokens, nothing will change, experts fear.

One could also say, that by not banning the financial betting office on having any effect on the real economy, the new mechanisms only mean that the next rescue missions will be quicker and better coordinated but hardly become obsolete. That's why 'The City' of London and Frankfurt am Main can live with it.

One thing is clear, though: over the past 4 years our leaders have either been incompetent or didn't want to tackle the problem, or maybe they don't have the power to do it.

PART 2

WHAT GERMANY WON'T DO:
FALL INTO OLD HABITS, NEITHER
COMMUNISTIC NOR NATIONALISTIC

I

A CLEAN, CLEAR CUT

First priority: to get rid off those stupid debts

In the first days of our government we will have to deal with the debts and will have to execute tough decisions. Many politicians, especially those of the neo-liberal block composed by Conservatives, Social Democrats and Green-Liberals who until recently advocated free financial markets, these days pretend to have had doubts earlier than the rest of us. Nevertheless, our leaders still pursue an economic system that has proven to be simply anti-economical. One economist proclaimed the rules of the present economic system to be as eternally valid as gravitation law in physics. Good comparison. The big crash is imminent and can be expected for autumn 2012 or sooner. While the debt bubble becomes bigger every day, it appears that the neo-liberals think that they can rescue capitalism by first nationalising the economy and afterwards privatising the Nation-State.

Democratically elected governments and parliaments authorise rescue packages and bailouts while putting the burden of these newly accumulated debts onto the shoulders of the taxpayers. Citizens are being told that unfortunately because of the terribly high debts there is no room for manoeuvring in order to save schools, hospitals, social subsistence, public life in general, cultural life from facing severe cuts.

As the central question these days is whether we will ever manage 'our' debts our state governments are creating it should be scrutinised whose debts these are. Also, one has to be aware of the fact that 'debt' on one side of the balance sheet means 'credit' on another balance sheet. Who are the beneficiaries?

The debts that are piling up trillion fold are disastrous in two ways: firstly these debts strangle our economies by creating a credit crunch and secondly by the accumulation of unreal wealth in form of a liquidity bubble that is hanging over us and that will, once it bursts and rains down on the goods markets, lead to hyper inflation.

So where are all these debts stemming from? Some, especially the most recent ones, were created in the virtual reality casino of the financial markets.

The way Goldman Sachs and other investment banks structured their business has been as if a car manufacturer produced cars of which it knew that the breaks will fail in a year's time while betting vast amounts on the collapse of the major car insurer companies. In the real economy this would be considered fraudulent.

Nevertheless, the advocates of exactly that sick economic model were, by a wilfully assisting media, hammering into our heads for 3 decades that public debt was the evil that had to be limited if not eradicated. Maastricht Accord and Lisbon Strategy were designed in the manner the neo-liberal movement needed it to justify public spending. Their goal was and is to force the state to withdraw from any engagement in the field of public subsistence while cutting down social expenditure thus entering a dreadful wage dumping spiral.

The debt-argument serves also as justification for rolling out the red carpet for private capital that has a constant hunger for ever more lucrative business deals in the field of public subsistence. Of course, privately managed public services are more expensive than those provided by the state because these need to be profitable and pay dividends to shareholders.

The public indebtedness in all industrialised nations has continuously grown since the mid 1970ies. The figures based on BIS working papers No. 300 from the Bank for International Settlement (BIS) from the Bank for International Settlement (BIS) reveals the weighed average of public debt in 21 OECD states and the development of their primary deficit (new debts minus interest).

The development of the public debt shows beyond doubt that the indebtedness of states are not the primary result from a classic Keynesian stirring of the economy in times of economic downturns, a legend neo-liberals always love to tell.

Instead, the primary deficit of industrialised nations between 1975 and 1997 has (except for 2 years) always been negative. Only in the years after 1997 one can see a cyclical up and down of credit-taking by the states which would support the theory of the states stirring the economy.

In reality public indebtedness already in the early 1980ies had nothing to do with Keynesian ideas anymore. The horrendous debts industrial nations began to pile up directly resulted from the neo-liberal trend that conquered most countries at the beginning of the 1980ies which led to the replacement of Keynesian dominated economic politics by an ideology of market radicalism and at the same time weak state à la Milton Friedman.

The aim of the Neo-Liberals has been the increase of the profit rate which required deregulations of labour markets, weakening of the unions, radical tax dumping as well as destruction of social systems. Wages got decoupled from the rise in productivity. Social benefits were axed mostly by Social Democratic or so called 'Socialist' governments under people like Lionel Jospin, Gerhard Schröder and Anthony Blair. The state's income shrank constantly because of tax dumping.

As a direct consequence purchasing power, the central pillar macro economic demand is resting on, collapsed. Without sufficient demand there are also no increased profit rates possible no matter how generously companies were relieved of their costs. The neo-liberal model had to deal with a major existential problem: it had to create sufficient market demand which should not automatically have a negative impact on the cost side of the companies balance sheets.

Higher wages or tax-financed social benefits were excluded by the Neo-Liberals, but not so credit-financed higher state expenditures.

Main problem of the public indebtedness is that it only for exactly that period of time will have an expansive, in other words consumption enhancing, effect during which the primary deficit is negative, i.e. the new credit-taking exceeds the expenditure for interest.

This is so because of the distribution of wealth in industrialised nations. According to Merrill Lynch in industrialised countries 1 % of the households own 50% of all cash deposits. That is why interest payments in their great majority end up in the portfolios of the rich upper class that uses it for further accumulation of wealth and not for consumption on the good's markets.

To the contrary, taxes are mostly paid by middle class and, as far as the steadily increasing indirect taxes such as VAT are concerned also by low income- and poor families. As interest payments are at least partly paid from the state's tax revenue the macroeconomic demand is further reduced.

A permanently negative primary deficit means that interest as well as principle repayment has to be financed through new debts. In addition a portion of new debt that effectively stirs domestic demand is required as well. The problem is that such a situation can not be upheld indefinitely. In economic terms such an unsustainable model is referred to as "Ponzi-financing" or snowball-systems that are based on exponential growth of the total debt and inevitably have to collapse sooner or later.

The higher the total debt, the higher is the amount of new debts at same interest rate that is required to cover the interest payment plus an eventually additional amount for stimulating demand. If interest rates are declining, a certain relief can be possible, but as long as the interest rates are determined by private banks and not a public institution the state won't have any influence on that important component.

When in the mid 1990ies the leverage for states to stabilise domestic demand because of extremely high public debts had reached it's limits a new strategy was quickly found. Foremost in the US the indebtedness of private households matched the general privatisation wave, in this case in form of a neo-liberal "Private Keynesianism" for which not the state borrows vast sums in order to help the economy by creating sufficient market demand, but the consumers themselves were deeply drawn into a debt spiral that they could never re-pay with their wages. That was the core of the American real-estate boom. Mortgages were mostly used to refinance old debts as well as new credit card debts. Fictitious evaluations allowed for ever greater loans to be handed out. Without this mechanism the American domestic demand would have had collapsed already much earlier as the average hourly wage of 16.57 US Dollars in the manufacturing sector today is, clear of inflation, on the level of the late 1960ies.

The trick to replace wages by debts has not been a purely American speciality, but was applied in Great-Britain, Ireland, Spain and many other EU countries as well, although less excessive than in the US. All the growth in the former Eastern European countries that joined the EU in the years from 2004 on is based on the private indebtedness of families. Without this motor, the neo-liberal model had much earlier reached it's limits and the current world economic crisis had started much sooner.

But, the private debt bubble didn't only consist of the aforementioned component. It has also been the increasing indebtedness of companies and corporations which hardly financed investment and innovation but expensive takeovers, dividend pay-outs and re-buying of stocks that only had one objective: to increase the shareholder value. Higher stock-listings and trading were 'bought' on loan basis in order to finance the wealth accumulation and luxury consumption of the upper ten thousand without them being liable for repayments as those debts were weighing heavily on the balance sheets of these corporations.

Following these developments the debts of companies as well as consumers in the US rose between 1999 and today by 12,904 billion Dollars, much quicker than GDP grew. This is evidence for the fact that those loans and mortgages were not invested into any productive way but were simply "eaten up".

Consequently, the relation of the non-financial private sector to GDP (clear of pension obligations) in the US has skyrocketed from 127 % to unbelievable 170%. And, in Europe similar developments can be noticed. The debts of private consumers and non-financial companies have risen from 114% by 8,066 billion Euros since 1999 to 170% of GDP, much quicker than public debt.

But, also consumers had to play by the same rules as credit-financed demand only works in an expansive manner as long as the new debts exceeded the interest payments due. Also the consumers had to follow the Ponzi-scheme and finance principle and interest of their existing debts by ever greater credit-lines. This, indeed, has happened in the US for many years. However, inevitably the day comes where the limit is reached here as well. In the moment that in addition to stagnating wages principle and interest payments reduce the available income for consumption above dynamism with all brutality turns the table.

Three decades of Neo-Liberalism on the one hand had by continuous re-distribution of wealth from bottom to top of society let privately held cash deposits explode and grow many times faster than GDP thus creating an enormous financial bubble. This has only been possible because at the same time a gigantic debt bubble began to blow up which turned the wealth bubble into real demand. This debt bubble had been carried until the mid 1990ies by the states, thereafter by the private consumers and companies.

It is obvious that these debts will never be paid back simply because nobody will be able to do that. The debt obligations which are held by rich privateers as well as banks, insurance companies and other financial investors naturally can only be written off. Logically, this means that also wealth that is based on those papers have to be declared null and void.

This may be relatively trivial in cases where the debt obligations are held by rich private individuals, but when these are resting in the basements of banks and insurance companies it will be rather complicated as in case of bank – bankruptcies shareholders are directly affected. The problem would arise to protect the personal savings of normal people. That's why so far major bank-failures (with the exception of Lehman) have been avoided by political rescue missions and the creation of "bad Banks". Technically these debts shift from the private to the public sector. The artificial wealth resulting from the artificially created debt that is standing on the opposite side of the debts remains unharmed.

The debt as well as the wealth bubble is not shrinking by this method, they are only shifted from side to the other. It is clear that this can not go on for long without a major, final crash, which comes closer every day.

Since 1980 "investments" in credit instruments and obligations has grown 20 times bigger and are now close to 43 trillion US Dollars globally while World GDP accounts for less than a quarter of that sum. In other words, if one wanted to bring the world economy back on track one would have to write off three quarters of that toxic foam.

But, our leaders are not brave enough to tell the rich upper class the bitter truth. They rather take on further debts these people have created. Within the EU state indebtedness between 2007 and 2009 has risen by 20% by 1.4 trillion Euros. It now stands at 8.7 trillion Euros. The indebtedness quota in the EU27 jumped from 59% to 74% of GDP. In the Euro-zone it is already at almost 90%. And, that is only the beginning because in the basements of the banks there are trillions more of the toxic assets.

It has become clear a while ago since the Maastricht accord but especially so after the enacting of the Lisbon Treaty, that in Europe the bridging of cyclical lacks of demand by the state employing expansive tools is not part of the "Lisbon Strategy of Stability and Growth". The harsh austerity programs will lead into depression. Deflation is likely but during a phase of deflation debts which will retain their nominal value will become even more pressing while the real interest will increase even though the nominal interest may remain low.

It is highly probable that the financial markets will demand higher interests from several Euro member states citing huge deficits, like they do already in the case of Greece and Spain. Germany could rescue Greece and maybe Ireland, but not Spain and Italy, as it can hardly rescue itself.

In real terms this means that even if no further bail-outs and transfer of private debts into the public hand was to happen the financial situation of all states is explosive. Given that suddenly all Euro-zone member states were able to present a balanced primary budget (which would be economically disastrous and which presently is obsolete anyhow) the public debt quota would still grow year by year in the amount of the difference between real interest and growth rate. In case of zero-growth and zero-inflation this would presently a debt – growth of annually 4 % of GDP.

In case the capital market interest was rising only by a tiny little bit, or if a new recession or deflation hit the economy, the deficit would be much worse. One has to note that this is the case already so under the impossible assumption that a balanced primary budget would be achieved, unthinkable at present even when more and more crazy budget cuts are brought in.

One doesn't need to be a prophet to see clearly that after three decades of Neo-Liberalism along the redistribution of wealth from bottom to top of society the resulting public debts led the economic model ad absurdum.

But, how to let the air out of this gigantic debt bubble without risking the middle class's personal savings?! There are several possible scenarios at hand:

1. The most likely and most disastrous one that EU Commission and the neo-liberal block presently undertake by applying the Lisbon-torture tools of strict austerity discipline and severe budget cuts. This inevitably will lead to depression and deflation. This will again bring down banks and financial institutions which need to be rescued once more by the state. Some Euro-zone states won't be able to refinance themselves under normal conditions and maybe the Euro-rescue-mechanism will help for a short while but as the debts are no longer shifted from private to public hands but only transferred from the weaker to the stronger Euro-zone states this is short-lived as well. Imagine 700 billion of debts from Spain

or Italy with somewhat 2 trillion Euros! Once the first country announces a payment – stop the interests for those who took over debts from others will explode so that these will be in a similar situation shortly thereafter. Bank crashes and runs on banks will be the beginning of the end at which the collapse of the Euro financial system stands. Rich people will lose some of their assets but the ones to be hit most severely will be the middle class like it has historically always been when it came to inflations and currency reforms.

2.   So what is the alternative? In the short term it would be feasible to have the state expand and jump-start the economy by massive public investment as well as higher minimum wages and increased social purchasing power, higher pensions and social benefits. In the medium term it is clear that the gap that was ripped into macroeconomic demand by the loss of consumer indebtedness can not be replaced by enormous public deficits. In the long term an economic balance will only be achieved by minimum wages that go in line with the rises in productivity, re-regulation of labour markets and a fundamentally different tax system that re-distributes wealth from top to middle class and bottom of society. If Germany applied those tools, this would also help level out the trade-imbalances that brought countries like Greece and most of Eastern Europe into trouble. As the GDP share of public debt in the Euro-zone is at around 90% and most likely will hit the 100% ceiling in a short while, it will be almost impossible for member states and the Euro-zone to 'grow' out of debt. As a rule of thumb one can say that a state can grow out of it's debts if the real interest is about 2% lower than GDP growth. Even Germany at present pays an average of 3.6% for its treasury bonds. At an inflation of 1% the economic growth needed to be at around 5% in order to have a chance to ever get rid of the debt. Even if inflation was 2% it still required a 4% annual growth, which illustrates how unrealistic it is to count on that option. But, also Japan lives with a debt of some 200% of it's GDP since quite a while. However, the Japanese situation can hardly pose as a role model since steadily growing debts and interest payments permanently restrict government action which leads to a continuous political crisis. The price Japan pays is high: a young generation that has never experienced real growth and times without recession and crisis.

3. Can old debts be reduced by higher taxes? It would be tempting to introduce a massive wealth tax and by this reduce public debt. At least one wouldn't hit the wrong people as the debts of a state typically ended up as wealth in the portfolios of the rich upper class. But, the tax system should rather enhance domestic demand by re-distribution of wealth from top to middle and bottom of society. Higher taxes on accumulated wealth and top income percentiles do not fulfil that task. Only an extremely high tax would let steam out of the bubble. Between 1998 and 2010 the German state debts had risen by 1 trillion Euros which can be regarded as the cap of the iceberg when taking into account the volume of the toxic assets which are still resting in the treasuries in many German banks. This trillion is countered by the trillion the German rich have accumulated in the same period. But, a "millionaire's tax" of annually only 5% would only create a revenue of 80 billion Euros for the German government that hardly touched the substance of that illegitimate wealth.

4. Devaluation of debt by inflation is a historically known method, but would hit foremost middle classes and the poor. The rich have spread their wealth between shares, stocks, real estate, capital goods as well as gold and other precious metals or germ stones. But, the average citizen usually has his savings on a bank or savings account, may have invested into life insurance or a pension plan. While the rich can easily afford the devaluation of the currency, the man in the street won't cope with that as pensions and savings would not be adjusted. On top of that any inflation is disastrous for people who are on a fixed income, such as pensioners, unemployed, sick and poor. It would simply be cynical to say there is one law for the rich and one for the poor. The strategy to eradicate debt by inflation would, however, only work as long as interest levels are low. If interests rose again, the level of old debts would decline but the refinancing would become more expensive. In any case, this scenario would punish the victim and not the beneficiaries of the virtual reality casino of recent years. The Butler would pay for the party.

5. Decoupling of state-debt from the capital markets instead could be the only realistic way out. Public finances would have to be strictly decoupled and separated from the capital markets, meaning that state deficits would solely be refinanced within a regulated

frame of low interest- or interest-free direct loans of the European Central Bank (ECB). This would de facto mean that money from the Central Bank only be brought into circulation by means of public investments instead of credit business of commercial private banks. The positive effect for the public finances would be that the amount of new debt would be drastically reduced because of the low interest rate. Also, the public finances would be calculable and reliable while the dependence on capital markets and it's fluctuations would be overcome. Speculative interests like in the case of Greece would be impossible. This scenario would be immediately possible if one only wanted to. It doesn't take more than a change in the European Central Bank's status as well as a few alterations in the European treaties, all of which can be done in only one afternoon. Previously, one had argued that the Central Bank financing of state debts would lead to irresponsible behaviour of the state controlled bank and that this would bear the risk of inflation. Compared with the recent excesses of private banks over the past 15 years this argument becomes totally invalid. All financial markets and private financial institutions have proven beyond doubt that they do not have the capacity to responsible administrate finances. No their own ones and certainly not public ones. Growth requires credit. The only difference would be that the funds needed would come from the state and not from private banks. This model would ensure that public finances no longer became subject to speculation of private banks. The verdict of financial markets and global players over politics of a country's democratically elected leadership would never again have financial effects. 'Credit ratings' for countries would become obsolete. Democracy would win.

6. Last and least, existing debt could be re-financed by the European Central Bank (ECB) The ECB already buys up older bonds and it would of course be thinkable that the state acquired the funds for refinancing it's debt when these were due, from the ECB directly. This would, however, step by step transfer state's debts to the ECB. Or, the ECB could buy all state bonds off the market. The problem that is buried in such a solution would be that the wealth bubble would not be eradicated but still exist into perpetuity, although the financial institutions would have one placement opportunity less. That would, indeed, only have a placebo effect as the liquidity bomb that is hanging over us because of 3 decades of re-distribution

of wealth from bottom to top of society would continue to seek lucrative speculation opportunities and would lead again and again to ever new debt- and speculation bubbles.

The only way out of the disastrous developments of the past 3 decades therefore can only be the politically controlled devaluation of the wealth and debt bubble by a concerted action of all industrialised nations, but at least of the member states of the Euro-zone and possibly also the entire EU. This scenario would require the nationalisation of the major financial institutions which of course means that their debts became public debt, but likewise would their valuable assets also be owned by the state. Following this, the majority of the public debt that resulted from the wrong development of the recent decades has to eradicated but with the restriction that also Argentina had practiced once: private investors below a certain level shall not be harmed. The financial institutions would then be recapitalised by public funds and by strict rules be forced to operate only within the framework of traditional banking business, i.e. classic credit and depository transactions. The state could acquire the necessary funds by a one-time wealth tax for wealth above a million Euros. By this, the old bubbles would be eradicated and the banks could return to their core business, become responsible credit suppliers for the economy.

A bit of Myths - busting

Critics and defenders of the old system will now say that in a globalised world it wouldn't be possible to do what we will do. But, which Globalisation are we talking about?! 100 years ago the World has been as "globalised" as nowadays, yet it led to catastrophe.

It has become fashionable in the late 1990ies and especially around the Millennium to talk about globalisation. Activists of ATTAC and leftist parties discovered that Anti-Imperialism and Anti-Capitalism could only be topped by Anti-Globalisation movements. "A new World is possible" shouted the scene but they were wrong. A new World is not possible. A new economic system would be possible if the old structures that for 400 years fill their pockets by scams and fraud by which they also organise power didn't stand in our way.

History doesn't repeat itself. It rather develops in form of a spiral. The spiral can point upwards or downwards. Today's decisions need to be made in the light of the question whether we want to live in a 1.0 World or a 2.0 World as Harvard lecturer Pankaj Ghemawat calls it. Nationalists like the French ultra-rightist Marine Le Pen advocates the first one, the latter is propagated by the American author Thomas Friedman who believes that we live in times of utmost globalisation. But, the World is more heterogenic, maybe we should call it World 3.0

It needs to be reflected in the light of the terror attack in Norway that the World today is not more 'globalised' than a hundred years ago. Maybe we feel different because of the internet and the ability to travel fast, but in reality we are still rather local and not that international than we think. Only 3 % of people live in a different country than which they were born in. Immigration and migration were much bigger issues a hundred years ago. And, only 2% of students study abroad.

Only 2% of all telephone calls are cross-border and less than 18% of internet communication is international. 95% of citizens digest the daily news from the media in their home country. 38% of news in Europe are international, but in most cases it is about issues in the EU, US, China, war zones or sports. The rest of the world is only covered by very few. Also trade in goods and services is less "globalised" than we are made to believe as only 20% of the World GDP is exported. And, most of the export of a country goes to it's direct neighbours. In case of Germany, the export nation number 2 in the World, 60% of it's goods are exported to EU member states although the GDP of the entire EU is less than 25% of World GDP. In 1914 Germany exported a bigger share of it's goods to other regions of the World than today.

One may think that because of the financial crisis and the size of the transactions the "globalization" had advanced in the world of finances but that is not true for the level and intensity of international investment only in terms of volume. Foreign direct investment (FDI) accounts for only 9% of all investments while only less than 20% of share capital is injected into investment funds outside the home country. Only 20% of stocks are held by foreigners.

Generally, one can say that our average level of globalisation in the most important matters such as telecommunication, trades of goods and services, news and cultural exchanges, as well as financial investments today is tumbling at around 20%. In 1914 the FDI-quota in relation to GDP was as high as today. This proves that national regulation can coexist with international agreements. The EU is a good example for the assumption that cultural diversity and integration are not contradicting each other.

But, it also means that our world is not that much different than 100 years ago. The dangers that result from the wrong economic decisions can lead to the same kind of disasters. In the United States of America we observe how the same old tools that hadn't worked well 82 years ago are debated between the corporate foundation of the so called "Tea Party" – fraction of the Republicans and President Obama. Back in 1929 when Andrew W. Mellon (founder of the Mellon Bank) as Treasury Secretary of the Hoover administration lowered taxes for the rich, he inevitably enhanced the bubble building.

It would be prudent for EU institutions to study the financial history of the 20th century carefully and not run blindfolded into a predictable disaster. The conservative Frankfurter Allgemeine Zeitung (F.A.Z.) noted in it's front page editorial on 2nd January 2008 under the headline "Die Systemfrage"('System-question') that "some people only now understand how much the competition with Communism as long as it existed, had also tamed Capitalism. Out of itself Democracy and free market economy are not more immune against self destruction than totalitarian systems. In contrast to the latter these do have breaks built in, but these have to be checked and serviced continuously….in order to sustain our society's vitality. Before others put the Systemfrage onto the agenda, our elites should do it." There is nothing to be added. In spring 1927 the Federal Reserve lowered the base rate from 4% to 3.5%, mostly because of pressure from Great-Britain, France and Germany. The "Gold standard" was also given up in order to help European money markets. More and more money backed by neither gold nor production was printed. Treasury bonds were bought by the Fed by bulk as banks and privateers sold and again profited from the cheap influx of cash by the central bank which they directly re-invested in stocks.

In 1929 like in 1987 interest rate – fixed obligations replaced traditional securities. In the 1990ies other "tools" to spin a big wheel with a minimal real capital injection were found, so called Derivatives. Like today, it has been vital to keep up the myth that everyone could and did participate in the boom but in 1928, like today, has been nothing but media brainwashing otherwise the entire system would have lost acceptance.

Of the 120 million people living in the United States of America in 1928 the 29 stock exchanges counted exactly 1,548,707 clients of which 1,371,920 by profession were either bankers, traders, brokers or agents themselves and by working for firms being members of the stock exchanges contributed to the financial incest. 600,000 of these "clients" bought stocks by collaterals and 950,000 paid for it by cash most of which had been lent to them. Also today, 83% of all stocks in the US are held by only 5% of society and are mostly inherited.

No dish washer ever got to that point and now even dish washers are automated – like money making. In Germany, only 8% of the adult population owns stocks. 248 multi billionaires control 50% of the world's economic output.

On 7th November 1928, a day after the re-election of President Hoover who offered tax-relief, the so called "Victory Boom" let stocks and shares skyrocket by 15% in one day. By 17th November 1928 Times sighted a cyclone-like dynamic.

Like later in 1987 (the Investment Trusts now were called "Mutual Funds" and today are called "Hedge Funds") and today in our "globalised" crisis this led to a devaluation of prices and wages, a logic consequence of economic excess which, again, like after excessive alcoholic consumption causes retraction. The brain shrinks. And, there is no reason why we should not do our own thing rather than clinging onto the American and Anglo-Saxon business model that always leads into the same predictable disaster.

Equal societies are more productive

This also means that we will build up an inclusive society which Americans will envy us for although they hate everything that looks a bit "socialistic". But, that is owed to the righ-wing propaganda and disinformation campaigns over the past 70 years. The majority of Americans already understood but aren't being heard by the political leadership that inequality is not only morally wrong, it is also anti-economical.

The extreme inequality that global capitalism creates is not only morally and socially wrong. It also is a major obstacle to productivity and innovation. Economic dynamism is at stake.

The theory that inequality let's people stretch to the ceiling is a myth that has been dismantled by tycoon John P. Morgan who once had it been investigated where the differences between the more and the less successful companies of his empire lay. In the company of the 'Mal-Performers' the differences between wages paid at certain levels were bigger than in the company with the best performers. In the latter the income-difference was never greater than 30%.

Kate Picket and Richard Wilkinson empirically prove in their book "Equality lays in Happiness" that in very unequal societies negative symptoms overwhelm the entire society: Alcohol and other drug addiction, obesity, psychotic conditions and diseases much more often are to be found than in more equal societies. Also birth and fertility rates are subject to the level of equality. An unequal society doesn't reproduce. But, also education and achievements in science are by far less good in unequal societies.

Last but not least, an unequal society has many more prisons than a more equal one. In the US, the number of prison inmates has quadrupled between 1977 and 2002. Under President William J. Clinton another sharp increase can be noticed. He had limited social security to five years one time per life. And, while the dotcom bubble laid the ground for the real estate bubble ultimately the financial crisis that cost the US it's global leadership, the income concentration in the upper quintile led to over-indebtedness of 4/5th of Americans whose wages today are (clear of inflation) on the level of the 1970ies.

Whoever believes in a free market society has to admit that markets can only reflect real demand when there is a more or less balanced income distribution in a society. What markets in a capitalistic model respond to is not the actual demand, but the ability to pay for such. Only if social purchasing power is sufficiently covered the market mechanisms will create a production responding to demand.

The opposite extreme of capitalism shows us every day that markets can be saturated while human beings are starving to death.

A high level of inequality also means polarisation of demand. Both, luxury brands as well as discounters, grow steadily but the latter not because people prefer cheap trash goods instead of high quality products but simply because they can't afford those.

As a result, less quality products are being produced which actually harms SMEs especially. Economic capacity that could provide for a higher standard of living for everyone, are wiped out from the market.

In essence one has to note that income concentration in the upper quintile of society while wages, pensions and social subsistence at best stagnate or even decline then also consumption declines. Parallel to this a dreadful money spinning cycle replaces the real economy. More and more funds are not invested into production but put onto the casino tables of the financial market. That has been so before 1929 and that is also so today.

The only way the capitalistic system can counter the income disparity is by debts. But, it is not only the state that gets indebted, it is the citizens themselves who pile up debts. This kind of privatized Keynesianism now collapses like a house of cards.

In Germany one tried to level these imbalances out by an aggressive export strategy that created huge surpluses which destabilized the entire Euro-zone. There is only one alternative: the inequality has to be reduced drastically or the economic substance will be destroyed and all will become poor.

The growing inequality has not only been the result of the wrong economic policy but foremost the predicament created by the distribution of wealth and power. Ownership cements an economic order that is totally undemocratic and mathematically unsustainable. The free-market ideology produces oligopolies that dominate public life and that manage to bribe and blackmail elected politicians who surrender the democratic state to a profit maximization principle that can not sustain itself because it only produces for profit and not for actual demand. The differences between Socialism and Capitalism become smaller when collapsing.

II
NEW DEMOCRACY – OLD PRINCIPLES

About the difficulties to become a conservative

If one asks a conservative German what makes him a conservative he (she usually is not asked) will respond that classicism and humanism were his ideals. She will stand next to him and add that she believes in God.

When one argues that His Son, Jesus, had been an anti-imperialist and anti-capitalist who had certainly been the first one to leave the Catholic church one may hear that although some criticism was justified especially when it comes to child-abuse one could not deny the fact that Christianity was the foundation of our society and that Islam wanted to wipe us out.

But, if I read the Bible correctly I find in the book of Acts quite communistic sounding passages:

All that believed were together, and had all things in common; And sold their possessions and goods, and parted them to all men, as every man had need.

(Acts 2:44-45)

And:

There was not a needy person among them, for as many as owned lands or houses sold them and brought the proceeds of what was sold. They laid it at the apostles' feet, and it was distributed to each as any had need. There was a Levite, a native of Cyprus, Joseph, to whom the apostles gave the name Barnabas (which means "son of encouragement"). He sold a field that belonged to him, then brought the money, and laid it at the apostles' feet.

(Acts 4:34-37)

Certainly, Karl Marx borrowed his famous line "From each according to his ability, to each according to his need" from the Bible. It is clear that Jesus Christ and no true Catholic believer could accept the present economic disparities in almost all societies. The conservative German then usually says that nevertheless he believed in the humanistic ideals that were represented by Immanuel Kant, Friedrich Schiller and Johann Wolfgang von Goethe, namely all the great classicists of German literature and philosophy. Somehow, German conservatism has managed to let it appear natural that all those old classic literature was seen as being the foundation of any conservatism.

But, considering the fact that we live once again in capitalistic and imperialistic times with wars over resources dominating the agenda that also axes social standards in industrialised nations while a barbaric poverty spreads over developing countries making rich richer and poor poorer, one might ask how that goes together with humanism and Catholicism?!

Goethe's Faust didn't want to lay around lazy but our present economic system excludes millions from participating in economy and social life while demanding from all others an ever greater "flexibility" that forces them to take up three jobs to survive. Faust had been restlessly searching for increasing his knowledge, finding beauty in arts and culture while longing for creativity, all which in our world today is being denied to 75 million Europeans who live below the poverty line while a rich upper-class bathes in Champagne and increases their portfolios by some 19% in every year of the financial crisis so far.

Whoever is responsible for this discrepancy in our inhumane society can not claim the moral leadership founded by Christianity and classical Humanism as Johann Wolfgang von Goethe described it as one of the first and profoundest critique of capitalism.

Goethe prophesized the threat to culture, civilisation and humanity that resulted from an entirely commercialised society and he strictly opposed an economic system in which human dignity had to be justified by economic feasibility.

Nevertheless, Goethe saw the enormous productive capacities of an profit orientated economy and it's benefits but he was wise enough to think of a post-capitalistic society while capitalism yet was seeking to establish itself.

Goethe's "Faust" dealt with the threat capitalism posed to the old structures in two ways, one destructive and one progressive: solely destructive has been the paper money by which Mephisto pleases the emperor of the rotten Reich that eventually declines rapidly because no investments are being made while only the decadent luxury of the upper-class is being financed by such artificially created wealth. Who wouldn't draw a parallel to our present casino capitalism?

But, Faust also is progressive in such sense as he acquires land that he makes useable by machines and modern technology that let's Faust advance as an entrepreneur par excellence but also as an barbaric person who can not control his desire to accumulate ever more wealth.

As economic pariah Faust doesn't require Mephisto any longer as his brutality is driven by greed and not productivity. Goethe had understood long before Karl Marx that Capitalism is not only about trade in a free market but always comes with greed, barbarism, war and piracy.

There is no doubt that Johann Wolfgang von Goethe had been disgusted by our present economic system that more and more pushed productivity aside and replaced creativity and innovation with profit maximization, greed and useless financial transactions degrading democratically elected politicians to instruments in a system that ultimately destructs wealth and society.

Today's society behaves exactly as described in the first Act of "Faust" in which everybody fights against each other while Mephisto miraculously creates the paper money scam. Goethe never accepted that we human beings were bound to neglect our most honourable attributes such as love, dignity and beauty while enhancing our darkest sides from greed to egoism and social ignorance.

At the end Mephisto loses out on his bet and in the grand final of "Faust II" the ever-female beauty leads us through all dark moments. Whoever read and understood Goethe has to feel that it can not remain as it is and that although a different world is not possible, a different economic system would be.

So why are conservatives claiming classic literature and religious moral for themselves while living it the opposite way? Or is it maybe that they haven't understood what is being laid in front of them?

The London School of Economics and Social Science in a study empirically proves that right wing and overly religious people usually have a lower than average IQ.

Maybe, all these conservatives who claim the bible and classic literature to be their fundament, in fact haven't even read and understood a single page of these works?

New Economic System

In the waning capitalistic system there is a lot of talk about "the neo-liberals" who were to be blamed for the collapse. One also hears every now and then, in Germany, especially, that a renewed social free market system needed to be reinstated, a *Neue Soziale* Marktwirtschaft referring to the West-German cushioned capitalism of the post WWII era.

Have the past 2 decades after the collapse of the Eastern European Socialism really been "neo-liberal" in the true sense of the word or is this just a misuse of terminology?

For leftists it is clear that 'neo-liberalism' is where all evil comes from, such as 'globalisation'. Globalisation existed since the first cross border trades commenced and on the dark side stood for colonialism, slavery, exploitation, but on the other side also for innovation, progress and internationalisation.

One could, a bit cynically, say that globalisation in the past 60 years was rather neo-colonial throwing so called "third world" countries economically back into the days when these nations won their independence. Debts multiplied each time when World Bank and IMF tried to do 'good'. Privatisations, deregulations and liberalisations are cited as the evil of a neo-liberal world order, but that is not correct. It is capitalism that led to such huge imbalances resulting in wars, not 'neo-liberalism'.

75 years ago the term 'neo-liberal' did NOT stand for a policy that provided for the utmost "business friendly" environment, tax- and standard-dumping by watering down any sensible rule set forth by democratically elected governments and destructing social subsistence and health care systems. 'Neo-liberalism' has been the opposite of a selling-off of the nation state's

table silver and it was diametrically opposed to the Laissez-fair Capitalism of unhindered profit maximization.

The term 'neo-liberal' has been coined by the German social science professor Alexander Rüstow who introduced it in 1938 at a conference in order to distinguish between the mainstream economic theories that in the aftermath of the Great Depression of 1929 led to fascist governments which had been brought to power by industrialists and rich aristocratic elites in Europe and subsequently to WWII.

The main principle behind the 'neo-liberalism' of that time has been to have the state provide for the framework in which the economy was embedded. Nowadays, it is the other way around.

For those who had survived WWII it was clear that the "economic liberalism had failed when assuming that free market was an automatism. Liberalism had neglected the political and economical inter-dependence as a governing framework as it regarded the price mechanism as fully functioning machinery but in reality this machine like any other requires to be given a sensible direction by human beings" Alfred Müller-Armack, founder of the Cologne School of Economics and one of the fathers of the West-German post WWII model of *Soziale Marktwirtschaft* (social free market) that had been the success-model for four decades.

The 'real' neo-liberal principles have vanished over the decades and since the collapse of the Eastern European Socialism in 1989 got replaced by brutal capitalism that has nothing in common with the original social free market – principle. Today's 'neo-liberal' policy conservative, green and social democratic parties pursue are to such an extent a result from a cushioned capitalism as Hitler's slogan "Arbeit macht frei" at the gates of Auschwitz could claim to have given work to everyone. Just, even Hitler himself would never had dared to refer to that.

The renewed neo-liberalism had evolved under Milton Friedman and his 'Chicago boys' once more resulted in blind market fanaticism while the state subordinated it's power to economic might and plight just like in 1929.

EUtopia versus Reality21

When regime - critical economists describe the probable collapse of the financial system that would mark the end of the present capitalistic system, conservative, liberal, social democratic and green politicians call these "horror scenarios". Whoever points out that media ownership and political power go hand in hand with interests of the beneficiaries of the financial virtual reality casino is branded as a "consipracy theorist".

Day per day more than 100,000 human beings die of hunger or it's consequences. A billion people are chronically under-nourished. At least an additional 100 million people were thrown into poverty because of the financial crisis. Globalisation critic Jean Ziegler points at the "owners of globalised capital who decide over life and death for billions of human beings". He cites the investment strategies along with speculation and political alliances in which these owners engage to make the decision on who may live on this planet and who is forced to die.

This is not a "horror scenario", this is Reality21.

Also in industrialised nations the dream of ever lasting growth and a constantly increasing standard of living has been an illusion as the dramatic decline proves. In the US the annual income of 90% of society is tumbling at around 1970ies levels. Of every Dollar of income increase between 1976 and 2007 exactly 58 cents were pocketed by the richest 1% of US households. In Germany it is not much better. Despite an export-leaning Aufschwung (up-swing) that slowly is bringing German industries back onto the 2000 level hardly any rise in primary employment but rather low paid mini-jobs can be noticed. The real net wages are locked into 1991 as if the past 20 years after German unification had not had any positive effect at all. Major corporations are reducing their engagements in research and development, private banks prefer to finance the financial merry-go-round rather than innovative SMEs.

Capitalism is in it's most severe crisis since the 1930ies. Reason for this is not the lack of a few tougher rules and regulations but the profit maximization principle. An economy which produces only for profit and not for actual demand will always fail. As long as privately accumulated wealth dominates the real economy it won't be actual needs of society but only the expected return on investment and profit share that will determine which investment is being made and whose job will be protected and whose social existence will be destroyed. The Financial Times Deutschland (FTD) justified the actions of oil giant BP which created an ecological disaster in the Gulf of Mexico. Even if he had wanted, the BP boss could hardly refrain from the deep horizon drilling as he is in his function not obliged to serve society but the owners of BP. FTD noted that if a company executed a morally correct decision that reduced the shareholder value would in the long run not be considered competitive anymore and be replaced by a less scrupulous rival.

It is more likely, however, that before that would ever happen the CEO would be fired by the shareholders. In that sense it only sounds logic what the former head of the capital market division of Dresdner Bank AG said in order to justify his speculation-orgies: "Can you imagine what had happened if I had said during the good times that these papers were dangerous? One would have fired me." The West-German cushioned capitalism that provided for a certain social security and in that sense a compromise between profit fixation and overall goals of the society as a whole had only existed because there was a socialist system in Eastern Germany. Right after German unification the 'third way' West Germans enjoyed for 45 years after WWII while their 'brothers and sisters' in the 'real existing socialism' in the East were paying for the lost war got replaced by an outright Manchester capitalism Germans in both states had never thought would be possible again after 1929.

West Germany's success model of a socially balanced free market economy and liberal society was sacrificed on the altar of a neo-liberal wave of privatisation, deregulation and liberalisation that emerged as the attempt to fight against a declining profit rate since the phenomenal growth rates of the past – WWII era could not be written forth. Neo-Liberalism managed to let profits skyrocket again but at the cost of wage- and social standard dumping as well as an ridiculous lowering of corporate taxes for rich multinational corporations while SMEs and ordinary taxpayers and citizens had to carry extra burdens by increased direct and indirect taxes and VAT as well as levies.

The steadily declining social purchasing power resulting from wage decreases was replaced by an incredible increase of public as well as private debt. Today, private as well as public households are over-indebted in a way that brings this system at it's limits. This is the reason for the current crisis. Parallel to this the global capitalism has led to an extreme concentration of economic power. Whereas socialism got crippled because of centralisation, capitalism suffocates because of concentration. 500 economic giants control half of this planet's economic output. The latter is reason for major corporations to replace democratically elected and controlled governments in order to push through their *Wirtschafts*-Stalinism holding our elected leaders hostage while blackmailing our parliaments to create an ever more profitable "environment".

In an absurd scenario that we are now to watch the assassins mutate to suiciders getting rescued by their victims. Sure, these Frankenstein-monsters have been created by the neo-liberal "masters of the universe" for who very often 'Social-Democratic', 'Socialist', 'Labour' or 'Green' governments rolled out the red carpet by allowing hedge fund – junkies, virtual reality casino 'Jedi Riders' and private equity - sharks to dictate their profit maximization conditions.

But, now that these monsters exist they block any groundbreaking change that is contrary to their interests. This wouldn't necessarily mean that politics can only act within the frame set forth by these monsters. It only means that real change can only be brought about if these cartels are denied their grip on the world's resources and capacities. Ownership determines power, economical and political one. The two go together. Political power is worthless without the power to make economic decisions, economic power is useless without a society defined by human rights, freedom and democracy.

Lately, we can observe how perverse the present economic regime functions. The financial conglomerates who had gotten it all wrong bring us into the absurd situation that the state is a house in which bandits of the organized crime have broken into. Funnily enough, the house owners then ask the same mafia to extend a loan for buying new furniture although it is clear that the gangsters return for yet another spree in the re-furnished house.

It is not utopic to overcome the corrupt structures of the financial capitalism that has proven to be anti-economical. It rather is utopic to believe under present conditions to force by a few new rules and tougher regulations major banks to suddenly support SMEs as long as more money can be made in the casino. Likewise it is ridiculous to think that global energy conglomerates will mutate to become the key promoter of ecological energy concepts as long as more money can be made by fossil fuel and nuclear fusions. Six of the world's ten largest corporations are energy monsters.

The above facts should not keep society from fighting for better rules and regulations for as long as there is no broad base in society for a better economic system. It does make sense to fight for minimum wages and social standards as well as tough legislation for banks and a change in resource management and the introduction of ecological energy solutions. But, one should not believe that these measurements will impose a different logic of development onto Capitalism. Every new regulation or law will be circumvented as effectively as possible by these conglomerates.

Most of the finance-innovation has got no other reason than to find loopholes to evade taxes and regulation. The imbalance between economy and politics undermines our democracies and can only be resolved by re-organization of economic power and thus ownership. Whoever is thinking that a smaller solution is possible is dreaming in Technicolor.

An economic model in which industries produce only for profit and not for actual demand is bound to collapse sooner or later. Our present economic model is not only being brought down by ruthless speculators, incompetent bank managers, merciless private equity sharks and hedge fund – Jedi Riders but foremost by fake mathematics.

One may be upset about our political leaders from Social-Democrats to Conservatives and Liberal Democratic-Greens who all rolled out the red carpet for the financial gangsters, but it is also the underlying economic theory that is fatally wrong but nevertheless is still being taught in our universities.

Mainstream economists, in a drive to help political leaders over decades to justify exploitation of citizens while allowing profit maximization dreams for owners and shareholders come true, manipulated mathematics in a fundamental question on which our present economic model rests in it's entirety.

The Neo-classical model, to a large degree developed by Milton Friedman and his Chicago School of Economics is mathematically incoherent.

In order to be able to record destruction as 'growth' the neo-classical model set's the axiom $\partial F(x)/\partial x = 0$. If it was $\partial F(x)/\partial x = 1$ this would mathematically mean that the function isn't a continuum. But, in the neo classical economy one wants to uphold the theory that the relations investment-wage, capital & labour, production and productivity, growth and consumption are continuing functions and for this reason set the axiom $\partial F(x)/\partial x = 0$.

This allows the economic model to substitute factors like 'capital' and 'labour' by whatever figures and assume that it is divisible. The neo-classical model in it's entirety bases on this assumption, making it possible that this model – in theory – shows even then growth rates if consumption declines because of shrinking wages leading to retracting production cycles while the profit rate increases amid declining production output.

Applying this model means that in theory even destruction would be measured as growth. But, the theorists of the neo classical model can't trick mathematics. The function $\partial F(x)/\partial x$ per se can not be a continuous one, only if one set it "0" but that defies any logic as non-continuous functions can not be differentiated.

The manipulated econometrics used by EU Commission, all member states and being taught at most universities also allows to declare the accumulation of wealth outside the production cycle and outside of the control of central banks irrelevant. According to the neo-classical ideology all the bubbles created by the financial market's chain-letter system wouldn't exist.

It has become obvious in the current crisis that a deregulated and liberalised global financial system had enjoyed the privilege of almost without limitation creating credit based funds. Under these circumstances central banks had almost no influence on the capital accumulation as well as the irrational movement and use of such liquidity.

The mathematically most elegant neo-classical model giving us the illusion of a balance has been developed by the economists Arrow and Debreu. Mathematically it is impossible to prove it wrong but a closer scrutiny reveals that it's underlying assumptions without which it's conclusions could not be upheld. It is, for instance assumed that in the Arrow-Debreu model every market participant knows exactly about the market conditions and is even able to predict the probability of future developments. The employee would know that by a 30% probability he could expect a pay increase in two years time while the likelihood that he be fired in the next year would be 70%. In this model a person would also know by which probability one would be married in the next ten years and how likely it would be that one died in the next 15 years.

In this wonderful model everyone has sufficient access to credit in order to bridge bad times or to invest and build up an own business. Even insurances against any adversities of life are possible within the Arrow-Debreu – Model.

Even more unreal are the assumptions of the neo-classical model when it comes to the behaviour of corporations. One assumes, of course, a perfect competition in which no company has the slightest influence on prices. This is only possible because it is assumed that regarding the production costs the scalar revenue would either decline or remain constant but in no case increase. Declining scalar revenue means that the bigger a company is becoming and the higher it's production volume, the more expensive every additionally produced unit would be. The revenue of increasing size of the company therefore is negative. If that was true there would be no danger of an overheating economy, there wouldn't be any mergers and fusions, take-overs and by this not the danger that economic monsters could pose an overwhelming economic power. But, that this is not true has become self-evident over the past decades of mega-mergers and fusions. Of course a big company will grow faster as any smaller competitor as it can re-finance itself cheaper, buy resources and energy at a better price and can sell at a higher price because it can, because of it's market dominance, influence the sale's prices.

In any case, increasing scalar revenues contain the danger of creating an oligopoly. Perfect competition in the true meaning of the neo-classical model is a factual impossibility.

But, big companies aren't only more efficient because they can be more productive but also because they can handle an increasing demand and also gain political influence.

If 3 or 4 or let's say even 20 companies determine the development of an entire industry, then the investment decisions of those companies become relevant for a region or even an entire state. No democratically elected representative can resist that power.

When in the 1990ies the European internal market got liberalised the strict cartel controlling mechanisms got watered down. The blind Laissez-Faire attitude towards major corporations that by European-wide mergers created mega-conglomerates had been justified by EU Commission and member state governments citing a bigger market that could still provide for competition.

But, we have seen that market dominance does not only develop when there is no competition any longer but already when just a somewhat limited amount of major corporations secured their share of the cake. Price fixing is at hand. This is evident in the EU for it's most important economic areas such as food, capital goods, car industry, energy and water.

The political problem that arises is that other than the markets the EU member states have not become bigger but are now confronted with major corporations that handle by far bigger budgets than what any elected government ever controls.

The biggest mistake committed at the founding of the European Community and later the EU has been that the economic power of major corporations got cemented that let the European Institutions advance to a lobby-machinery governing against the declared will of the vast majority of European citizens. The same applies to the WTO, G8 and IMF sponsored so called "Globalisation" which sole purpose is to manifest a world order that provides for unhindered investment and capital accumulation opportunities on a world wide scale regardless of what would be in the interest of citizens. An economic model that produces only for profit but not for actual demand in the end, we witness today, becomes anti-economical no matter how much it's protagonists try to manipulate it's scientific base.

Public and Private Ownership

In the new economic system the question will be answered who may own whom? Of course one priority of our government will be the confiscation of misused economic wealth as well as the unbundling of conglomerates that are not working effectively. It is a thin line we have to walk on in order to revive the economy.

No alternative to capitalism has ever worked - so far. Socialism got crippled by centralisation, corruption and nepotism, capitalism by corrupt nepotism and concentration. The neo-liberal bloc these days along with the EU Commission advocate so called "unbundling" as the solution to the crisis of the system. But, is that really feasible and why should one not rather than trying to keep a system proven to be anti-economical and inhumane alive think about a mathematically sound, ecologically wise humanistic new economic system?

In history it has never worked to return to old systems. There is no danger that the world falls back into Soviet style of Stalinism, but repression that in previous times when the capitalistic system failed (5 times in 400 years!) led to the at the various times to date known biggest ever catastrophe. Fascism has been a result of the Great Depression that led to WWII.

History does not repeat itself, but it rather develops in form of spirals. Whether said spiral is pointing upwards or downwards is in our, the people who live in the present time, hands. We all influence history's course by what we undertake to do and by what we refrain from doing.

By continuing to adhere to an unsustainable economic model that destroys capacities we are obstructing new developments like ben Ali, Mubarak and Gaddafi did. It is our duty to think about the time after the financial capitalism as it is clear that the old system is rotten and can not function much longer.

The German Philosopher Ernst Bloch once pointed out that one of the greatest challenges for human beings were to imagine a society that in reality did not exist yet. Mass media is owned and controlled by private oligopolies and for this reason makes the economic predicament appear inevitably be without an alternative. A predicament can not be changed. But, a problem resulting from a predicament can be solved. The predicament of the present economic system is that wealth is *created* but not *produced*.

Ownership is the key to solving the problems of our times. In capitalism political power is subordinated to economic power. In order to rescue their system, the neo-liberals propose to "unbundled" conglomerates, but it is striking that wherever they govern, all EU member states while they dominate European Parliament and EU institutions they have not made any credible steps into that direction.

But, a mere shrinking of major corporations that would guarantee that these privately held companies would not pose a threat to democracy while still being able to serve the economy with their investment decisions dominating the social existence of millions of people will be impossible because it will simply not be feasible.

Modern technologies require a certain capital to operate mass production that is higher than what a classical SME has available. Industrial scale production below a certain minimum of pieces being produced wouldn't justify expenses for research and development. Major corporations are a pre-requirement to produce on a high level, but they do not need to be owned privately.

It won't be possible to build cars or produce innovative electronic goods, pharmaceutical products, energy and telecommunications on SME-level. The argument that publicly owned companies would not be efficient and profitable is led ad absurdum by countries such as Sweden or China. Their major corporations are all state-owned and obviously by far more sustainable than in the western free world. Incentives for managers and workforce will keep innovation and profitability up.

The advantage of such corporations clearly is that they have to be profitable but don't need to produce an additional profit that is being paid out to shareholders who do nothing but enjoy the fruits of other people's work.

Unbundling and downsizing won't do. That's why the key to any solution of the present crisis is the question of ownership. But, whoever only mentions this is immediately under suspicion to wanting to confiscate private family homes. This is of course ridiculous but mainstream media always makes it appear as going hand in hand. Reason for this is to make ordinary citizens instinctively reject any suggestions regarding ownership of huge economic capacities.

But, whoever believes that by defending the present economic system and it's dreadful distribution of wealth he protects his own property as well is being mislead as it is this economic predicament that currently deprives the vast majority of their standard of living and in ever more cases their own family's home.

The aim to protect wealth that has been worked for is counter-caricatured by the present economic system that created artificial wealth posing as privately owned economic power that in a dreadful spiral ever faster deprives the vast majority of everything they have worked for.

A major, market dominating, corporation is not a matter of private affairs and should have an obligation to serve the community and the interests of the majority of people living in it. Anything else is anti-economical.

Therefore, Common Law at the end of the 19th century defined that some ownerships are related to 'business affected with a public interest'. This is even reflected in the EU treaties, but nobody seems to care about it although it would be high time to consider this matter.

Moreover, the EU Commission under President José Manuel Barroso changed the status of those services of general economic interest by letting commercial services advance to the same level and by this allowed ever more exemptions from competition rules.

If a company of public interest is owned privately and by this is subject to profitability this will automatically pose a problem. In lieu of the fact that private economic concentration is choking our entire system one should immediately draw consequences and nationalise major corporations.

Since the next move will be for the taxpayer to 'rescue' the real economy from the banks previously 'rescued', this move will only be logic. No compensation to shareholders does needs to be paid as it is their own fault to have speculated and trusted the 'masters of the universe' who manipulated the system and nevertheless got it all wrong.

The most famous case in history is when the US's Supreme Court ruled that one can not own a human being. At the same time the judges ordered that no compensation ought to be paid to the keepers of the former slaves. 150 years ago it had been unthinkable to many that slavery ever would be abolished. Ernst Bloch was right, so let's now think of our future!

The Third Way

After financial capitalism, what will be next? Soviet-style of "Socialism", or rather an entirely new model?

In the long term it will be required to overhaul the entire economic system. This will not be possible without unbundling of conglomerates and restructuring ownership of market dominating major corporations. At present, no such thing as a "free" market exists. As said before, global players, (6 of the biggest 10 are energy conglomerates) are standing in the way of ecological innovation and sustainable development.

It is hardly possible for any democratically elected leader to stand up against their power and it is impossible for any smaller competitor to win a market share even though the product is more innovative or the underlying business idea much better because banks are hardly financing any SMEs but only their own gambling.

In Germany, it would be less than 200 companies which needed to be led into public ownership as they are too big to be administrated in a good way when private profit maximization dreams dominate the agenda. The owners of those majors in most cases have inherited their shares anyhow and in almost all cases don't even work in the management of the company but derive their wealth from the work of others.

Since these major corporations have continuously received public funds in form of subsidies also from Brussels one should simply turn such taxpayer's money into shares of the relevant company.

The usual argument against public ownership that neo-liberals bring into play is that a publicly owned company was less efficient and less profitable than a private one. That is bullocks and does in no way stand up empirical studies.

First of all, a publicly owned company is free from the chains of producing profit that feeds some rich heir that never worked for the company. In this sense, a publicly owned company will always have more resources available and for this reason be much better prepared for innovation and re-investment than a privately owned company that additionally to it's operational costs needs to produce a profit that is being distributed to shareholders and rich family-clans.

Adam Smith and John Locke would turn in their graves if they could see how major corporations today operate and fail to invest into new technologies. What both instead would certainly like to see is a modern economy-democracy in which the employees control production and investments in a way that the Czech economist Ota Sik envisioned in 1979.

According to Ota Sik "the corporation is not for the shareholder but for the employee a living social institution" for which he developed the model of a continuous neutralisation of share-capital by transferring all additionally accumulated production capital into a foundation owned by the employees of the company as the ownership of a company is defined by the continuing accumulation of innovative production capacity and results derived from such.

The foundation and it's capital shall not individually be liquidized or sold. This is highly beneficial for the company as it is under no pressure to pay dividends or please shareholders by distributing profits but can use the accumulated wealth for innovation and re-investment within the company.

And, the benefit for the employees lays in the fact that they participate in the vital decisions of the company. This concept is much different from the usual practice by which major corporations ever since threw a hand full of shares at their employees instead of wage increases or social rights and which were never significant enough to make a relevant difference to the ownership structure of the company.

To the contrary, the common practice has been to lay the burdens of wrong decisions by the management onto the shoulders of the workers. What shall not be the main issue is the question of distribution but that of production in order to increase the creation of wealth.

Under this predicament of either public or (the third way) economic-democratic ownership no shareholder value needs to be created as neither public hand (ultimately the taxpayer) nor the employees (including the top management of the company) would plunder the company's assets and not re-invest in the best interest of the company because it would simply not be possible.

No private equity - shark or hedge fund - junky could make fortune on the back of employees and production capacity of the company. And, no heir would be able to sit on the sun roof zipping away champagne without working.

After all, this concept is the only solution to ever establish a truly free market as only such company will be successful in the long term that is innovative and re-invests into new technologies, ecologically sound and beneficial to society.

The motivation for management as well as workers to stretch to the ceiling and work better couldn't be greater than by providing for a safe and socially just working environment with fair, productivity-orientated, remuneration. All of which our present economic system does not provide for.

The US - American sociologist and 1978 - Nobel Prize laureate Herbert Simon has empirically proven that the differences in competitiveness between privately and publicly owned companies were less grave than always maintained since most producers are employees and not the owners of a company and according to the classical theory have no reason to maximize the profit share of a company unless being controlled and forced by the owners to do that. Controlling a public company in that way is even easier than a private one as an audit by the state will always be more stringent than that of a private entity being paid by the owners themselves.

The big scandals of private audit companies and rating agencies that brought down our present economic system are evidence enough for that. One may have wished to have had more control by the public hand especially in the past decades that led to the insane merger & take-over excesses.

Herbert Simon had pointed out and proven it beyond doubt that there is no difference between profit-orientated and publicly owned companies or organisations in regards to the manager's and employee's motivation to produce effectively and efficiently. The only difference is, in fact, to set different priorities. In private companies the priority is the generating of profit that can be paid out to shareholders while in publicly controlled companies innovation and sustainability are the priority.

The German economist Helmut Arndt, an evolutionist of the Schumpeter-tradition, asserted that a competing economic model doesn't function better because a company is privately owned or not, but solely because companies independently have to compete in a free market to win the same customer. Neither the ownership nor the legal frame of company make any difference as long as their independence and market-orientated free decision making is guaranteed.

The German economics professor and consultant Hermann Simon, not related to Nobel Laureate Herbert Simon, made it absolutely clear in his book 'Hidden Champions' that "the phenomenon of the success of the 'hidden champions' are not primarily questions over the ownership by family clans but that over the strategy and leadership of a company".

Strategy and leadership of a company has to orientate itself on economically meaningful goals for which incentives will have to create the right motivation among all employees, workers as well as management.

There are no guarantees but the likelihood that the right priorities are put forward by a publicly owned or economic-democratically controlled company is much higher than it presently is by any privately owned, stock market listed, major corporation that is feeding heirs of family clans rather than putting profit generated back to work.

Europe after the financial capitalism will have to revisit the issue of ownership for the sake of a truly free market and ecologically sound economic system that serves all people.

The Heir Apparent

The economic system has to serve the people, not vice versa. At least this has been the resolution of any liberal and free market apologist. Over the neo-liberal age of the past 2 decades we have left behind this principle with every new speculation bubble for good.

The resignation of Germany's top aristocratic "copy-paste-delete" - Minister of Defence 'Dr.' 'Freiherr' Karl-Theodor zu Guttenberg raises the question why a democratic society still bathes heirs and shareholders in champagne while the economic future of the western world is at stake.

Many founders and owners of successful enterprises seem to have doubts about their heirs. Latest example is the German HARIBO corporation that ageing founder Hans Riegel wishes to be managed by outside experts rather than his nephews. He is not the only one as the dramatically rising number of foundations in Germany proves.

None of the foundations created by the founders of ALDI Nord, Thyssen-Krupp, the 'empire' of Ferdinand Piech, Bosch, Bertelsmann and LIDL have any social or humanitarian aspirations but solely shall administrate an until then successful company by protecting it against being split up or ruined by incapacitated heirs.

The latter of course still derive their income from such foundations. Nobody can explain where the use for the innovation of industry and productivity in general lies when billions are transferred to a degenerating class of heirs.

To the contrary, these corporations would be more productive and innovative if the funds could be used within the company rather than financing champagne parties. But, it is not only economically useless heirs but also shareholders whose guaranteed right to draw blood from company gains and profits is counterproductive as it amounts to semi-feudalistic privileges as the great US American economist Kenneth Galbraith in his book "The new industrial State" wrote.

The aforementioned cases of course only relate to major corporations of thousands of employees and not a classical SME. The latter usually has to fight hard to sustain itself and maintain a safe position in the market. Competition is a pre-condition for any vital economic system but it is also brutal and any wrong decision by the company's management can cost it it's existence.

SMEs do not blackmail elected governments and also don't write laws and regulations to make these suit it's personal interests, but major corporations if these are privately owned do exactly that as it is proven by the EU Commission in any and all deregulations every day.

There is a huge difference between major corporations that hold a market- and society dominating position and those 99.7% of SMEs. As long as democratically elected governments and parliaments but also EU Commission and Council are adhering to what the major multinationals are dictating, there won't be any economic recovery in sight.

Ownership rights cover four important issues in a company, namely the goals and criteria of how the company is being led, the use of funds in other words also investments and employment, the right to own and control the company's profit and last but not least, the right to sell the company.

The justification for the state to hand over economic resources of society to private owners initially had been the free market whose invisible hand was to lead selfish interests into an efficient and productive direction. This principle does not work anymore with major corporations.

One could draw the conclusion that it would be sufficient to limit the owner's discretion of making decisions on how to use profits and force them to re-invest those funds in order to make a sustainable development possible that serves society best. The alternative would be to confiscate shares and nationalise major corporations.

But, a study conducted on European level in 1993 under the title "Industrial Democracy in Europe Revisited" (Oxford 1993) came to the conclusion "that institutional norms may have a more limited impact on worker influence than was indicated in our earlier study... For workers, the general state of the labour-market appears to be a better predictor of influence than is the institutional framework of participation – the higher the unemployment rate, the lower is the influence which workers have over organizational decisions."

Whoever dreamed that a social-democratic 'Third Way' was possible can see that it is rather not as the study finds that "neither *de jure* Participative Structures nor *de facto* Participative Behaviour are very highly developed in the majority of our countries."

Only utopists believe that one can change underlying priorities of the management of a company by allowing employees to participate in a democratic way in the key decisions of a company because as long as the owners concentrate the economic power in their hands they will always dominate the management and use their funds to let it always get their way, if not legally, then illegally by bribing the worker's representatives the latter for which there are countless examples to be found in history.

The case of Volkswagen where managers bribed and blackmailed unionists to agree to for employees unfavorable terms has only been the tip of the iceberg.

For the same reason it is an illusion to think that better regulation and tougher laws will force major corporations back on the path of doing good for society. The reality check reveals especially during the financial crisis that any of the EU's new legislation is immediately being counter-caricatured and undermined by circumvention, re-naming or re-branding.

The truth is that the socially somewhat tamed capitalism of the post WWII era rested on the fact that major corporations and their owners at that time have not been more powerful than the industrialized states themselves.

This balance of power has shifted completely in favor of global players that combined an ever bigger concentration of market dominance with every de-regulation EU Commission and World Trade Organization conferences had pushed through.

Even if one limited the owner's direct influence on any decisions on company decisions they would still enjoy one important privilege: to sell what they own. But, as long as production is being made dependent on private investor's and shareholder's investment decisions their power will always set the priorities of any major corporation.

Unlike a small or medium sized enterprise, usually a classical family-business, where the owner and the employees are tied together working collectively to produce quality goods on highest level while being forced to be profitable, a major global player will only produce what promises the highest profit rate and not necessarily what is the highest quality-level.

In addition, the major corporation not only has to be profitable but also produce a high return on investment to please shareholders and owners who would, if a higher return is promised elsewhere, withdraw their funds. The flaws are built into the system by a ludicrous profit dictate that makes investment decisions by the falling blade of a guillotine.

Without the promise of a significant return on investment no Euro will be ever invested into any company anymore. This fact has led to an economy that only produces for profit and not for the actual demand. That is why our economies only produce such an incredible amount of trash and not long lasting products in a sustainable and ecologic way. Profit maximization has led to a dreadful investment – stop as we have seen in all our countries that are falling back in comparison with China, India and Brazil.

Unless we manage to have ownership rules that combine public interest with productivity and innovation, the so far industrialised nations will rapidly decline and never come up again. The alimentation of heirs and useless shareholders has to be stopped right now.

The free-market – myth

Competition in a free market only exists for SMEs, not for major corporations.

What is the deeper sense and meaning of an economy? Certainly not to make the people living in it poorer but richer. An economic order that results in a lower standard of living for the vast majority while leaving existing economic capacity unused and deprive millions of people of participating in a productive work as well as public life according to their abilities and qualifications thus contributing to economic and social wealth, such an economic system has completely failed big time. And, an economic model that destroy the natural habitats as well as human existence like a bulldozer has no legitimacy, but is rather a danger to life on Earth.

There are no objective reasons for a constantly declining standard of living. So called "globalisation" opens new production capacities in emerging- and developing countries and there is absolutely no reason for this going hand in hand with the loss of jobs and subsequently impoverishment of millions in industrialised nations. Globalisation is not a process that is happening to us like a *Deus ex Machina* and it is anything but a natural development that we would have to adjust to, it is rather the other way around: we have to make it be useful to us human beings and our long term goals.

Globalisation under the auspices of major corporations and financial institutions doesn't play along the lines of humankind's long term goals as the living conditions of the vast majority of people on this planet are worsening day by day.

An increased life-expectancy in industrialised nations is also not the reason for increasing poverty as productivity rises much quicker than the share of seniors in the population. Even the ecological that requires different technologies and new, renewable, resource management, doesn't lower the standard of living at all but forces us to change our production patterns, away from short term useable products that waste resources for a quick turnover and huge profitability towards a sustainable production of long lasting quality products.

Up to now the necessary ecological change has not been pursued radically enough so it can hardly be seen as the reason for the decline of standard of living.

So what is it that deprives us of increased wealth if it is not modern technologies, the internationalisation of production structures or the natural givens and demographic developments? It is the way how our present economic system is organising the production of goods and provision of services, the criteria that govern economic decisions and goals to which these are subordinated.

Whoever still maintains what the German initiative for a new social market economy (a kind of right-wing think-tank) upholds as their ultima ratio, namely that "private ownership and private economic, competition-driven, entrepreneurial activity most favourably warrant an efficient use of resources and the adjustment to a changing environment"[14] is either blind or a lobbyist.

For a longer historic period there had been reasons for believing in this dogma and for a few tiny areas of our economy it may still be valid, but it the less true the bigger a company is.

In Germany, officially, the definition for SMEs (kleine und mittlere Unternehmen ‚KMU') cover companies of up to 250 employees and/or a total turnover of 50 million Euros. These are 99.7% of all 3 million German companies. Of all German employees 65.8% are working in a KMU / SME which account for only a third of the total turnover by German companies.

These companies usually face tough competition in an open market. Not so the 8,500 major corporations in Germany who account for two thirds of all turnover. The 8,500 German majors are mainly owned by the same structures leaving some 3,500 really independent major corporations.[15] A third of the 3,500 corporations are owned by family clans of which the top 100 are the actual power structure in Germany.

---

14 Gutachten im Auftrag der Initiative Neue Soziale Marktwirtschaft; Ch. Kaserer, Staatliche Hilfen für Banken und ihre Kosten – Notwendigkeit und Merkmale einer Ausstiegsstrategie, April 2010, S. 11

15 ZEW, ifm, Stiftung Familienunternehmen, Die wirtschaftliche Bedeutung von Familienunternehmen, 2009

Absurd priorities set forth by managers of stock market listed companies make the maximisation of profitability the highest criteria for economic decisions and not the quality of the product or service. That's why precarious work replaces qualified labour leading to immense pressure on the workforce and wage dumping while social standards are axed by the political leadership. Lay-offs and redundancies create a climate in companies as well as the entire society that let's the motivation of the workforce shrink at the same pace rate that it's productivity and efficiency declines.

Exorbitant bonus payments and dividends draw liquidity from the companies' substance and minimise the required funds for investment, innovation, development and research.

Free market and competition no longer discipline major corporations because the power of a few global players is too overwhelming. This power allows the unsanctioned pursuing of the anti-productive strategy by imposing pressure on SMEs who produce the intermediate capital goods.

On those markets selfishness and profit maximisation are not, as Adam Smith had hoped for, be guided by an invisible hand leading the economy to be beneficial to all of society.

For the conservative management – theorist Fredmund Malik the underlying reason and "use of a company is to create by it's market performance satisfied customers"[16]

In sharp contrast to the prevailing shareholder-value – philosophy of our present times, Mr Malik is convinced that "profit as highest goal" destroys the profitability of a company and inevitably leads it into bankruptcy[17], because the real reasons for good performances of companies are "innovation, marketing and productivity" by which one should be guided long before any profit or even gain could be envisioned. Fredmund Malik expressly writes that "profit shall never be the highest aim for management decisions" as profit has to be understood as the measurement of how good an enterprise fulfils it's task while it is clear that profit may only be seen as such an indicator in a truly free market based on a functioning real competition.

For Fredmund Malik the most important question is not the one for profit-

---

16   Malik, Corporate Governance, a.a.O. S. 83
17   Malik, Corporate Governance, a.a.O. S. 126

maximum but for profit-minimum: "what minimum of profit requires a company to be in business also tomorrow?"[18]

"Real entrepreneurs", Fredmund Malik says, "maximise the value-added producing capacity of the enterprise by the best-performing product and service for customer and maximise their market position and not their growth. They maximise the use for the customer and not the dividends. They maximise the innovation and not the shareholder value."[19]

But, it is the owner of a company, the shareholder, who determines under which criteria the enterprise is being managed. Therefore, the most important question nowadays has to be whether the present ownership structures benefit the economy under Malik's criteria or do they make it impossible and by this let our system become anti-economical?

The fact that a few major corporations control most of the economic output of this planet while economic capacities are destroyed proves that there is no free market but only dreadful concentration

Thanks to these major's ability to manipulate the most important variables of economic life such as investment decisions and labour conditions, the global players hold the public hostage and dictate national politics and not vice-versa, resulting in the macroeconomic disastrous developments that we are currently living through for the fifth time in 400 years.

---

18   Malik, Corporate Governance, a.a.O. S. 129
19   Malik, Corporate Governance, a.a.O. S. 143

PUBLIC BANKS

It won't help to nationalise banks without closing the casino

It is true, also public banks have indulged in the financial craziness of the past years but first of all not to such an extent as the privately owned banks and secondly they have still fulfilled to a large degree their task of supplying the real economy with liquidity. But, it is also true that it wouldn't help society if private banks were only nationalised without a thorough and complete closing down of the financial virtual reality casino.

Nevertheless, the EU Commission's dirty task for many years has been and still is to break up the public banking structure in Germany and allow private banks to get rid of competitors and secondly to eat into the market share these leave behind. The EU Commission tried to slaughter German WESTLB, split it up and throw it into the open mouth of private banks.

Over many years German public Sparkassen and Landesbanken had a bad reputation being branded too bureaucratic and 'unsexy' because they only reluctantly were willing to follow the trend private banks did in kissing their core business, providing liquidity for real economy and households ‚good-bye‘ and turning to what Wall Street called 'investment banking' producing skyrocketing profit rates.

Deutsche Bank AG in the past years fed their record profits almost exclusively through their ‚investment banking‘ division that made fortunes gambling with Greek state obligations by trading Credit Default Swaps. And, when this turned sour the German government bailed out Hypo Real Estate (HRE) where Deutsche Bank AG had dumped those toxic assets.

Taxpayers could have handed over their money directly to Deutsche Bank AG - shareholders without allowing CEO Josef Ackermann to ruin Greece beforehand.

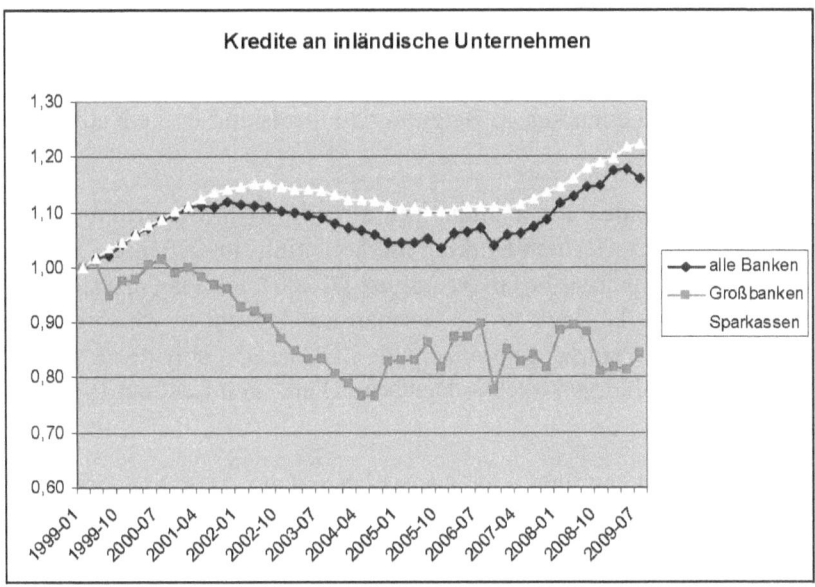

Kredite an inländische Unternehmen

reference: above graph shows that from 1999 on the "Großbanken" (major private German banks) had left the path of sustainable traditional banking business and heavily engaged in gambling with CDOs, credit Default Swaps, and Derivatives instead of concentrating on their core business: lending to businesses. Public Sparkassen only in a minimal way got involved in that kind of 'investment banking' but increasingly handed out loans to the 'real' economy. Private Banks in Germany instead accumulated an estimated amount of 600 billion Euros in 'toxic assets' by their "investment banking" branches for which the German taxpayer is providing comforting guarantees.

The EU Commission had been lobbied since the early 1990ies by German private banks, namely Deutsche Bank AG, to attack the German government over the country's 'inflexible' public banking sector. In Germany there are more than 500 rural Sparkassen that own 12 Landesbanken, 11 Landesbausparkassen and employ 350,000 people who by a network of 17,000 branch offices administrate 70 million accounts.

Public Sparkassen are, because they are not stock companies that have to satisfy any shareholder's hunger for ever bigger dividends, more efficient in serving average citizens and SMEs. Their market share is steady at around 36%, whereas private banks in Germany only account for 28.4% of which the four major banks control more than 50%. Deutsche Bank AG dominates this segment by almost 50% but with it's 7% market share is still well behind public Genossenschaftsbanken that are owned by municipalities and communities.

Logic, that private banks in Germany are eager to break up the market dominance of public banks and use the EU Commission for that purpose. In Great-Britain for instance, the market is reduced to only a few highly profitable private banks and also in France the biggest 5 private banks control 50% of the market, in Belgium two thirds and in the Netherlands even four fifth.

The IMF demanded for a long time already to break up any public monopolies in the German banking market citing 'inefficiencies'. Lately, since the financial crisis began on August 11, 2007, German private media was banging on the flaws of the German Landesbanken which also got engaged in some stupid gambling with CDOs and Derivatives and lost billions in the Goldman Sachs-, Deutsche Bank- and Lehman Brothers - Ponzi-schemes

But, truth be told, the time span over which and the extent to which public German banks got involved in highly speculative transactions are at best laughable in comparison to the damage done by private banks for who the taxpayer has to guarantee now. Nevertheless, media concentrated on the failings of Landesbanken and Sparkassen although these are rather minimal in comparison to the big wheels major private Banks were spinning.

On top of that it were the public banks and Sparkassen which supplied the real economy with liquidity and increasingly stepped in for the private banks that over the past decade withdrew from that business segment and put almost everything onto the casino tables of the financial markets.

The fact that major private banks in Germany account for the least ratio of profitability in the loan segment proves that Sparkassen and Genossenschaftsbanken, both owned by the public, are doing by far better in this important core business than their reputation suggests.

This, of course, raises the appetite of private banks who whish to pick the raisins from the pie and would like to eat into that segment. That is the only reason why Landesbanken came under attack by EU Commission and German government as well as mainstream media as only by discrediting the institutions it will be possible to create public sentiment for privatizing one of the most lucrative and stabile businesses in Germany

After all, we are talking here about a 50% market share in the private client's segment that Sparkassen were able to build up also because private banks had continuously pulled out of this field while concentrating on the seemingly more profitable 'investment banking' which, to put it mildly, has not been such a good idea.

In order to win back this important market share, it has become a prerogative to destroy public banking in Germany completely. This unpopular move could never come from the German government itself, so that's why the EU Commission is employed for this dirty task. For the re-structuring of WESTLB government money will be needed. Such state-aid is always subject to the EU Commission's approval.

This, however, is a sensitive issue as over the past years Germany's private banks have received far more public money than the Landesbanken - without interventions from the EU Commission. Also Deutsche Bank AG, especially, had benefited from taxpayer's money big time when the rescue mission for HRE had been completed. Without state aid Deutsche Bank AG would not have had a dividend to pay out the following year but to eat it's losses resulting from Unicredit- and HRE-engagements.

Instead of throwing more big privatization deals to that monster bank one should rather think of demanding taxpayer's money back which might result in Deutsche Bank AG's nationalisation. Germany's major private banks have evidently not fulfilled their obligations by providing liquidity for the real economy. The tendency clearly points to be symptomatic as the financial experts of Germany's SME federations cite a 63% more difficult access to re-financing sources.

Obviously, private banks in the EU are clearly acting pro-cyclical and by this put fuel to the fire as they are not fulfilling their obligations Across the EU a similar development is noted as Ireland, Spain and Greece are tumbling into state-bankruptcy. The credit crunch is hitting SMEs especially hard as re-financing is crucial for those companies if ever there shall be a recovery. The question which banks are primarily responsible for the credit crunch is not on the agenda of EU Commission and member state governments, it appears, as one also avoids raising the question how much more privately owned banks were to be made responsible for the drying out of the re-financing market in comparison to publicly owned banks such as the German Volksbanken and Sparkassen.

This may only be logic as the EU Commission over the past years had continuously undermined the German Landesbanken, state-controlled banks that are owned by public rural Sparkassen that were targeted by the federation of the German private banks (Bund deutscher Banken).

The aim was, it seems, to discredit such publicly owned banks by citing inefficiencies as well as a certain bureaucratic appearance. The role of the EU Commission is at least questionable, too, since it had adopted the position of the German private banks which couldn't wait to take over the profitable parts of such public banks once these were forced into privatisation under EU rules.

In fact, the suspicion seems legitimate to say that potentially the EU Commission conspired with private banks to abolish any public financing sector that has always been a strong competitor when it came to SME-financing in Germany.

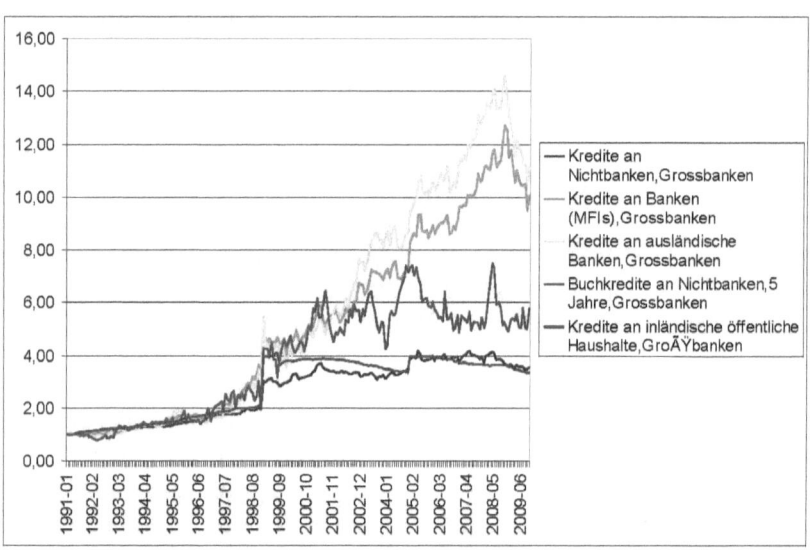

reference: above graph shows that from 2001 on the "Großbanken" (major German banks) had left the path of sustainable traditional banking business and heavily engaged in gambling with CDOs, credit Default Swaps and Derivatives while public Sparkassen only in a minimal way got involved in that kind of 'investment banking'.

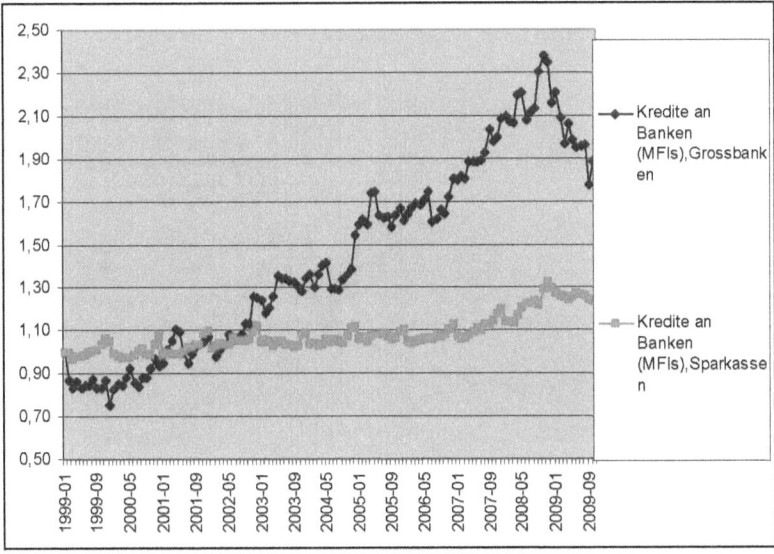

the bulk of all capital has been absorbed by major financial institutions and banks not the public institutions such as Sparkassen and Volksbanken.

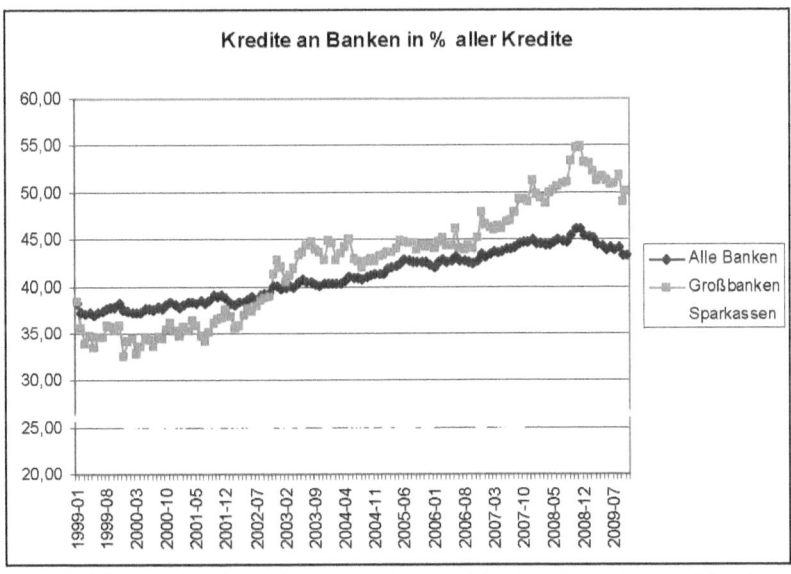

the total of all credit-lines handed out proves that especially since the beginning of the crisis on 11th August 2007, private banks were the major receivers, not the public banks

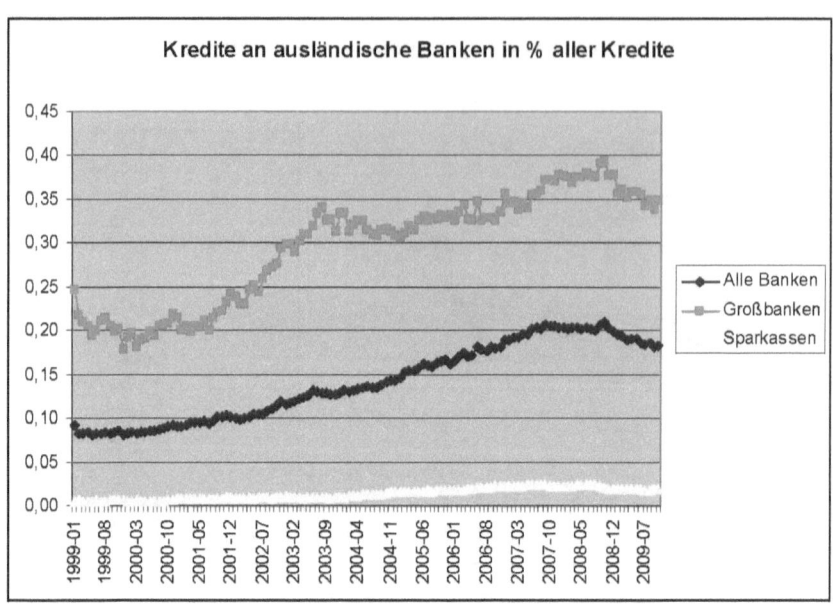

foreign major banks were also the beneficiaries while Sparkassen stood steady.

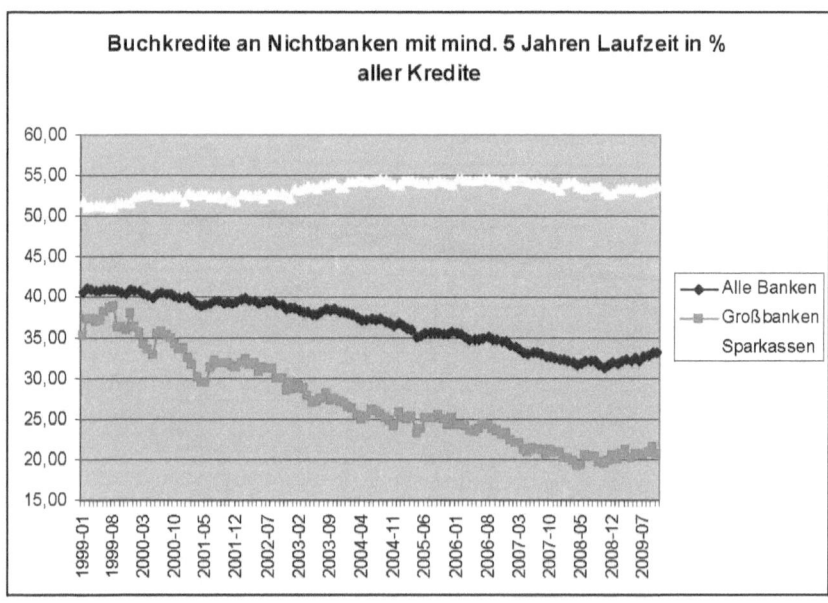

whereas public Sparkassen still handed our credit-lines to non-banking businesses and by this helped the real economy, SMEs especially, major private banks did the opposite

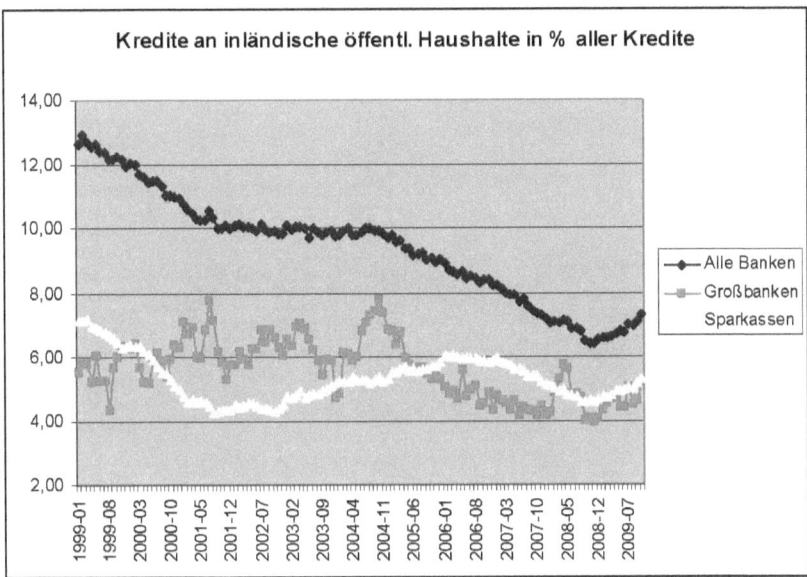

also during the crisis Sparkassen are still lending to public households at the same rate as private banks do so.

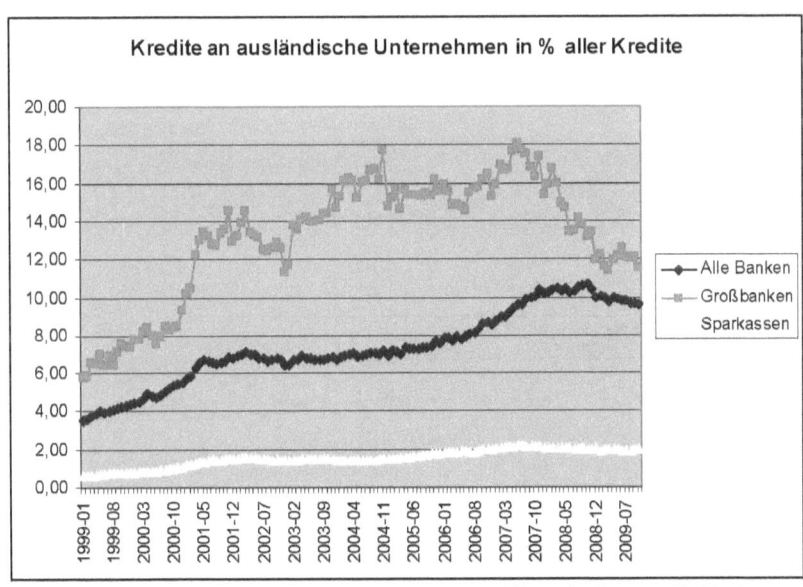

Sparkassen increased their loan engagement with SMEs while major banks pulled in the umbrellas when the rain started to set in.

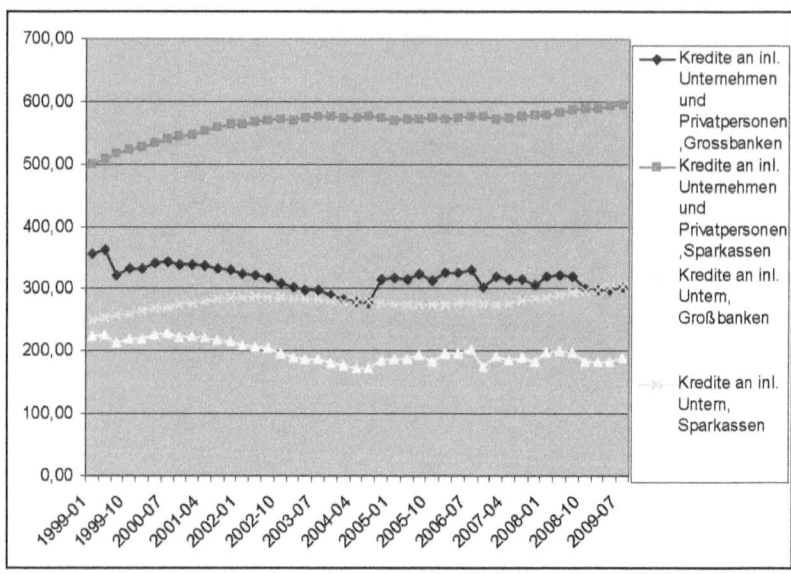

at all times the major private banks got the bulk of all credit-lines handed out. They then went to gamble with it.

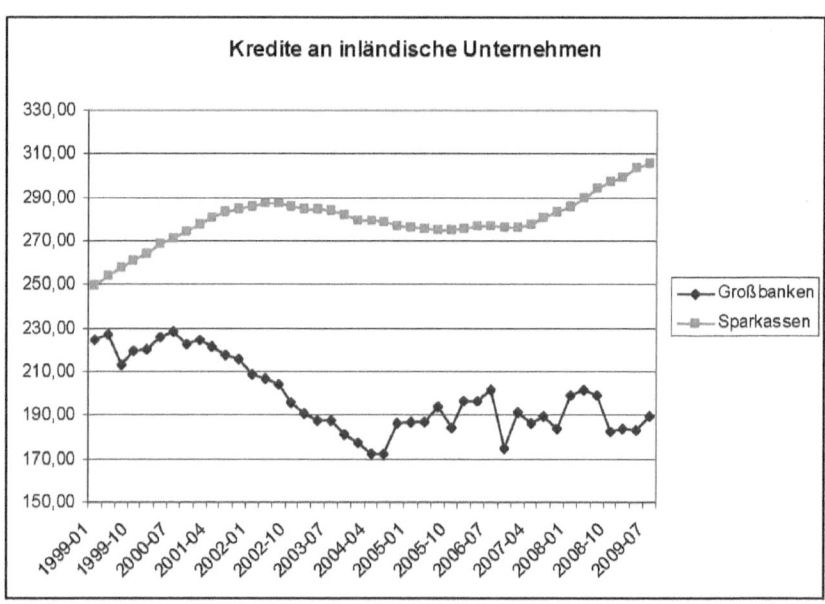

the public Sparkassen especially during the crisis supported the real economy while major banks noted a constant decline despite their pledge to do good and help SMEs.

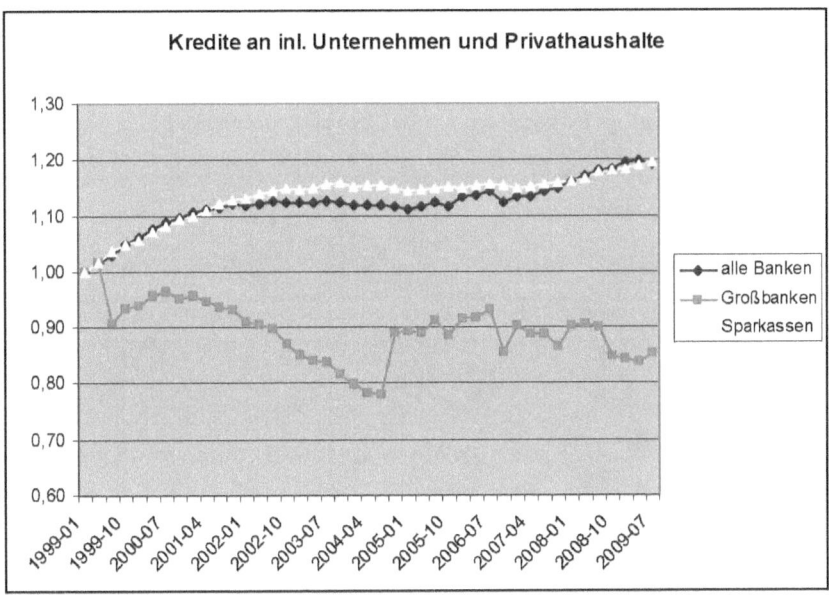

having by far received less funds the Sparkassen steadily increased their SME-engagement

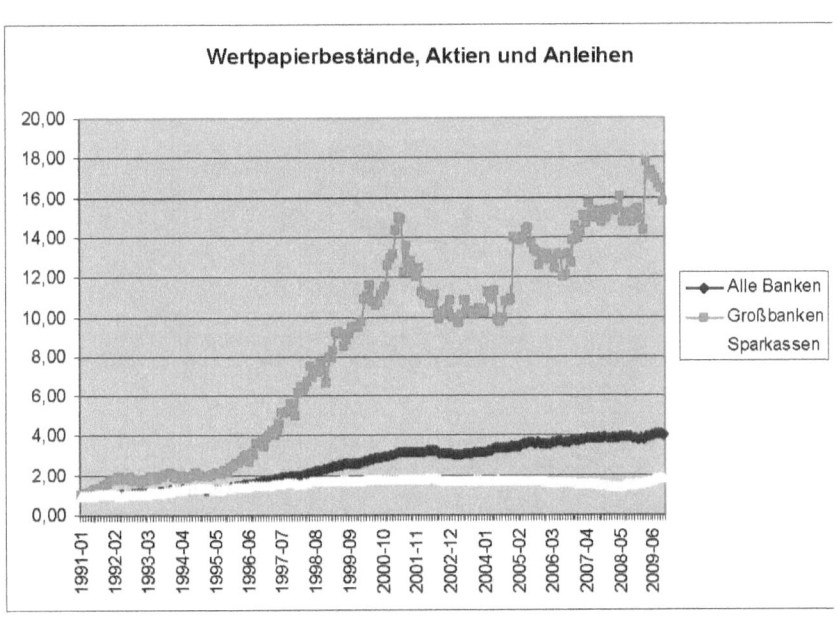

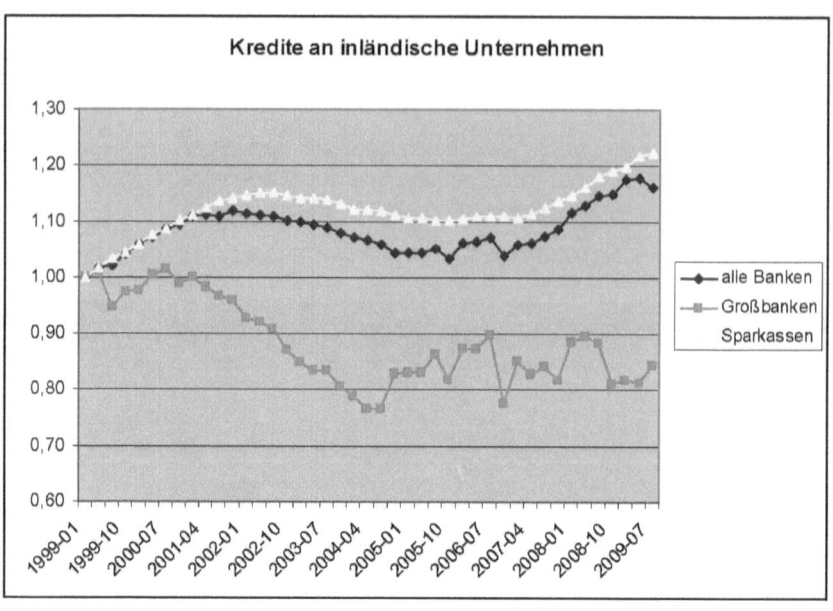

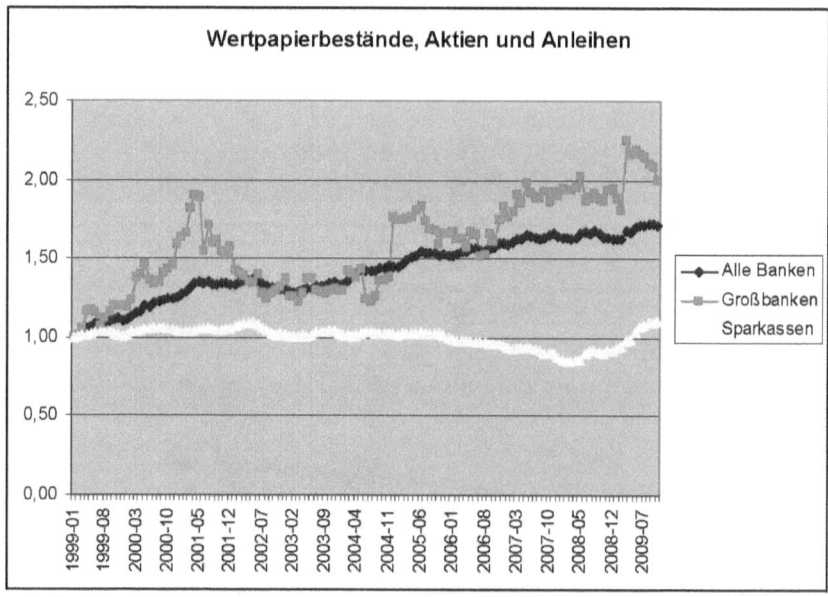

major banks used the funds to buy dubious financial products, stocks and shares that turned into toxic assets. Only at a much lower level and at the height of the crisis in 2008 and 2009 the Sparkassen got engaged in the virtual reality casino as well, foremost because they got tricked by private banks who managed in a fraudulent manner to dump their toxic assets by selling them short to naïve Sparkassen directors.

The Junkie's needle

It is quite laughable that MEPs have asked for guarantees from the Council and Commission on the independence and resourcing of the EU's new financial supervisory authorities as the mere 'supervision' will hardly stop any of the financial junkies to stick the needle ever more often in until it becomes a direct infusion from the ECB.

Former IMF-chief economist and MIT – Professor Simon Johnson said in 2009 "that the finance sector has effectively captured the government" and concluded that "recovery will fail unless we break the financial oligarchy that is blocking essential reform".

We should not allow our political leaders to put us to sleep by introducing some half-hearted dubious 'control mechanisms' as long as the financial oligarchs have their grip on our economies.

Dictators like Ben Ali and Mubarak are not allowed to live in luxury any longer while they let their peoples become subject to exploitation by US American and Western European major corporations. Their Swiss bank accounts are frozen.

American and European banksters instead still enjoy the financial merry-go-round to pick up speed again with every round of government "stability" packages that let the liquidity bomb that is hanging over us be fed by further debts owners and shareholders of financial institutions hold. These oligarchs, who of course have never worked for such extreme wealth, can only be deprived of their illegitimate profit maximization dreams by taking away the tools from them.

The hot steam needs to be let out of the debt bubble because otherwise the liquidity bomb will drop and when it bursts flood the good's market and cause hyper inflation. The only way to solve the crisis in a controlled way is by nationalisation of all banks, insurance companies and financial institutions.

The question of shareholder-compensation is absurd as the crisis has shown beyond doubt that the private banks had not survived until today anyhow without taxpayer's help pumping hundreds of billions into the arteries of an ailing system.

Once Greece, Ireland, Portugal, Spain and Italy will start the next round of re-financing of their sovereign debt by forcing their debtors to accept a hair cut, the debtors, international financial conglomerates, will again request massive support by EU and last but not least the taxpayer. That will be the right moment to simply nationalise the whole lot without any compensation.

In any case it won't hit anyone who has worked for his wealth and one should only refund someone up to 500,000 € if it is beyond doubt that those funds have been legitimately earned and did not result from speculation. Savings accounts should also be protected up to that ceiling which is a reasonable life-time achievement if someone managed to work that hard and honestly earn such n amount.

Insurance companies will have to be kept alive, but nationalised, especially because of millions of clients who hold a life insurance policy or other form of life time savings with those companies.

Especially Deutsche Bank AG had benefited from taxpayer's money big time when the rescue mission for HRE had been completed. Without state aid Deutsche Bank AG would not have had a dividend to pay out the following year but to eat it's losses resulting from Unicredit- and HRE-engagements.

Instead of throwing more big privatization deals to that monster bank one should rather think of demanding taxpayer's money back which might result in Deutsche Bank AG's nationalisation.

Small private banks will neither be required to be rescued nor to be nationalised as they will anyway run out of business when the rich upper class whose wealth these banks administered will lose most of their casino-tokens once the dreadful income distribution and wealth concentration that crippled the real economy has been reversed.

But, taking from the rich and giving to the poor has never been a lasting solution to any crisis. And, of course it won't help to simply nationalise the financial institutions without changing fundamentally their business model.

The casino capitalism needs to be replaced by an economic system that produces not for profit but for actual demand. Banks in this system will be limited to the traditional core function they have in an economically sustainable system: to supply the producing industries and SMEs with liquidity. Any deviation from this good old principle will lead to yet another creation of virtual reality money outside of the control of the central bank.

Nobody, other than financial oligarchs, need the betting offices of investment banks who place toxic assets over-the-counter and which Paul Volcker rightly so branded as useless operations.

Of course, not all financial instruments are toxic and have been, other than Collateral Debt Obligations (CDOs) and Credit Default Swaps (CDSs) which Deutsche Bank AG made billions with over the Greek-crisis, solely invented for speculation purposes.

But, other than the classical treasury bond there are not many solid financial instruments out there and one should have public oversight over those. Only what is allowed as a trading instrument shall exist and only those instruments that enhance the real economy by loans and guarantees that do not hide risks shall be allowed.

The casino capitalism creates bubbles over bubbles and destroys with every bursting bubble capacities in the real economy. It can not be controlled and has to be banned completely.

As long as above reality is not acknowledged by MEPs, EU officials, political leaders and central bankers, it doesn't matter who is put into the seat as 'supervisor'. Parliament did better not copy the helpless gestures of Ben Ali or Mubarak but reject the idea of any 'supervision' outright and ask for shutting down the casino for good as this is what the vast majority of Europeans want.

In our present economic system of shareholder-value driven capitalism the goal of any investment is not to reinvest but to distribute newly accumulated wealth.

That's why important and necessary investments aren't being made. That's why the economic system declines and may even collapse.

It is not only the fault of the casino capitalism of the financial markets, but rather the basic principles which define our economic system. A system that only produces for profit and not for actual demand is bound to fail.

Major corporations target a 20% return on investment. Anything below that figure will not be considered justifiable for any investment. But, this means that any investment of 10 million in stock capital has to justify the expectation to create a return of 2 million per year. If not, no investment will be made.

It doesn't matter whether the beneficiaries are planning to reinvest or do anything else with their miraculously accumulated wealth, it is only important that the return is steadily growing even if the GDP is much lower than the profit expectations of hungry shareholders.

Then, one let's wages, social and public subsistence decline.

The price that is being paid is a declining standard of living for the great majority of the population.

But, the problem what shall happen with that newly accumulated wealth transferred from the working population to the shareholders becomes ever greater.

That's the real dilemma of our economic system as only in a phase of a self-enhancing extensive investment dynamism that provides for steadily renewed profitable (!) investment opportunities for the fresh shareholder value such problem wouldn't exist.

It's like the choice between pest and cholera: if the profit share is diminished the investment ratio declines. If the profit share is high then there aren't enough profitable investment opportunities at hand and the vagabonding billions pile up on the financial markets creating a bubble because of the low wages and poor social standards that allow for a higher profit do not provide for any sensible investment opportunity.

Only way out is the increased indebtedness of the state and the consumers. After WWII Keynesianism provided the base for an artificial investment dynamism.

In the last 30 years in the US where wages shrank dramatically consumer debts piled up. Keynesianism, it seems, got privatised.

Not the state took out the loans to jumpstart the economy, but the consumer. The same happened in Eastern Europe after the former socialist countries opened their markets and joined the EU.

At the same time ever more funds flow onto the financial markets. No goods are being produced or traded.

Especially because the "investment" banks kept the snowball system alive by generating virtual money in form of toxic assets the catastrophe has become inevitable: one day, the immensely inflated bubble will burst and when it rains down on us will flood the good's market and cause hyper inflation.

No sensible and necessary investments are being made, only debts are piled up while artificial wealth is created on the other side of the equation. But, wealth can not be created, it has o be produced.

Production in capitalism is stagnating since a long time already. The world economy today is resting on two very fragile pillars: firstly, public and private debts.

If these debts grow slower than shareholder's hunger then the real economy's profit motor chokes. Because of a continuously increasing portion of interest payments less and less capital can be used to finance consumption.

Secondly, the money spinning financial merry-go-round needs to be kept going otherwise the snowball system with it's virtual returns on investment collapses.

The two pillars of our economy, indebtedness and money printing, has to continue into perpetuity to prevent the under present conditions sole engine of our economy, the profit, from collapsing.

It becomes clear why since the beginning of the crisis on August 11, 2007, our political leaders have engaged in revitalising this vicious circle at whatever cost.

As long as present economic system has been regarded as being without alternative there was no other concept and EU Commission as well as democratically elected governments dumped taxpayer's money in some Frankenstein-banks without any remorse.

The truth is that central banks and governments print trillions to flood the financial markets and fail to regulate the financial sector in any way that could bring this craziness to an end.

In fact, this 'simsa-la-bim' - finance policy of European Central Bank and Federal Reserve has for a brief moment created something like a recovery or up-swing, but of course not for long. The German economy, after it took a dive, is now back on the level of 2005, but as this owed to it's export strategy, one may wonder who in the US will be able to buy German cars?

Again: is the investment requirement of a society high and are the markets open, the profit orientation of companies will create growth and will direct the capital into the right areas while profits are being reinvested.

This would maintain a high investment level and would enhance innovation while high profits are being made. Wages could rise and a dynamic and innovative economy would create a higher productivity resulting in a higher standard of living for all.

The declining economic system of our times is the opposite of the above. It's investment motor doesn't keep pace with the profits and kills any dynamism.

A crisis like we live through right now provides for no other way out but to destroy such an amount of capital that the required investment will absorb the entire capacity to let the process start all over again.

In past centuries wars had this function.

We still have the possibility to reverse this mechanism and avoid the tragedies of the World Wars. All it needs is to abolish the profit principle as the sole engine of our economic system as it let's the standard of living decline while it kills wealth, innovation and productivity and last but not least human beings.

Outside the Box

"Money can not create capacities but merely is a resource. With money or money-capital one can not produce anything. But, one can by using money mobilise capacities of the real-economy." Professor Joseph Huber wrote in his book "Vollgeld"[20].

Since mankind started to develop economic structures and built empires on those theories on how best to distribute wealth accumulated in a society have provided for heated discussions, fights over distribution and last but not least revolutions. Since mankind had found ways to evade hard bodily work there have always been some who understood how they can make others work for themselves and make a profit from those other's hard bodily

---

20   Joseph Huber, "Vollgeld" (Berlin 1998)

work, or, since the industrial revolution, by making those others operate machines and lately robots and computers in order to generate wealth. It fell in those early days of the industrial revolution that philosophers, human rights activists and economists, from Maximilien Robespierre, Thomas Hobbes, John Locke, José Ortega y Gasset, Jean-Paul Sartre, Tsvetan Todorov, Lucian Blaga, Adam Smith, Karl Marx, Friedrich Hegel and Immanuel Kant had all given their best to define a lasting equilibrium between Humanism and Economic power, progress and efficiency. Tremendous upheavals and achievements by society, rulers and those who were ruled upon had to be made and not seldom it has been necessary that not too little amounts of blood had been spread.

The thought that a fair distribution of the wealth a society in it's entirety accumulates by the sweat and blood of hard working people, the genius innovations by inventors and scientists as well as courage entrepreneurs who take a commercial risk are in a fair way split between future innovation, production and social subsistence while it can be shared in solidarity with those who for different good reason can not participate in such economic life but shall at least participate in the life of society as they are part of such, at least in Humanistic societies.

Because of this constant struggle, and especially in times like ours where the difference between rich and poor becomes more than ever visible, leftist and rightist propagandists find all kinds of "solutions" for a fair distribution of wealth.

Wealth can't be created, it has to be produced

As we are witnessing the bubbles of the financial markets ruin our real economies while an ever greater amount of citizens are excluded from the production process and while the majority of citizens have to endure a constantly declining standard of living a new formula would be badly needed. That's why populists from right to left to demand the introduction of a "citizen subsistence" a certain minimum payment every person would receive from the state irrespective of age, social status as well as whether the person is unemployed or sick. At fist sight this may sound enticing as it would simplify the whole debate about the fair and just distribution of wealth in our societies, one may think. But, in reality the problem we would face is much deeper rooted: The wealth we see today being created is predominantly created in the virtual reality casinos of the financial markets and not by industrial production. Therefore, it doesn't make sense to start distributing all these electronically created and stored numbers and zeros which do not relate to any production output. Under the present economic conditions it is impossible to distribute wealth as once the foam hits the real economy inflation goes into orbit. The basic principle has to be that only what has been produced can be distributed. Until the Bretton Wood system collapsed in 1971, this has been more or less the underlying rule for the creation of money. Long before, a currency had been covered by gold which limited the emitting of bank notes and coins. For a good reason central banks had to obey this principle. Whenever it has been neglected it led to disasters.

Traditionally, our economies are based on a dual reserve system, the central bank on the one side and the commercial banks which are obliged to keep a certain reserve but other than that are free to multiply the money they keep in their bank by whatever means. If one prohibited the artificial creation of virtual money by enforcing a rule that banks need to hold a 100% reserve on current accounts, the so called *"Vollgeld"*, the money in the books all of a sudden became real money and the inflationary creation of virtual funds once and for all would be stopped. In today's reserve system only an ever decreasing amount of circulating cash is actually emitted by the central bank. The vast majority (almost ¾) of circulating money (M1) today is put into motion by commercial banks. For a good reason it has been the privilege of the Central Banks to emit and control the amount of notes and coins. It has always been one of the key tools of any central banker to fight inflation by controlling M1.

Income justice won't be achievable under present economic model

Let's go back to the noble idea of a basic subsistence income for all citizens.

Based on today's price levels one would need for the German population some 55 billion Euros in order to provide for basic subsistence of all citizens but under the present reserve-system this is simply not feasible as the European Central Bank currently only emits some 7 billion Euros per year in Germany while the German private banking sector accumulates more than 80 billion Euros which it let's enter the monetary cycle. This doesn't correlate with the nominal GDP growth as it doesn't reach the real economy's capital and consumer goods sector. Nevertheless, the money which is being created artificially, is somewhere in the system and is used for bubble building. That alone would not pose as a big problem if it had not at the same time an impact on the real economy which is often lacking funds for fuelling consumption, production output and demand. Therefore, the goal should be to guarantee subsistence without a secondary re-distribution of wealth and without increasing the state-quota. We have seen lately in the U.S. that additional credit doesn't result in investing but directly in increased consumption. In a way, the new model would not create a new credit tower, bearing interest, but it still would result in a re-distribution of wealth as what the beneficiaries of the model would consume on the one side would not be available on the other side anymore. This would mean that the top incomes have to be lower while the subsistence income has to be adjusted to inflation. At least that is the theory according to Professor Huber.

Let's assume that all taxes were used for social transfers and the consumption quota from those transfers was 1:

$$C_t + I_t = Y_t$$

$$C_t = c\,(1 - tax_{t-1})Y_{t-1} + tax_{t-1}Y_{t-1} + CC_t = c\,Y_{t-1} + tax_{t-1}\,(1 - c)\,Y_{t-1} + CC_t$$

$$I_t = Y_{t-1} - C_{t-1} + CI_t$$

CC_t is consumption credit and CI_t additional, not by previous savings covered investment credit; if a part of CC_t was not credit but subsistence income and instead tax_{t-1} becomes $= 0$, this would mean that this subsistence income would match the nominal consumption growth. The real value of the subsistence income logically would be reduced to the real consumption growth. If the increased demand results in real production increase the model would work perfectly.

Mathematical Impossibilities of our present Economic System

But, when the entire growth would be distributed as subsistence income CI_t will become Zero which means that investments would have to be made from previous savings. This would not be sustainable for long. So the model rather should be as follows, assuming a growing society without taxes:

$$C_t = c\,Y_{t-1} + SubsistenceIncome_t$$

$$I_t = (1 - c)\,Y_{t-1} + NewCredit_t$$

$$Y_t = Y_{t-1} + Subsistence\ Income_t + NewCredit_t$$

$\Delta Y_t = \text{SubsistenceIncome}_t + \text{NewCredit}_t$

As we assume a constant capital coefficient this means:

$Y_t = k\,K_t$ leading to: $\Delta Y_t = k\,\Delta K_t$, requiring nominal equal growth:

$I_t = \Delta K_t = 1/k\,\Delta Y_t = 1/k\,(\text{SubsistenceIncome}_t + \text{NewCredit}_t)$

If NewCredit for Investments equals Zero:

$I_t = 1/k\,\text{SubsistenceIncome}_t\ (k < 0)$

Equilibrium requirement is:

$(1 - c)\,Y_{t-1} = 1/k\,\text{SubsistenceIncome}_t$

The nominal income grows in exactly the way the additional money accumulation does. SubsistenceIncome plus NewCredit, provided that entire growth is distributed as SubsistenceIncome meaning that investment financing solely is conducted from previous savings which indeed will work perfectly fine as effective demand grows which leads to sufficient growth of production, but on the other hand a sufficient savings rate is required otherwise the investments can not sustain a real growth rate which shall finance the SubsistenceIncome. This is what had gone wrong in the past Socialism.

So, the idea to have SubsistenceIncome be financed simply out of production growth may only work if what used to be distributed by taxes would in this model be required to be saved otherwise inflationary devaluation will destroy the model.

Let's assume k equals a third and the SubsistenceIncome $1/20 = 0.05$ of the previous income (which would be very low) than we would get:

$(1 - c) = 3 \times 0.05 = 0.15$

Which means a Savings Rate of 15% was required in order to finance a SubsistenceIncome increase of 5% which today the ruling class sees as no problem since their growth rates are well above the 5%. The truth is that because inflation is already at 4% according to EUROSTAT (although for food and basic goods it is well above that rate) an annual 5% increase would really be the absolute minimum under present conditions in order to ensure a life in dignity. As the Deutsches Institut für Wirtschaft (DIW) reported[21]

---

21   Spiegel online 25th August 2008

the income of the vast majority of German citizens has declined over the past ten years by 14% while the top of society had double digit increases. It may be a political debate about the justice or injustice of our economic system and this shall be discussed on political level, but as an economic scientist one can only come to the conclusion that an income increase of more than 5% per year is mathematically impossible unless the Savings Rate of all citizens was 15%. In reality, the savings rate in Germany as well as in most EU member states tumbled at lowest levels and stagnated for years. But, as the elites still wanted to bath in lukewarm rains of Euros giving them income increases beyond sustainability, someone had to save, so they went stealing, social security, pensions, health care, education, culture, public subsistence.

According to neo-classical model all these bubbles wouldn't exist

Not only is the current economic model unfair, which one can debate if one is cynical, but what is simply un-debatable is the fact that it is unsustainable. More than 2 or 3 % of growth are hard to achieve year by year, so where shall the double digit profit rates and income increases of the upper class come from? Someone got to work for it and eat and drink less if at the same time shareholder value shall be increased. The funny thing is that the advocates of our present economic model always are quick to say that we have to save, but from what?

It has become clear that all the talk about the necessity to save is not because our economies were not able to provide enough and high quality goods for all, but that the term "save" takes a different meaning. It should rather be replaced by "sacrifice". It is hard to explain to working people or anybody in the production cycle why one should sacrifice standard of living to finance speculation, bubble building and by this destruction. Even more funny is that according to the neo-classical model all these bubbles wouldn't exist. The economic model can not be reformed as it is rotten. If some people think that excessive growth is a good thing then one has to ask whether they have a second planet at hand. But to demand the continuation of the present economic model is as sick as Casino junkies who ask for credit at the Black Jack table.

Above all, one should ask the question whether such a growth at pace rates would be achievable over a longer period of time. It is more realistic to have 2% growth but this would also mean that SubsistenceIncome would not exceed 2% of total national income which hardly can be seen as sufficient. The problem of our present economic system is that the amount of money has grown much faster than real GDP. Only because of that it may appear as a possibility to finance the SubsistenceIncome from the growth of the amount of money. But, the amount of money can only grow that long faster than real GDP as long as this money doesn't in any way be it by consumption or investment reach the capital and consumption good markets, otherwise it leads to inflation. That's what has happened recently and this is the mathematical impossibility of our present economic system which only creates money but not economic capacity. So, the best way still would be to simply introduce the rule of *Vollgeld* and make financial bubbles history. Then, we can go and distribute income on a fair basis by what has been produced by all parts of society.

Basic non-conditional Subsistence - model: Bedingungsloses Grund-Einkommen (BGE)

"Ever again the standard national-income accounting identity is marshalled to emphasise the tightness of the investment-saving relationship; yet, the identity doesn't tell us anything about causality" writes Stanford-Professor Dunmore "DM" Gordon[22] who is famous for analysing the behaviour of ants. "Concerning a sensible definition of investment: it seems appropriate to exclude from consideration inventory investments and residential investment, since neither significantly effects longer-term improvements in productivity, hence, one would be led to concentrate primarily on real fixed domestic non-residential investment, measured either gross or net." D.M. Gordon writes but neglects to mention that the savings rate in the U.S. as well as in the EU stagnated for quite a while, though, and has only been boosted slightly by the increasing privatisation of pension schemes forcing more and more people to put money aside for a private pension plan. Other than that, the savings rate is rather declining than stagnating or increasing.

"It is certainly true that the division between net investment and depreciation is somewhat arbitrary, reflecting accounting practices at least as much as economic behaviour, however, if we are interested in exploring temporal and behavioural relationships between investment and saving, concentration on gross values may introduce a near tautology into the discussion: since exactly the same flows measuring depreciation ("capital consumption

22   D. M. Gordon. Must we Save Our Way Out of Stagnation? The Investment-Saving Relationship Revisited

allowances") are included in the value of both gross investment and gross saving, and since depreciation is fairly large relative to net investment (and net business saving) an extremely high correlation between investment and saving is simply the consequence of definitional conventions" Professor Gordon continues making the assumption that "if the change in saving rate respectively change investment rate is regressed to lags in the investment-saving gap (investment minus saving rate) by using quarterly data, the causality should become more clear: if investment is responsive to saving, we should find that a higher past period's gap should cause investment to decline, resulting in a negative coefficient of the gap variable, if saving is responsive to investment, a lagged gap should boost saving resulting in a strongly positive coefficient of this gap in the regression to the differentials of the saving rate. In fact, Feldstein and Bachetta (1994) pursued those regressions although they draw different conclusions the coefficients in the investment regression are nowhere negative and significant, while the coefficients in the saving equation are always positive and significant."

This is certainly right, but only within the framework of the model. It depends entirely on the investment priorities of a society whether or not savings will be possible. This is the problem of the still-present economic system and its theories. In theory it all looks fine, but it doesn't match reality.

"Also if one analyses correlations of investment to more far away leads and lags of (private or national) saving the results suggests that (normalised) real net fixed investment appears to have a stronger influence on leads of (normalised) real net national saving than vice versa." D.M. Gordon explains and later writes that "in Keynesian Macroeconomics investment rather than saving is the key variable; Firms decide the level of investment, and income and saving then adapt to bring about the *ex post* identity."

Then, Professor Gordon focuses on a much debated model: "more recently many heterodox economists have begun to construct an alternative macro perspective that seeks to synthesise crucial insights of both neo-Keynesian and Marxian Traditions; many of us refer to this perspective as *structuralist macroeconomics*" he writes and continues with saying that "in this heterodox perspective, the distribution of income between classes plays a decisive macroeconomic role:

→ A reduced – form structuralist model of a real open private macro economy:

$$\varphi \equiv C + I^n + d_k + X^n + Z\varphi \tag{1}$$

$$C = C(\varphi^+, r, i^-, Z_C) \tag{2}$$

$$I^n = I^n(\varphi^+, r^+, i^-, Z_I) \tag{3}$$

$$X^n = X^n(\varphi^-, r^?, i^-, Z_X) \tag{4}$$

$$r = r(\varphi^?, Z_r) \tag{5}$$

$$S^n \equiv \varphi - C - d_k \tag{6}$$

$$\pi \equiv r/(\varphi \cdot q_k^*) \tag{7}$$

$$d_k \equiv \lambda \cdot K \tag{8}$$

$$K \equiv K_I + I \cdot Q^* \tag{9}$$

$$g_K \equiv K' \tag{10}$$

$$q_k^* \equiv Q^*/K$$

K' – logarithmic rate of change
φ – capacity utilisation (Q/Q^*)
C – real consumption expenditure
I^n – real net Investment
d_K – real depreciation
X^n – real net exports
r – Rate of profit
π – profit share
i – real interest rate
S^n – real net saving (net of depreciation)
q_k^* - potential output-capital ratio
K – real fixed capital stock
g_K – growth of real fixed capital stock
Z_i – vector of exogenous variables affecting variable i
flow variables and Z_i as well as K normalised on potential output"

But, if that really was so, then q_K^* is defined incorrectly, as it would rather have to be $1/K$ which means that also the definition of K is not correct as K obviously is not normalised in the equations.

D. M. Gordon finds that "this is a *reduced-form* model for two reasons: it relies on an equation, in which the profit rate is determined directly in a behavioural equation rather than a algebraic function of the level of productivity, real wages and other deductions from total output; it implements the heterodox Cambridge savings hypothesis through a consumption function in which consumption is a negative function of the profit rate rather than a direct function of the (normalised) flows of wage and capital income." Later, he writes that "in order to control for the size of the economy, all flow variables are normalised for scale by dividing them by potential output; aggregate output normalised this way generates a measure of capacity utilisation (...) referring to Z_r in the profit rate equation: in the post Keynesian/Kaleckian radition, the key exogenous variable is likely to be one or another index of monopoly power; in the classical Marxian tradition, the key variable would be some measure of intensity of competitive pressure" D.M. Gordon concludes but neglects to mention the power of classes, for which here variables as unemployment are very important.

He is right in saying that "this model differs from neoclassical analogues in three main respects: it places distributional concerns at its core; it carries no presumption about full labour employment when the economy is at 'full capacity'; there is no theoretical presumption that the equilibrium path generated from such an economy will reach or only approach 'full utilisation'". And, it is certainly also not too far fetched to say "that business saving is definitional close to what structuralists constitutes the flow of profits differing only in netting out dividends; thus in this single respect a neoclassical economist might claim that business saving leads investment, while a structuralist claims that profits lead investment."

However, what D.M. Gordon as well as the inventors of above model totally neglect is the fact that the state could force by law and by setting let's say ecological standards to invest. This is left out of the equation as it is not within the frame of the thinking of scientists who have probably resigned on the idea of changing the system in its entirety. But, the New Economic System will make us all think outside the box. Never have been the times and conditions that favourably for investing into innovation protecting nature. There are plenty of pressing tasks that we can not afford to postpone. And, there is a lot of capital which cries for productive usage and there are millions of people who look for work. What is lacking is a sensible political management which brings all these components together.

Never has one succeeded in history to overcome a crisis by mere re-distribution of wealth and by paying basic subsistence instead of fair and sufficient wages for work. The state ought to create jobs and not arrange for people who could work retire before having reached a certain age. Of course social benefits have to be provided for everyone irrespective of his ability to work but the first task should be to find a person work.

IV

10 RULES OF THUMB FOR THE
NEW ECONOMIC SYSTEM

1. Regulated Money markets and currency exchange controls need to be re-installed

Many economists today demand a "common growth strategy of the industrialized economies" as John Kenneth Galbraith calls it. But, a global Keynesianism also requires a non-restrictive monetary policy of the central banks and this should also include the German Bundesbank and European Central Bank whose hobby it seems to be to press inflation permanently under 2% although one knows that anything below this border-inflation any innovative industrial society destroys its economic growth. The only reason why the Frankfurt based banks still adhere to that principle is because they are beholden by the interest of shareholders who do not want to see their virtual wealth be eaten up by inflation. Neither Bundesbank nor ECB ever were a 'people's bank' but designed for manifesting income distribution from bottom to top of society. But, this is our own fault as we let our private financial sector like in 1720 John Law not only emit worthless toilet paper but also generate the money for the purchase of such. Central Banks are sidelined in the whole process and have to re-establish their role.

And, a worldwide coordinated monetary and interest policy consequently requires a World Central Bank in order to make sure that countries aren't competing with each other about attracting capital by offering interest premiums and other favourable conditions which only let the cost of money supply go through the ceiling. This, however, is a dream and in a deregulated and liberalised money market it is hard to see it come true and if, how effective would it be?

Truth is that the IMF and World Bank already exist and have a terrible record when it comes to providing stability. Unforgotten is the IMF demanding South East Asian countries like Malaysia to open its market during the 1998 crisis. China was not affected during that crisis only because its currency was not convertible. The demand for a world central bank which shall also take over the risks private banks is frequently repeated these days, but it has been Josef Ackermann, in 1998 board member and today CEO of Deutsche Bank AG who is dreaming in Technicolor that a world central bank would put up with all the mis-sepcualtions of his and other banks and without regulating the markets simply let them continue do their business. It amounts to allowing banks to regulate themselves and if it goes wrong have the world stand together to shoulder the risk.

The only reasonable and achievable way out is indeed to have regulation and currency control restrictions in place which have always been proven a good tool to manage markets. And, as said above, the Vollgeld – rule would make bubble building impossible. It only requires these two simple regulations and laws to be agreed upon internationally and no new body of a world central bank or world reserve system would be necessary.

The institutions are already there, the mechanism is there, so why not make use of it?

2. Corporate and income taxes to be harmonized, offshore places taxed at 25%

As the financial direct investment which comes into the EU from off shore places has doubled over the past 5 years, and since it is clear that those funds have previously legally or illegally circumvented national taxation of member states, any transfer from such black holes of the financial markets should be taxed at a flat rate, let's say 25%. If at least all EU member states apply this rule, one will notice that the money is staying in the place where it is accumulated and also spent. The reaction of EU Commission, EU Council and European Parliament citing that it was impossible to tax international financial transfers as this would hurt the economy in EU member states is simply not true. The money our major corporations produce here and transfer to these offshore places under palm trees would not leave the EU and therefore would also not have to be brought back.

The reaction by member state governments to the tax evasion of major corporations who entertain finance companies in Panama, Liechtenstein, Tobago, Bahamas or Panama and others so far has been to lower corporate taxes at home. A dreadful tax dumping competition is also in full swing between member states. This can be stopped by one single law or regulation fixing the corporate tax across the EU at a certain minimum level one may debate and negotiate politically. The fact that any other taxes, such as VAT are harmonized proves that it is indeed possible to harmonize taxes, so why not capital gains-, corporate- and income taxes? It is the political will that is making it possible.

3. A thumb – formula for the distribution of wealth based on Capital co-efficient

Since productivity had risen over the past 25 years by some 50% while per capita income has skyrocketed in the past 10 years as well, the question arises why the standard of living of the vast majority of citizens has declined. The level of wages is (clear of inflation) down to where it has been in 1983. So people on an average basis lived better 25 years ago. Reason for this is the income distribution from bottom to top of society. The economic development of the past quarter of a century has bypassed most citizens. Technologies make it possible to increase productivity rapidly. A higher productivity means that higher quality goods could be produced in less time requiring less labour- and energy input. Theoretically, the average person should have today a much higher standard of living, have more money in the pocket than 25 years ago or work less but still have the same income. The truth is that the rise in productivity has only benefited the top of society. Not only the increased productivity should lead to an increase in standard of living but especially also the phenomenal growth rates of the 1990ies and early 2000s. One can, of course, argue that an investor in 1983 had to put relatively less capital up in order to have certain return on investment, whereas today this would be significantly more. But, that is a mere capitalistic problem, as it could be avoided if the capital coefficient was adjusted. Within the economic system it won't be possible to eliminate this problem. This can only be fixed when one thinks outside the box. What remains, is the fact that increased productivity allows us to use resources more wisely, work less for the same reward and enjoy a better standard of living, better healthcare, better pension systems, better education, a better and cleaner environment and better public subsistence and life. In order to achieve this, a rule of thumb for the distribution of wealth generated from the rise in productivity and growth has to be negotiated. This is a matter for politicians to sort out, but an idea could be to say that those rises are equally split, i.e. a Third shall be put on an annual basis behind a better Education, increased welfare and healthcare, the second Third behind innovation and science, while the last Third shall be reserved to entice investors to put their money behind start-up's, innovative production lines and environmentally friendly technologies. Wouldn't that be a fair deal?

4. Productivity-rise - defined increases of wages, social-, health-care-, innovation-, education-spending

As it is clear that only that fur of the bear can be distributed that has successfully been hunted, the annual increases of wages as well as social expenditure has to be determined by a clear formula that assesses what the rise of productivity and growth had achieved. The old formula of the old economic system which we see in these days end in disaster was obviously mathematically incoherent and based on the misunderstanding of a few of our elites that all that needed to be done was to create wealth by whatever means even if that destroyed production lines. And, it has been the cynical approach of our political leadership to think that as long as they themselves enjoyed an ever increasing standard of living all they needed to do was to listen to the shareholder's who told them that as long as they made huge profits the economy was fine and eventually some of the fruits of the earth they squeezed would trickle down to the masses. Then, when the world economic crisis could no longer be denied, some of the same elites started to revive old ideas, some from the old Socialism, some from Keynesianism but these models won't save our economies anymore as a few peanuts here and there don't do anymore. It would mean to fall back into the old habit of distributing what in reality doesn't exist. It doesn't help the people in the street who sees purchasing power decline to give him a few tin cans full of hot air and some deadly foam from financial bubbles. Let's say that wages shall increase by 2 % per year if social expenditure will increase by the same and assuming that economic growth is at around 2%. This, of course, implies that bubble – building no longer will be counted as economic growth but is only allowed in casinos.

5. Incentive-based system for paying of employees

One of the biggest problems of every economy, be it socialistic or capitalistic, is to motivate people to work hard. There are only two major driving forces behind any economic activity and innovation, the goal of profit and the fear of competition. Likewise, there are only two forces which make a human being work, the goal of being able to afford a better standard of living and the fear of not being able to make a living at all. In a perfect scenario a mixture of goal and fear keep the balance. What people in the Eastern European Socialism were deprived off had been both: goal *and* fear. Unless one had been an oppositional activist in the East, there was nothing to fear which would make someone stretch to the ceiling as the basic subsistence had been provided for by the state. On the other hand, there hadn't been many goals as the centralised economy had proven inefficient and static, producing only goods one either didn't really care about or couldn't buy because the output quantity had been insufficient. Socialistic Centralisation suppressed innovation, Capitalistic Concentration destroys economic capacities. In our –still- capitalistic economic system any goals are replaced by fear. It is the fear of not being able to survive in dignity as an unemployed or sick or old person. Any goals which once existed for the masses have been put into jeopardy by elites who shrug their shoulders when being asked how a single mother shall survive on a few Euros per day for food or how parent's shall afford to pay for school books and university enrolment even though they already hold down 2 jobs. The reason why the majority of people still endure the economic system is for the sole reason of fear. It is the fear to loose even that little bit, they got. These people do not stretch to the ceiling anymore either. They walk around depressed. In a society which wants to sustain economic lead by innovation goals are inevitably necessary. The goal for an engineer to be paid a good salary from which he can sustain himself and his family, pay for a house and a car without being over indebted or the goal for an uneducated worker who feels challenged to qualify for a better position by evening courses which enables her or him to climb up the ladder and enjoy life even more are the driving force in any economy, be it organised socialistically or capitalistically. The biggest mistake the past Socialism made probably has been to believe that human beings would, if all were paid equal in a classless society, not develop apathy or even greed. The Socialist economy could have become quite successful if only in addition to the basic needs some incentives were given for those who wanted to stretch to the ceiling and work more and become innovative and if the economy had not been centralised. The biggest mistake the ailing capitalistic model presently undertakes is to believe that fear alone will make masses continue to push the wheel in the treadmill and create mega concentrations. The New Economic System will make sure that every person can lead a life in dignity even if there is no place found for him or her in the production process. And, the New Economic System will guarantee economic growth by strictly applying an incentive scheme for innovative and more productive employees. At the same time, the New Economic System will not allow anyone to sit around being bored to death doing nothing but cutting interest coupons while zipping away Champagne other have to work for. That ought to be the sole fear one shall have in the new society.

6. Corporate taxes defined by Wertschöpfungsabgabe rather than static figures

The backbone of any economy are Small & Medium Sized Enterprises (SMEs) which also are the largest group of employers in any EU member state, but it is very often made difficult for those companies to be flexible in their employment decisions. In Germany, 65% of all new jobs are created by SMEs while more than 80% of apprenticeships and educational programs are conducted by those small and medium sized companies, from which major corporations as well as multinationals indeed do benefit a lot, too.

Too often decide entrepreneurs against employing a person because of the high social security and labour costs combined with any new employment. Static regulations make it hard for smaller companies to decide pro-employment. On the other hand, the American model of Hire & Fire can not be recommended either, so how to balance in the New Economic System the necessary flexibility for the entrepreneur with the reasonable interest of an employee to have a certain security to keep the work for a certain time and be protected throughout the engagement and also not to fall through any social net after being laid off? Notably, smaller companies are more labour intensive than let's say large banks and insurance companies. Accumulation of added value in relation to labour intensity shall define the contribution a company shall pay into the social security systems as this would take a burden from SMEs while at the same time lay a reasonable cost on the shoulders of those corporations whose production is streamlined and less labour intensive. A person which is employed by a small company thus will have the same protection and benefits as a person being employed by a major corporation while the entrepreneur benefits from the burden sharing between his SME and a multinational corporation which generates value in a more automated way or even entirely by machines. The *Wertschöpfungsabgabe* (Accumulated Value Contribution) is the only reasonable and fair equilibrium between the interests of the employed, the SMEs as well as major corporations and it will ensure in the New Economic System that a free, social, market economy will be sustainable. It will be, however, extremely important to make sure that the system can not be led ad absurdum by companies hiding profits and by this circumvent the *Wertschöpfungsabgabe*. In order to ensure that such can not happen it is vital to establish also a system of taxing profits before these will be distributed to shareholders. Also, one needs to relate the amount to be contributed to the social system to the number of jobs in a company as the wage-share total can not be that easily be brought down by balance sheet manipulations as the profit rate. By an increased wage – share contribution, the state could guide the wage-development which in times of ever weaker unions would be a must. And, last but not least one has to tax dividends at a flat rate of a significant minimum amount as these also can not be hidden and manipulated by balancing tricks like the profit can and certainly would be by the company's management. And, by charging high taxes on the dividends one really hit at the right ones, the rich owners and shareholders, rather than an SME or family business that barely survives.

7. Un-bundling of conglomerates

The EU Commission's credo when it came to energy market liberalisation has always been to "un-bundle" the major providers. Theoretically, this should lead to more competition, better quality, lower prices, etc. The usual nonsense the neo-classical model promises. The reality, however, is the opposite. Prices went up by more than 39% within a year's time in Germany, the networks were not safe anymore as the privatised energy conglomerates failed to invest into the networks. In short: it has been a disaster. When the EU Commission ordered ENSA, the Spanish national energy provider to be split up as the monopoly would violate European free market, the buyer, the German RWE already stood ready to take it over. This was rather an example for bundling than unbundling. In Germany, the de-regulated energy market was left alone from any effective supervision and of course price-fixing was ripe. What all these neo-liberal ideologists don't want to spell out is the fact that they and their friends are after the profit from a privatised company. As greed is their drive they do not invest into maintaining the network. On the other hand, those who are controlling a network are sitting on a classical monopoly and therefore ought to be nationalized as otherwise it can not be made sure that the situation is not exploited in the interest of an increased shareholder value bearing higher costs as well as certain security risks for the end-user as we have seen several times. There are a few things one can not be administrated and managed well by private ownership. Some of them are energy providers, national railway systems, public transport, postal services, schools, hospitals, libraries, prisons, police and security forces, motorway, airports and, last but not least, the central bank. The deficiencies of state owned corporations has all along been pointed out and in many cases rightly so, but private companies are not much better but when governed by the profit maximisation goal are unable to make reasonable decisions. In the New Economic System we will have state owned companies where necessary but their employees will have to abide by the same rules as private companies in order to be more efficient and innovative. Again, the driving force behind it shall be incentives and not apathy. There is no natural law that says that state controlled or state owned companies can not have competition among themselves and within their departments. It should be easy to install those mechanisms. But, what the New Economic System will not allow is the cynical arithmetic's of private insurance corporations who find thousands of excuses not to deliver under the terms and conditions they set-forth. Insurance companies need to be regulated in such a way that they predominantly serve the client and not the shareholders. There won't be many shareholders probably if insurance business is conducted responsibly. What all insurance companies fail to spell out when they sell a pension plan is that it doesn't matter whether or not one agrees to an automatic inflation dynamism in the pension contract as neither the mathematicians of the insurance company nor anybody else will be able to predict what the Euro or whatever currency in the future will be worth. Nobody can tell today, even is provision is made for compensating inflation, what one will be able to buy for a Euro in 30 or 40 years time. It is ridiculous to speculate how productive future generations will be. Whatever one may wish to buy in the future for money saved today solely depends on what is produced at what cost in what time and nobody can guess how good that will be in the future. The 21st century society needs to be built on solidarity. Solidarity requires that all citizens are enjoying the same privilege of having their subsistence be guaranteed even when becoming sick and old. Therefore, one should not allow private companies to take care of such important issues like ones pension. One can not make business with healthcare, pensions, social security and education as this, under shareholder value – conditions can only mean to gamble with other people's life.

8. Calculate GDP growth also by quality of life measurements

Let's forget for a moment about money. It is only a tool anyway and as we all know, it is maybe sexy to have a lot of it, but then again, it also only is so because it represents a certain value which doesn't create capacities but may move those. The still economic system we endure in its final stages engaged in creating enormous wealth but at the same time destroyed its capacities. The elites of the declining economic and political system hadn't understood that wealth needs to be produced not created. That's why they believed in their own model and managed to interpret even it's destruction as "economic growth". The New Economic System will calculate GDP growth not only by measuring wealth and production output, but also by other factors which are relevant for our societies, such as standard of living, quality of life, public subsistence, health, environment and last but not least, cultural life. All these factors ought to be weighed and adjustments have to be defined to make sure an as accurate as possible picture can be drawn. It is of course important to know how many healthy years after 65 men and women in the member states on average basis can enjoy, a statistic which is available but not part of any economic theory although it is so vitally important. The New Economic System will set the axiom on which the whole neo-classical model had been based on and which until now has been $\partial F(x)/\partial x = 0$ not ZERO but ONE so that it doesn't allow the economic model to substitute the factors like capital and labour by whatever figures and assumes that it is divisible anymore. The old, neo classical, model in it's entirety had been based on this assumption, making it possible that their models – in theory – show even then growth rates if consumption declines because of shrinking wages leading to retracting production cycles while the profit rate increases amid declining production output. Applying this old model means that in theory even destruction would be measured as growth. In the New Economic System the axiom will be put right as we can not afford to dream of growth that doesn't exist. And, we need to be able to calculate the consequences for wages, social expenditure as well as production output correctly and realistically.

Furthermore, GDP growth in the New Economic System will deal with the most pressing question of our times: what is Time *worth*? Since productivity constantly rises, more time is gained for many of the citizens. Time is not money, it is wealth.

9. European wide minimum standards prevent exploitation

Instead of a dreadful spiral pointing downwards when it comes to all kinds of standards, the New Economic System will be based on high standards across the European Union. Worker's protection, social security, health care, education, public subsistence will be given the highest priority while at the same time SMEs and corporations will benefit from an as widely harmonised standard as possible. It wouldn't benefit enterprises in the long run to have an ever declining industrial standard. The Bolkestein Service Directive and all similar attempts by the EU Commission to set the lowest standard will be replaced by a directive which will set the targets for doing better. In this way member states and companies can very well compete with each other. Innovation is the only principle which shall govern the setting of standards. Exploitation will be made unprofitable and true and honest competition let the best companies succeed, not the most ruthless ones. The New Economic System will set priorities for science, healthcare, ecology, education and sustainability. A society in which a sports-star is paid multiple amounts of what a scientist who develops a treatment for a disease earns definitely didn't get its priorities right. Sport's and tabloid entertainment are welcome distractions from real life, but they aren't the priorities of Europe's new societies. The New Economic System is not aiming at a so called "classless society" but rather a *classy society* giving everyone equal chances to succeed and find ones personal felicity.

10. Resource management and Fair trade

It has become impossible now to deny that planet Earth is about to become uninhabitable. It is the profligacy and wanton destruction of natural habitats which result from the false economic system.

Fair trade is free trade, but this is not a one way road. Emerging economies and developing countries need to be given access to the world market, not kept out of those by Doha Round and WTO rules. Our New Economic System will be able to deal with the challenges of a truly free trade and free market as EU companies produce high quality goods and services. A vivid exchange between all continents and countries won't be counterproductive to anyone except for the greedy. Resources shall be traded at market value on the world's markets and no blackmailing by EU countries shall be allowed for acquiring such products. It is overdue that we buy the resources of Africa, South America and Asia without making pressure on the sellers. It will pay off or our societies in Europe that we will have normal trade relationships with the rest of the world without exercising political or economic pressure. The 'Wealth of the Nations' always meant to say this. In return, we will see that we will be granted access to resources and markets without investing into war machinery. And, we will see that products we have thought of being overpriced suddenly appear to be quite reasonable. As productivity in the world rises by some 2.5% per annum while economic growth is relatively constant around 2% but population grows only by 1.75% annually, there is no need to see anyone go hungry and not be able to drink clean water, be protected from diseases and enjoy life. The New Economic System will take account of the fact that productivity rises faster than the world's population and will set free capacities for sustainable, not excessive, growth and management of resources in environmental friendly manner. Our ever richer and more productive economies have the ability to rescue this planet and all beings on it, human and non-human, North and South, Rich and Poor must get their act together. We have to cut down on emissions, not human beings and nature.

Germany after Capitalism

A new business model ought to be developed for Germany immediately after the final collapse of the financial capitalism. This will first of all require to undo the privatisations of the past two decades and secondly reverse the commercialisation of those areas of public subsistence that are still owned by communities, city councils and the state but are already managed in a way a private company would be.

We don't need a private major logistic company with more than 500 holdings and daughter companies that doesn't want to invest anymore in the maintenance of the tracks and trains so that the passengers reach their destination even when the sun is shining or when it is snowing in winter. We used to say, when the Deutsche Bundesbahn was still owned by the federal government, that when there were adverse weather conditions one should rather take the train to be safe. Nowadays one would hardly suggest this to a passenger who pays twice as much as when going by car because in winter German trains are either immensely delayed or don't run at all.

The German railway company has to provide for nothing else but safe and efficient railroad service for passengers as well as freight at home and to Germany's neighbouring countries but not on other continents.

Of course, an extensive railway system that provides for a good service also in rural areas can hardly be profitable. That's why it is for the state to operate it on a non-profit – basis. The losses accumulated in the railway-section of state operations can be easily compensated by huge gains that are being made with enhanced telecommunication services and new technologies that should also become an obligation for the state to introduce.

Public subsistence areas such as water-, energy- and waste management but also health care and education will be strictly dealt with by the public hand as private companies have proven not to be able to provide efficient service at affordable costs while obeying tariffs and wage standards as well as providing social security for the workforce. If public enterprises in those sectors are not profitable, private one's won't manage better but usually only lower the standards and increase the prices in order to fill the pockets of shareholders or pay bonuses to their management.

At the same token, one has to reiterate that it is not in the interest of the public to have a public service company that engages in cross-border take-over bids in other countries. Public subsistence is by far too important in order for it to be left in the hands of private companies that do not concentrate on their core business and on what the public expects from them because their management is busy with maximising profits.

The social and ecological tasks and standards for public companies have to be guaranteed by law and democratically controlled. This will only be possible if the public is owner of the enterprise. Public sovereignty over key areas of subsistence are a first step towards restoring democracy. By giving power over infrastructure, resources and public subsistence to democratically elected and controlled (!) representatives of the citizens is the way that leads out of the private economic power that avoids any democratic control like the devil the holy water. Communities and parliaments will no longer be left out of decisions as to the level of rent, water and electricity prices and by this correct the dreadful developments resulting from privatisation and liberalisations in these sectors that created private conglomerates which are impossible to un-bundle because whoever owns a network is sitting on a classical monopoly.

In order to execute control over bureaucratic and administrative structures that might become inefficient or cancerous when left alone it would be a key element to not only have elected representatives be sent into the controlling bodies of these public enterprises but also integrate a statuary right of the citizens to launch initiatives and be heard when directly being affected.

Public basic subsistence for the citizens for the most essential requirements for life quality is not automatically the only solution to all problems but it is the pre-requirement for democracy and for an economy that is being rewarded for ecological and socially sound production.

In order to find the best way for the future it is prudent to analyse the experiences from the past.

Other than Germany, France after 1945 has not only been confronted with the task of reconstruction but also with the necessity for modernization as industrialisation had gotten stuck in the 19th century and had not reached most areas of the economy leaving France in a disadvantageous position in comparison with it's neighbours. With agriculture in 1945 being the strongest sector of the French economy employing more people than any industrial sector it became common sense that the required modernisation could not be left to the market and private entrepreneurs who actually had been responsible for the lack of industrialisation.

Instead, the state was to give impulses and guide the modernisation and industrialisation. Based on the union's decision of 1919 the Congress of the Résistance in 1944 defined the post WW II economic policy which General Charles de Gaulle promoted and that made clear that the treasures of the nation could not be exploited for the profit of a few. This has only become partly real. Wide ranging nationalisations Jean Monnet proposed especially also of the insurance, banking sector as well as the coal mines, heavy industry, gas and electricity were designed to expand the capacities.

In the following years France enjoyed during the fifties and sixties a phase of phenomenal growth of 5.6 % annually. While agricultural dominance shrank, industry until 1970 and services grew and transformed in only 3 decades a traditionalist society into a modern industrial and services economy.

Key to the success has been the ownership of the resources as well as existing major companies and of course the banks which were directed to finance the investment projects. The state owned car manufacturer Renault became a rapidly expanding internationally competitive corporation which managed to secure market shares also in Germany although until the mid 1980ies never received direct or indirect state subsidies. Every year has ended profitable. Half of the profit was paid to the state while the other half was distributed among the employees.

The socialist government of Francoise Mitterrand from 1981 on pushed through further nationalisations in industry and banking sector in order to protect the French economy against the economic decline that had set in during the 1970ies in the world economy. But, the newly nationalised industries, especially the major steel manufacturers, all had financial difficulties and needed to be rescued by an increase in the investment into research and development. The investment in the newly nationalised industries were much higher than in privately owned companies. In 1981 the difference was 44% in 1984 still 26%. In total, the public enterprises that generated in the first half of the 1980ies 29% of the total economic turnover and employed 20% of the workforce accounted for 52% of all investments.

President Mitterrand's had been very successful as the French growth rates rose higher than the EC average at that time. Only the opening of the market towards the European Community lowered the trade balance and put the Franc under pressure to depreciate which accelerated because of capital-flight. At the end, France had to agree to a restrictive fiscal corset in order to keep the Franc within the European monetary system.

By these measurements the attempt to find an alternative way out of the crisis to the neo-liberal policy of the neighbouring countries had proven illusory. From 1986 onwards a privatisation wave set in during which the state sold it's silver cutlery in order to achieve short term effects. Tragically, Mitterrand's concept didn't work because of a malfunctioning of the state owned industries and public sectors but solely because he had been isolated among the EC leaders in his socialist approach and had more than once clashed with the German Bundesbank and it's restrictive course. To continue with the "French way" would only have been possible by re-introducing capital control measurements while pulling out of the European monetary system.

All this although one can say that the nationalised industries had nevertheless continued to increase their investments that made them ever more profitable and allowed them to pay fair wages and also provide for better working conditions than any private enterprise could.

Also in Great-Britain a wave of nationalisations in the years following WWII had swept through the kingdom. First 'victim' of the Labour government had been the Bank of England that, although it had been central bank-functions, like the American Federal Reserve, been in private ownership.

Coal mines, the telegraph company, civil air transportation, electricity and gas, almost any and all transport companies except for shipping companies, and, in 1950, heavy – and steel industry got nationalised. The latter got quickly privatised by the following Tory government in 1953 and in 1967 re-nationalised under the next Labour government and re-privatised in 1970 by the conservatives.

British state companies were organised in form of public corporations and were neither being directly subordinated to the parliament nor were they in any way included in the government budget or played a role in the state finances. The state's influence, however, was limited to the relevant department defining the corporate governance and overall strategy for major investment decisions as well as appointing the directors. One important issue the government had influence over was the price structure. Other than that, the public corporations were bound to satisfy the demand and to grant producers as well as consumers the right to participate in the decision making processes. In order to guarantee this, the nationalised industries had to allow consumer boards which never played a significant role in British society. In heavy and steel industry the corporations remained separate entities that were competing with each other.

The National Coal Board was intended to unite some 800 privately and utmost inefficient operating coal mines that were working with old technologies and were because of their size not able to make any of the required investments. After nationalisation the coal mines got modernised and reorganised.

Labour productivity at the public corporations on an average basis was as high as in private sector industries and significantly higher than in private American infrastructure industries as the British economist Robert Millward wrote in his article "State Enterprise in Britain"[23].

Like in France, the capital accumulation in the nationalised sectors had been higher than in the private sectors. Another advantage has been that the investment activity of the public corporations remained steady even during economic downturns and by this stabilised the entire economy. All in all,

---

23 Millward, Robert: "State Enterprise in Britain", in: Toninelli, Pier Angello (Hrsg), "The Rise and Fall of State-Owned Enterprise in the Western World", Cambridge University Press, 2000

the nationalisations of old as well as new industries had led to economic surpluses that the private industry was never able to achieve.

Reason why the coal industry had outlived itself after a few years had to do with the price policy dictated by the state that had the mines sell for much below market value. For private households this had the advantage to save on heating costs, but this price policy was nothing else but a more or less direct permanent subsidisation of the private industry that also availed of the cheap coal which the conservative governments enhanced also because of their general anti-socialisation sentiment as well as their aversion against the powerful unions. By this, the profits made in the public sector de facto got privatised.

Other than the coal mines the public electricity and gas corporations remained profitable despite keeping prices affordable. Robert Millward noted that the gains at the public corporations in the 1950ies already had been sufficient in order to cover operational costs and even the interest they needed to pay to capital investment from the outside. In the 1960ies the gains were big enough to allow the public corporations to work entirely without any state subsidies. In the seventies, however, the losses escalated which had nothing to do with the form of ownership but had been a direct consequence of the European-wide steel and coal crisis that made all European heavy industry become reliant on the state. Since the mid eighties Prime Minister Thatcher shut down entire sectors of the industry and privatised the profitable parts.

Not every public corporation is working for the public interest, that is only the case when it is being given a certain task by the state. On the other hand, if public companies are commercialised and as a result will be ordered to become as efficient as a privately owned company and stand in competition with the latter, then the public corporation will follow the same patterns. The public interest is then left behind.

But, in contrast to the commercial private companies a public corporation can be ordered to follow other principles than the profit and shareholder criteria. And, last but not least, a public company will always be more efficient and have greater resources for investments as it does not have to put money from the profits aside to pay dividends to shareholders.

Germany after Capitalism will only nationalise those sectors of industries that can hardly be operated as small private entities providing services and public subsistence under non-profit criteria. Banks, transport, infrastructure, resources, major industries, telecommunication, energy and resources, hospitals, education and anything bearing a public interest will be operated by public corporations, and democratically controlled by councils and parliaments, last not least consumer boards.

V

THE NEW GERMANY'S RAISON D'ÉTAT

New Raison d' État

Since WWII we Germans are struggling with coming clear with our nation's dark past. Even for us who have been born after the Holocaust the long shadows are thrown in front of us, foremost but not exclusively when we are to deal with issues of peace and war, the suffering of Palestinians and Israelis or when debating how to build a peaceful European Union.

After WWII it has become a *raison d'état* for us in the Federal Republic of Germany to support Israel although we knew that the conquering of Palestine through the United Nations in 1947 bore the same unhealthy side effects which had occurred in the case of Ireland after it had been conquered by King Henry II in 1171.

Not seldom is it overseen how nasty an occupied people may behave.

Nevertheless, we Germans, united again under one nationhood since 3rd October 1990, and by incorporating the former Eastern Germans who were taught throughout Soviet rule an adverse stance in the question over Palestine and Israel, are still confronted with the 'collective guilt' - syndrome our nation has accumulated. I for my part think that there is no such thing as 'collective guilt' but that there should be a collective responsibility never to let it happen again. Not in Germany and not elsewhere.

Post – WWII and post-unification *raison d'état* has been and still is to stand by our foes and defend Israel. But, also when Israel oppresses and commits war crimes? What about our morale, our democratic values and humanistic principles?

An undemocratic, inhumane *raison d'état* as basis for the European Union?

What does *raison d'état* really mean? It is usually attributed to conservative political doctrine. Quite cynically comes along a remark by Prussian king Friedrich II: "You may reason as much as you like, as long as you are obedient."

This is certainly a misinterpretation of what *raison d'état* should constitute. Machiavelli wrote in 1525 that *raison d'état* authorised the ruler to make or not make use of morale whatever suited the purpose.

Modern society in a democracy should carefully weigh its options when it comes to defining a *raison d'état*.

We are able to observe the self-determination of statehood applying all, even immoral tools over and over again from neo-colonial wars and destruction of social structures to profligacy and wanton destruction of natural habitats.

Our democracies should not only resonate and be locked in a subaltern relationship with the state-power that until recently has benefited multinational corporations and banks by rolling out the red carpet for tax evasion, downsizing and deregulation. To allow a *raison d'état* been drawn up by state power which so clearly has failed in our own crisis and to let it determine our attitude towards the Palestine – Israel conflict pre-destines it to fail as well.

In Germany, for the past 20 years, the *raison d'état* implied that Anti-Imperialism was literally dead after the Eastern European Socialism had imploded and the Berlin Wall be brought down. Ever since are we told that *Globalisation* was not imperialistic but brought freedom and democracy and will eventually bring peace to all nations. And celestial choirs will be singing...

The reality is rather different.

EU institutions did better to adopt an Anti-Imperialistic position if Humanism mattered

Why should we denounce the necessity for an anti-imperialistic fight right now only because previous sympathy for national liberation movements had been disappointed or because the imperialistic appearing approach of the US – led Israeli government is directly connected with the traumata of the Jewish being under threat and persecution over hundreds of years?

Moshe Zuckermann said on 14th April 2008 that "whatever ideologies may determine the Israeli Shoah-commemoration, it can not be denied that the Shoah remains the basic Matrix for the foundation of the state of Israel." I fully agree, but wish to add that in lieu of that the events immediately after the founding of the Israeli state tragic mistakes have been made as the progressive movements in the Arabian population of Palestine had supported the UN resolution on the British troop withdrawal and the founding of two independent states despite the insurgence of Arab league nations after 15th May 1948 and despite of horrifying terror.

The Arab population of Palestine fought for the withdrawal of the Arab interventionist forces and in favour of the founding of a Palestinian state as it had been advocated by the United Nations, and for a democratic and independent government in such state which in a perfect scenario would cooperate and negotiate with the Jewish state on equal level.

It came the other way.

Lost illusions and myths

But this does not justify the injustices carried out against the Palestinian people over six decades. It rather is an argument dictated by history to grant Palestinians as well as Israelis, the Arabic as well as the Jewish, lasting peace and a humane society along a prosperous economy.

This will be impossible without the Israeli withdrawal from occupied territories while finding a humane solution for all Palestinian refugees.

Back to lost illusions:

Anti-Imperialism doesn't result from illusions and disappointments won't let it become out-fashioned. And, also where a black-white scheme is especially useless, one has to ask where the various interests lay. Although the wars against Iraq, Afghanistan and the repression against Iran clearly aim at imperialistic goals it is not about creating colonies. Also, one can clearly say that the term *Imperialism* doesn't describe Israel's policy correctly although Israel indeed does play a significant role in the imperialistic aims of USA and some NATO states.

The question should be asked why would Anti-Imperialism require the component of a contrary power in order to exist? The imperialistic colonialism of previous centuries ultimately has been replaced by imperialistic *hegenomism* which is fashionably coming along under the cover of pseudo-humanitarian Western-Free-World lead *internationalism* which nevertheless still uses the same barbaric tools as in all the centuries before.

Legendary remains the speech by chief delegate Andrey Gromyko on 14th May 1948 at the UN. "One should not oversee the fact that Palestine is inhabited by two peoples, an Arabic one and a Jewish one. Both peoples have their roots in the very territory. The historic past and especially not the reality created during our times do not justify any one-sided solution of the Palestine-question, neither by erecting an independent Arabic state which doesn't suit the legitimate rights of the Jewish nor by erecting an independent Jewish state which defies the legitimate rights of the Arabs. (...) A just solution would best be expressed in the founding of an Arabic-Jewish independent and democratic state, (...) however, should it transpire that because of the shattered relationship between Jewish and Arabic Palestinians has become impossible then one has to consider another solution, namely the secession and division of the country into two independent and self-determined states, a Jewish one and an Arabic one."

This is the solution my fatherland should pursue in an honest approach to guarantee that the existence of the Israeli state which shall not be questioned can not be at the expense of the Palestinian Arabs. Such can only be achieved without a complete troop withdrawal from the occupied territory, an end of the settlement policy and a humanitarian solution for the refugees.

That's the essence derived from the history of the Middle East conflict.

The terrible role the British colonial power played enhanced the conflict between Jews and Palestinians but also the protagonist's of Zionism and the Arabian reaction let things get out of hand. There are no easy solutions to the most complicated and longest conflict in human history but it is clear that as long as the rights of the Palestinians are kicked around like a football there will neither be peace for Israel nor for the entire region. The Israeli peace movement 'Gush Shalom' recently advertised in the daily *Haaretz*: "Only when the first independence day of a sovereign Palestine will be celebrated, will the future of the sovereign Israel be secured."

There is nothing to be added.

The Mid-East conflict can neither be solved by phrases like "Death to Israel" nor by employing anti-German rhetoric. Those who deny the oppressed solidarity can not claim to have learnt any lesson from fascism and the Holocaust. To justify settlement policy and occupation on the grounds that the rulers of Israel pretend to fight for the legitimate rights of an over centuries persecuted minority can not be the policy of a European Union based on human rights, freedom and democracy. Likewise can the EU not sympathise with religious fanatics who employ the suffering of the people in the West-Bank and in Gaza for their own interests. Our solidarity as Europeans shall be with the peace movement in Israel as well as the oppressed in Palestine.

If that was the official stance of the German government one should use German influence to promote such position among the EU member states and institutions. Unfortunately, the official stance of the German government is the unequivocal support of the Israeli policy citing a moral obligation resulting from our nation's dark past. But, history obliges us to fully commit to Anti-Fascism, Anti-Imperialism, Anti-Racism, including the disgust about Anti-Semitism and Islam-phobia, and it obliges us to commit to a humane policy towards refugees and asylum seekers and an at least principal criticism of capitalism. All the above does not characterize German and EU policy. It is rather so that government and predominantly private mainstream media focus on reducing the crimes committed by the fascists to their sick race-ideology which indeed has been unprecedented and horrific. But, the crimes of the NAZI regime don't allow to be reduced to that. The industrially organised most brutal mass-murder of Jews, Roma, Sinti, Communists and many other people who stood in the way of the fascists would have been impossible without WW II that has been initiated by Germany. For quite some time now the German mainstream media report about this war that has been directed against many peoples in the world, but foremost against the Soviet Union and the direct neighbours of Germany, Poland and France, especially, by focussing on the suffering German civilians had to endure when the war returned to from where it started. Not much is told the new generation of Germans these days about the unimaginable suffering of the peoples in the Soviet Union, Yugoslavia, Poland, Czech, Slovakia, Romania, Greece, France and many others who were occupied by German forces and fascists.

Totalitarism – Doctrine, a comforting explanation

The question arises whether the official stance of all West-German- as well as the post-unification governments had been that of a split tongue when dealing with Germany's past: on one side the historic obligation resulting from the Holocaust and on the other side the permanent relativity of the fascist perversion foremost through the so called *Totalitarism Doctrine*. It is also hard to explain the legality and existence of neo-fascist parties like NPD, DVU and REP if the German government really wanted to deal with the NAZI heritage. This deliberate un-clarity of the German *raison d'état* sparks new Anti-Semitism and 'theories' about a "Jewish world conspiracy". Nothing justifies such positions. Nobody should serve the evil tradition of suggesting Jewish provoked Anti-Semitism. It is obviously quite difficult to determine where a line is crossed and where criticising Israel may feed Anti-Semitic resentment. Those who either don't have their guts tell them where the line that shall never be crossed is or those who do not have a comprehensive knowledge about the facts better remain silent. This is especially so as Israeli war hawks invite Anti-Semitic reactions.

But, that is no reason for Anti-Semitism.

Vice-versa, it is rather that the existence of Anti-Semitism can not pose as a reason for accepting Israeli politics without criticising it and to acknowledge the hypocritical official stance of the German government and mainstream media as *raison d'état*. Knowing about the latent existing Anti-Semitism and the possibility for Anti-Semites to live such in supposedly criticising Israel doesn't oblige anybody to remain silent but rather to measured responses which shall not cast any doubt that Anti-Semitism is not acceptable in a democracy based on civil liberties, human rights and freedom of speech. Especially in Germany any comparison between Israel's policy and the NAZI regime must not be allowed. Not one single supposed 'argument' or cliché by which the NAZIS had ideologically tried to legitimise murdering more than 6 million Jews can be a valid comparison. And, because the preparations for the war against Iran are under way, there shall be no doubt that a conference in Tehran supposedly 're-examining' the Holocaust is counterproductive for world peace.

It is not the right time to accept Germany's *raison d'état*. For such, our state is too much that of banks and major corporations; it is also not the time to make wars subject to careful consideration as for such wars have become far to common; and it is definitely inappropriate at the height of times to allow the security of the people in Israel and the entire resource-rich region become a football on the field of Imperialism. It *is* high time, instead, to say 'No' to war as a profitable continuation of policy goals of states dominated by banks and major corporations.

HUMAN RIGHTS, let's begin at our own shores!

There are some deadly loopholes in the Lisbon treaty as the capitalist's ultima ration seems to be capital punishment. Officially, the death penalty is abolished but the question arises whether one will shoot at Greek demonstrators, students, ordinary citizens?

Why is Amnesty International turning a blind eye when it comes to Lisbon Treaty & Death Penalty?

Amnesty International is urging the EU to strongly and publicly condemn the two executions in Belarus from earlier this month. In a letter to High Representative of the Union for Foreign Affairs and Security Policy, Vice President of the European Commission, Baroness Catherine Ashton, Amnesty International also calls on Spain to take a stronger lead in promoting an immediate moratorium of the death penalty worldwide.

Amnesty International's annual report Death Sentences and Executions 2009 published today, shows that no one was executed in Europe last year. This important milestone did however become obscure when two individuals were executed in Belarus around 18 March. The fairness of the trials has been questioned and both had appealed for clemency to president Lukashenka. The reaction from the EU on these two killings has been also been muted.

"Spain has for a long time been a leader in the worldwide abolitionist movement and it was encouraging to see that Madrid made a strong commitment to set the death penalty as a top priority during its presidency. Yet, the death penalty has not been mentioned on a regular basis in high-level political statements and the deafening silence after the executions in Belarus has made the issue of the death penalty look even less like a priority" says Nicolas Beger, the director of Amnesty International's EU office.

Even if worldwide progress towards ending judicial killings by states has been made, 58 countries still retain capital punishment and 18 of those were known to have carried out executions in 2009. Amnesty International documented at least 714 executions last year but this total don't include figures from the world's largest executioner, China, which would inflate the real global total significantly.

All EU member states have abolished the death penalty, making the EU a vital global force against its practice. The establishment of the External Action Service (EAS) should also guarantee that the EU has the ability to act decisively in all cases of imminent execution but this can only happen if the death penalty features as one of the EAS' top priorities.

"The EU is a key player in the fight for a global abolition of the death penalty and it is time to really push for more progress. There are no excuses anymore as to why the EU, as a global actor, can't continue to keep up the pressure to achieve a total ban on capital punishment," concludes Beger.

It is interesting to see how persistent Amnesty International criticises the death penalty outside the European Union while the organisation turns a blind eye when it comes to the Lisbon Treaty.

The International Herald Tribune (IHT) noted on 21 February 2010 that "European officials have said privately that China's recent hard-line policies on issues like human rights have made it politically easy for European governments to toughen up on tariffs."

In other words, Western leaders only publicly brand China for it's executions while then turning to business. One may be reminded of the hypocritical stance of US- and Western European governments in the 1970ies when dealing and wheeling with Latin American juntas and the South African apartheid regime.

But, also the EU doesn't have a clean bill of health when it comes to potentially allowing 'elimination' in state of war or in case of up-risings. Loopholes in the definitions are probably intended, critics say.

According to Professor Dr. Karl Albrecht Schachtschneider the EU's Lisbon Treaty provides for the reintroduction of the death penalty. In an interview with the German "Focus-Money" magazine he said on 19 August 2009 that the EU Charta's article 2 which prohibits capital punishment is led ad absurdum by the definitions contained in the Human Rights Convention of 1950 that became an integral part of the Lisbon Treaty.

Article 6, clauses 1 and 3 of the treaty governs that article VII of the Charta that had been proclaimed in Nice in 2000 but until the Lisbon Treaty became effective had not been enacted automatically the "definitions" of the Charta gain validity. Article 52, clauses 3 and 7 clearly make amendments become part of the Lisbon Treaty and by this make it possible to (re-) introduce the death penalty in case of war or up-risings, Professor Schachtschneider explains, warning that a the definition when the EU was at war could be stretched.

Some EU member states were at war with Yugoslavia and still are engaged in Afghanistan, Professor Schachtschneider argues, adding that in case of up-risings no law or court order would be required to justify killings: "The Monday-up-risings in Leipzig in 1989 or other non-authorised demonstrations like in Greece could be interpreted on that basis as up-risings. One just needs a few 'autonomic' activists who throw stones in order to justify such a state."

Quelle: Focus-Money 35/2009 vom 19.8.2009[24]

---

24   Artikel 2 der Charta der Grundrechte – Recht auf Leben

1. Jeder Mensch hat das Recht auf Leben.

2. Niemand darf zur Todesstrafe verurteilt oder hingerichtet werden.

Quelle: Charta der Grundrechte der Europäischen Union in der Fassung vom 14.12.2007,

Amtsblatt der Europäischen Union C 303/1

Erläuterung zu Artikel 2 – Recht auf Leben

1. Absatz dieses Artikels basiert auf Artikel 2 Absatz 1 Satz 1 der Europäischen Menschenrechtskonvention (EMRK), der wie folgt lautet:

«1. Das Recht jedes Menschen auf Leben wird gesetzlich geschützt [...]».

2. Satz 2 der genannten Vorschrift, der die Todesstrafe zum Gegenstand hatte, ist durch das Inkrafttreten des Protokolls Nr. 6 zur EMRK hinfällig geworden, dessen Artikel 1 wie folgt lautet:

«Die Todesstrafe ist abgeschafft. Niemand darf zu dieser Strafe verurteilt oder hingerichtet werden.»

Auf dieser Vorschrift beruht Artikel 2 Absatz 2 der Charta.

3. Die Bestimmungen des Artikels 2 der Charta entsprechen den Bestimmungen der genannten Artikel der EMRK und des Zusatzprotokolls. Sie haben nach Artikel 52 Absatz 3 der Charta die gleiche Bedeutung und Tragweite. So müssen die in der EMRK enthaltenen «Negativdefinitionen» auch als Teil der Charta betrachtet werden:

a) a) Artikel 2 Absatz 2 EMRK:

«Eine Tötung wird nicht als Verletzung dieses Artikels betrachtet, wenn sie durch eine Gewaltanwendung verursacht wird, die unbedingt erforderlich ist, um

a) jemanden gegen rechtswidrige Gewalt zu verteidigen;

b) jemanden rechtmässig festzunehmen oder jemanden, dem die Freiheit rechtmässig entzogen ist, an der Flucht zu hindern;

c) einen Aufruhr oder Aufstand rechtmässig niederzuschlagen.»

b) b) Artikel 2 des Protokolls Nr. 6 zur EMRK:

«Ein Staat kann in seinem Recht die Todesstrafe für Taten vorsehen, die in Kriegszeiten oder bei unmittelbarer Kriegsgefahr begangen werden; diese Strafe darf nur in den Fällen, die im Recht vorgesehen sind, und in Übereinstimmung mit dessen Bestimmungen angewendet werden [...]».

Quelle: Erläuterungen zur Charta der Grundrechte in der Fassung vom 14.12.2007,

Amtsblatt der Europäischen Union C 303/17

Artikel 52 der Charta der GrundrechteTragweite und Auslegung der Rechte und Grundsätze

[...]

(3) Soweit diese Charta Rechte enthält, die den durch die Europäische Konvention zum Schutz der Menschenrechte und Grundfreiheiten garantierten Rechten entsprechen, haben sie die gleiche Bedeutung und Tragweite, wie sie ihnen in der genannten Konvention verliehen wird. Diese Bestimmung steht dem nicht entgegen, dass das Recht der Union einen weitergehenden Schutz gewährt.

[...]

(7) Die Erläuterungen, die als Anleitung für die Auslegung dieser Charta verfasst wurden, sind von den Gerichten der Union und der Mitgliedsstaaten gebührend zu berücksichtigen.

Der Abdruck erschien am 31.08.2009 in der Ausgabe Nr. 35 der Zeitschrift ‚Zeit-Fragen', Redaktion und Verlag, Postfach, CH-8044 Zürich

Planet of the Millennium

United Nation's COP 17 – climate change tourism hardly covers up neo-colonialism.

It becomes more and more obvious that the climate change hype, although officially being the underlying reason along with the dramatic climatic calamity owed to waste of resources going along with wanton destruction of natural habitats only served two purposes, firstly the revival of the nuclear energy and secondly to have an excuse to dictate to emerging economies not to grow too fast while the trade off of carbon emission credits plunders the developing countries once more in a kind of neo-colonial style.

To achieve the first goal seems to be more difficult as it has suffered kind of a backlash after the Fukushima meltdown. It is a bit like when the West told President Gorbachev to introduce perestroika and democracy along with the opening of the Soviet market and the Berlin wall and at the same time demand that he should do it slowly as if he could dismantle the wall brick by brick.

For 40 years we told the East Asian countries to introduce western life style and free market capitalism and then tell them to do it slowly. That's what COP 15 was about and that is what COP 17 is about.

It is the clash between China and the West but also an awakening of the emerging markets that rub their eyes in disbelief as they are being told by the North that their industrial development was not in line with emission reduction targets.

The UN's conference in Durban reveals that one can not solve the problem of 'Climate Change' without seriously debating the economic model our world is made run by these days.

This leads us to the fundamental question whether the economic model, the profit based production and it's shareholder capitalism is still sustainable.

Resource management has to be rethought but an economy that only produces for profit and not for the actual demand is not sustainable.

Instead of long lasting high quality products our industries produce an incredible amount of trash because the highest profit rates are being achieved with an ever faster turnover.

This wastes resources.

On top of that, the EU Commission continues with the absurd subsidization of major corporations that would hardly need state aid but who are benefiting by both the ownership of vast farm land that draws huge amounts of tax payer's money while at the same time the distribution channels with major retailers are eliminating any serious competition.

Food safety and democracy go together. As long as the food production is only directed to satisfying the rich North one can not speak of a fair distribution of wealth. We feed fish to fish to make Sardines become Salmon and in topping every thinkable perversity livestock that consumes grain to cows to get filet mignon on the plate that the better off in the rich countries can afford. But, by this we are shrinking the supply and although there would be sufficient market demand but as the majority of citizens on this planet is living below the poverty line one can not make profit on supplying food for those of us who go hungry.

To ask this question, the UN are not brave enough as this would ultimately lead to the abolishment of shareholder capitalism and a closing down of the Wall Street casino. The UN did better to listen to the "Occupy" activists as these seem to have understood what is at stake.

But, this will be the only democratic way to save this planet's climate. It is not true that the declining wealth of the majority in industrialised nations would at least be compensated by an increased wealth for vast populations in other parts of the world, i.e. emerging markets.

This is the mantra of the globalisation-ideologists which the Swiss Sociologist and former UN rapporteur Jean Ziegler had called a major scam as also in the developing countries and emerging markets only the top 1% really benefit from the new productivity and new wealth.

A small, compared with the size of the population, middle class profits unless it jeopardises it like it happened in the South East Asian crisis in 1997 but the vast majority of the population is being sidelined.

The bulk of the capital that is streaming into those countries is invested on a short term basis and is subject to immediate withdrawal should the profit rate not increase steadily.

Usually such a retracting mechanism destroys more than what it previously had encouraged. Even foreign direct investments of the major multinationals, their takeovers and job transfers into low-wage zones do not create a lot of wealth on a local level especially because of the terribly low level of social purchasing power and net wages and corporate tax rebates blackmailed from the respective government.

Very often existing and long time established 'home-grown' structures are being destroyed while the local suppliers and manufacturers are being ruined.

In reality there has never been such globalisation of the world economy that has always been advocated. Instead of that there is a globally distributed small segment of business in which the major corporations, banks, insurance companies and distribution agents as well as retailers conspire in order to cut deals for themselves and by this to create wealth for those who manage to be part of it.

For the majority of the population the situation deteriorates and leads to despair.

The gulf has become wider by "globalisation" not narrower. In about 81 countries of this planet the per capita income has declined sharply between 1992 and 2002 while life expectancy took a dive, too.

The discrepancies between top and bottom of the poorer societies had grown bigger, too. Whereas the poorest 20% of the planet's population had accounted for a share of 2.3% of World GDP, it is today only 1.4%.

In 2009 for the first time in mankind's history more than a billion people were starving. Since 1945 about 600 million people died of hunger, ten times more than the WWII – toll.

In addition to that in wars more people die through weapons than by starvation. The goal of the UN's "Millennium Summit" to halve the amount of hungry people could very cynically be understood in a way that the wars do the job. The EU's export to APC and developing countries is massively subsidised and by this undermines the agricultural competition in those countries.

On top of that, industrialised countries subsidise their agricultural sectors with 1 billion Dollars per day and create dumping situations on the world market. It is a known fact that receivers of EU funds through the "Common Agricultural Policy (CAP)" for farming are foremost major corporations, but also rich private individuals. Parallel to this, the 2011 Global Hunger Index reveals that 26 countries have levels of hunger that are "Extremely Alarming" or "Alarming". Moreover, the EU is robbing the western Sahara region of the fruits of the sea by the implementation of the "Fisheries Agreement" with Morocco that neglects Saharwian people completely while oppressing the population in the Western Sahara.

Human Dignity dies when each and every move of a person has to be efficient, economically justifiable and sustainable. Where only profit maximisation rules, there is no room for Democracy. The 'survival-of-the-fittest – credo' is the opposite of Freedom and Equality. The new Germany will engage in a world wide equilibrium and fair trade.

Conclusion

The above facts are nothing else but a declaration of bankruptcy of our political and economic system. A society in which children become a poverty risk won't reproduce itself. It becomes cold and lonely. The disappointment of people with a system that provides no security, because only shareholder values matter, will provoke anger and hatred. The European Institutions are proud to claim that they are in power, but they are only in government. Even as a government they are only transitional, but do a lot of harm to our democratic system.

Our Union is in a crisis. Our European society is in a crisis. The crisis is an economical, political and cultural one. Our system does not work anymore. It has been the victim of exploitation by the rich, not the poor. While we should be richer than ever before, because we have worked hard to achieve an ever higher productivity, some parasites bribe and blackmail our politicians to change legislation the way they need it in order to make it look legal, although it will never be legitimate.

Despite the fact that the 'Constitution' as well as the EU Commission's plan B, the Lisbon Reform Treaty has been overwhelmingly rejected by the citizens a plan C has come into play: one went ahead with so called ratifications and by imposing a regime that cements an economic system that does not work and which is directed against the majority of EU citizens.

To draw up a new treaty or fiscal compact that is only being enacted by violating an existing treaty automatically makes it become null and void under international law.

We need an understanding between member states that the economic model applied is wrong and can't be legitimized by legalising it against the declared wish of the majority of the citizens. To flood the European Parliament with lobbyists who camouflage themselves as lawyers, PR agents or even Journalists is the wrong approach to win back public trust.

To have EU Commissioners and staff be selected by the European Round Table of Industrialists doesn't secure legitimacy either. Not the institutions, not the framework of the EU is wrong, it is the underlying economic model.

Unless we question the legitimacy of the present system, we will in a short while be confronted with a right-wing populist who may lead us into a future that we had believed was our continent's dark past. To say that because I am able to voice my criticism proves that I am wrong, is the threat with Fascism.

Article 20 of the German Basic Law, our constitution, states that "the Federal Republic of Germany is a *social, federal, state* based on the rule of law. The legislation is bound by the constitution, the judicative branch by the law and the executive branch by legislation. The German people have the right of resistance against whoever intends to abolish these principles."

We, the peoples of Europe, have not authorised our leaders to execute treaties creating a regime of *Wirtschafts* – Stalinism, *EURO*-Apartheid and *ECO*-Fascism.

Whether history repeats itself is entirely in our hands. Our political leaders could avert such disastrous consequences. We all in a way influence history's course by what we undertake to do and by what we refrain from doing. The resistance required to avert the catastrophe from happening should be directed rather against the financial system as well as the sick economic model our elected leaders worship than institutions headed by opportunists and incompetent wannabe – statesmen.

I would prefer to not see it become necessary to invoke Article 20 of our constitution.

www.ingramcontent.com/pod-product-compliance
Lightning Source LLC
Chambersburg PA
CBHW061359280526
45784CB00001B/307